W9-BNQ-674

999=

HOW TO BE A BUSH PILOT

02-14-11-12-56-57-01-01.

C Collins

HOW TO BE A
BUSH PILOT

A Field Guide to Getting Luckier

★ **CLAUDIA DEY** ★

Illustrations by Jason Logan

DISCLAIMER

Bush Pilots,

You are smart, sagacious fellows who know better than to believe everything you read. E.g., there is stuff in here about smoking and drinking. Totally bad for you! And there is stuff in here about sex. Totally good for you! And there are many celebrity names repurposed to be your hardware. Totally playful. My caveat: In this book, I am presenting one truth that I cannot promise, as much as I would like to, is the only truth. As I am not a high-wire act, a surgeon or a farmhand, I am not a certified sex educator. I am a lady, a researcher and a writer. This book is not a substitute for medical advice, nor is it a stand-in for your own independent research. I encourage you now, as always, to use your man-wiles.

Onwards. And upwards.

Published by Collins, an imprint of
HarperCollins Publishers Ltd

First Edition

HarperCollins books may be purchased
for educational, business, or sales
promotional use through our
Special Markets Department.

HarperCollins Publishers Ltd
2 Bloor Street East, 20th Floor
Toronto, Ontario, Canada
M4W 1A8

www.harpercollins.ca

Library and Archives Canada Cataloguing
in Publication

Dey, Claudia
How to be a bush pilot : a field guide to
getting luckier / Claudia Dey.

ISBN 978-1-55468-552-3

1. Sex instruction. I. Title.
HQ31.D54 2010   613.9'6
C2010-903246-2

Printed and bound in the United States
RRD 9 8 7 6 5 4 3 2

FOR MY MOM AND DAD

CONTENTS

(OF OUR PANTS)

PART FOUR: THE LAY OF THE LAND

PART FIVE: (YOUR WINGS) GRADUATION

I know, I know. Your babe bought you this book and it's made you misty-eyed. Admit it: You're crying a bit. Not because you are chuffed. But because you are wondering: "Whoa. Do I suck? Am I a subpar lay? Do I screw the way Steven Seagal runs? And wait a minute, if I gave you a book like this, about sex and being sexier and all the sex stuff you don't do or maybe can't do, you'd kick me in the shins and close shop for like at least seven nights. Actually, you'd dump me, and then you'd call your sister and you'd come up with some terrible name for me. Not even a name. A sound. Like a fart or a burp. That's it. That's how you'd refer to me for the rest of time. As a fart. Or a burp. Or maybe even a yawn. This is totally unfair. What about that time when you were like, yes. Eh? What about it?"

What about it?

Unlock the bathroom door. Stop playing "Redemption Song" on your saxophone. Put down her Chardonnay. Torch blankie and, for your babe's sake, take that black band off your melancholic willie. Here, my young bucks, my elegant hard-ons of the future, is your one-way ticket to Screwtopia. How to Be a Bush Pilot. Chin up. Package too.

INITIATION

Bush Pilots,

Lace up your combat boots, cinch your flight suits and stand at attention.

We love you. We really do. We love your eagerness and your good intentions. We love your awkward charm—like when you served us beef jerky, frozen peas and Five Star for dinner last night. In camping pots. Cute. Primitive. But cute. And then you showed us your weight room— or, I guess we should just say it: closet. And then you showed us your record collection. And then you put on *Led Zeppelin IV.* Good choice. And then you sang the wrong words to "When the Levee Breaks" while doing a really slow head bang. It got to us. We fooled around in your sleeping bag. It went well—so well, you got to try out your new, patented move. The Woodpecker. Just that morning, you'd drawn the steps and mailed them to yourself to copyright them. Phew.

Then, wood-pecking, you heard us moan, and it sounded a lot like "come," so you did, and then you fell into a deep, untroubled sleep. Until you woke up crying, "No good! Wide right!" It haunts you still. You looked around, wanting to be held. But we were gone. No note. No lipstick smudge on your cheek. No forgotten really tiny underwear. Spooked, you tried to console yourself. You looked in the mirror and kissed your biceps. A few times. But that didn't work, so you pulled out the fail-safe GOB: "Come on!" and that made you feel better. For a while.

Let me explain. We love you. We really do. But, you see, despite The Woodpecker and your other patented moves, Nights on Broadway and Richard the Contortionist, when we fall asleep together tangled up in your Star Wars sheets, you silently farting, there is something missing. Something is not quite what it could be. Yes, there is that thing you do with your tongue while doing that other thing with your hands while doing that other thing with your boner—thank you for that. It's good. It really is. But it could be better. And last longer. A while longer.

Come now.

I am here to help you, to train you, to make you the ace I know you are. I am to you what Mr. Miyagi was to Daniel LaRusso, what Paulie was to Rocky, and yes, what Viper was to Maverick. Only I have longer hair, higher heels and a harness in my purse. I am your Zen Master, your coach, your Commander Mistress. And you, Bush Pilot, you are my unruly star.

So listen up. Here is my promise to you (and your babe in hot pants, reading this over your hirsute shoulder): I will teach you how to be a better lover. Of the bush. With the bush. In the bush. For the bush.

Take it to the bridge.

In the following pages, you will evolve from a man with a few patented moves into a man with unparalleled technique. Your sexual willingness will become your sexual prowess. Your medieval sword, a light sabre. Your musket, a six-shooter. Your name will be written across bathroom walls, tattooed to backsides and held hushed on the ends of tongues. Leonard Cohen will picture you when he meditates. So will Jenna Jameson. So will your babe. You will have more sex. You will have better sex. You will have epic sex. You will be a certified Bush Pilot.

But first, you will study and sweat and dare yourself. You will accept that jerky is not an aphrodisiac and that the woodpecker is an idiot bird. You will fart elsewhere. You will stop soaking your shirts in Drakkar Noir. You will memorize the fifteen thousand nerve endings in your babe's lady parts. You will give them each their due. You will do push-ups with your tongue and pull-ups with your fingers. You will talk dirty to your *Sports Illustrated* swimsuit issue until you are hoarse. You will recognize that the G-spot is not an emcee, the kit is not to be surprise-mounted and that sex toys are not for inferior dorks. You will understand that a moan is just a moan. You will reassess your package. You will stop calling him Simple Jack. You will train him. He will take over your weight closet. He will pump. He will flex. He will condition. And just when you both want to throw in the towel, and go back to the bathroom and gasp "Don't Let Me Be Misunderstood" into your melodica, you will think about Braveheart. You will see yourself in his kilt and furs, his man-bangs and braids and you will stand up and yell, "What is it going to be: layman or legend?"

I know you have it in you.

Somewhere.

Let me show you the way.

PART ONE
Understanding the Instruments

FLIGHT MISSION:
BUSH PILOTS,
SURVEY HER TERRAIN
AND ASSESS YOUR
LANDING GEAR
BEFORE ATTEMPTING
TAKEOFF.

A HUDDLE WITH
CAPTAIN GOODSCREW

Captain Dylan I. Goodscrew

EVERY BOY NEEDS A HERO. And every Bush Pilot needs an ace to look up to and think, "I wish I screwed like you." Well, Bush Pilots, on the cusp of your boner's further education, it is my honour (and my pleasure) to introduce you to that ace.

Boys, meet the most highly decorated Bush Pilot flying the low altitudes today. He has done search and rescue. He has done extreme. He has landed on a glacier and taken off from a sandbar. He has found the maximum performance in his craft. He once fixed his rudder with pine gum and a toothbrush. He knows his grasses. He does not have a bank account. He can start a bonfire in a rainstorm with a piece of shale and a tattered copy of *Papillon*. He fears dishonesty more than death. He keeps an apartment in Dallas. His favourite place is an unnamed lake in Alaska. He would rather land on floats than wheels. He finds comfort in the word "remote." He has fallen asleep in a motorcycle helmet and a kimono, and woken up next to a lioness and her trainer. His parachute has a naked lady on it. He has been in love more than twice. He really pulls off the beard-and-dinner-jacket look. He can play the electric guitar and sing Boston's "More than a Feeling" note perfectly. Bush Pilots, your captain: Captain D. I. Goodscrew. (That's right, Bush Pilots, his initials are D.I.G. Gold star!)

Captain Goodscrew will be present throughout your training; he will add his self-described "sluttery" to your schooling. By the time you finish reading this book, you will carry Captain Goodscrew's likeness in your wallet. You will cop his haircut. You will make a Captain Goodscrew action figure out of chiselled wood. You will tuck your Captain Goodscrew action figure into your Pilot pants for good luck. You will have secret conversations with him. How did you survive that storm cell? That crash landing? That tailspin? That overshoot? That steep turn? That time your battery quit? What, Captain Goodscrew, did you do? You will memorize his flight missions and use his misadventures to complete your own. You will dust off "More than a Feeling."

Bush Pilots, Captain Goodscrew will swear a lot. He will use all those four-letter words I don't. He will say things like, "At one party, I was fucking a lady I knew socially. Both of us were watching the lady who was being fucked beside us. There were three dudes in housecoats fucking this lady in the mouth, ass and vagina. It looked like a lot of logistics, but they were pulling it off"—with a straight, unsurprised face. But mostly, in a really charming and informed way, Captain Goodscrew will make you want to be him. You too will want to be an action figure in someone else's Pilot pants. You too will want to be an Ace.

Also making frequent appearances throughout your Field Guide: many, many babes. About the bush, and the pilots who travel the bush, they will present their insights and their outtakes, unabridged and uncensored. You ask yourself, "I know this high-speed pass is sexy for me, but is it sexy for both of us?" My den of foxes, your air traffic control, will tell you. (But to save us all time, the answer is no.)

Where to start? In this, Part One: Understanding the Instruments, we will decode your babe's lady parts, your man parts, the toy department and, most important, Bush Pilots, the safety dance.

Break.

CHAPTER 1
THE LADY PARTS

NOTE FROM THE FIELD:
THE GIRL NEXT DOOR

It's summer, 1979. Lee lies back on his parents' plastic lawn furniture, baby-oiled chest near blistering in the noonday sun. He is thirteen. He is Chachi. Terrycloth headband, jean shorts, faintly moustached. He is king of the backyard. He is king of the boner. His day consists of masturbating between chores.

The sprinkler does its lazy drawl across the grass, the sky so blue it looks shined up, for sale. A family has moved in next door: a daughter, his age. Fascinating. He has seen her baby-stepping on her white roller skates, striped bikini, braces. He looks up at her bedroom window, blinds drawn. What is she doing? Her hair? Origami? Naked back arches in front of the mirror? Sucking on fresh cherries while thinking about his flexing torso? Rod Stewart's platinum scratch flirts from her transistor radio: "Da Ya Think I'm Sexy?" He considers the proposition and retreats to his bedroom for the third time that day.

XANADU

Bush Pilots, we know all about your furtive dates with your man parts, on your bottom bunk, between Spider-Man sheets, with a grinning and nippled Farrah Fawcett lording blonde above you. We know all about your sexual awakening, puberty, that awkward slap, coming in the form of gym-shorts erections, three minutes in a bathroom stall after shop and before band, skin magazines and Sears catalogues stuffed between your mattresses. But what about us? The girls next door? What did we do between lemonade stands and modern dance, sleepovers and figure skating? What did we do when we were listening to "Xanadu" over and over and over again? What was our sexual awakening? Get this: Our first step was the same as yours.

Want a peek?

PEEPING BUSH PILOT

Follow me, over the fence, up the trellis and through the window. Follow me into our bedrooms and into our bodies. Let us begin with an anatomical roundup—for how can you expect to land a high-winged bird if you cannot locate the runway? Sit up straight, sharpen your pencils and put your hands where I can see them. We will start with your babe's lady parts. Whoa, you say impetuously, but I know those parts. I visit those parts. Often. I have pet names for those parts. Those parts love me.

Yes.

But they could love you more.

Get to know

The Breast

INTERIOR VIEW

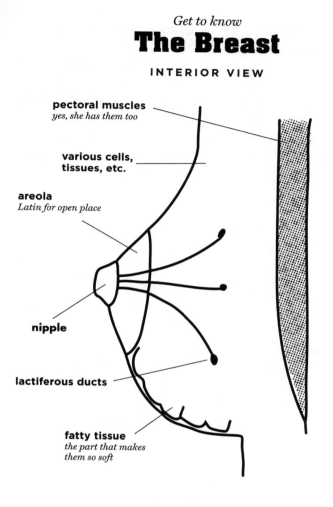

pectoral muscles
yes, she has them too

various cells, tissues, etc.

areola
Latin for open place

nipple

lactiferous ducts

fatty tissue
the part that makes them so soft

TWIN PEAKS

Your first obsession, your first subject: her breasts.

Breasts are composed of connective and fat tissue and, belying their most overt raison d'être, mammary glands; these flare and taper into an elaborate and circuitous delivery system of ducts. In short: fat on the outside, milkmaids on the inside, eye candy all around. The standard, non-milk-making breast weighs in at two-thirds of a pound; translation: the perfect handful. You will find them under your babe's Clash T-shirt, above her navel and below her collarbone. If still lost, locate the mound-like twins punctuated by those exclamation marks of the body: her nipples. Nipples, surrounded by the circular areola, are bright with nerve endings and connected to the intricate and ingenious web that also lights up your babe's brain and bush. Pilots, take note: Her neurological artistry is your good fortune. If you turn one on, the others are sure to follow.

AN AERIAL VIEW
should you be so lucky

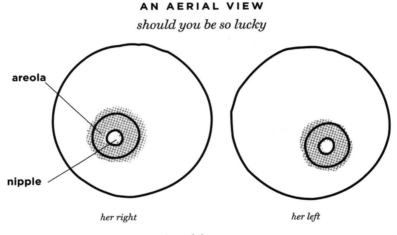

areola

nipple

her right *her left*

size and shape may vary

Pinned as he is, his hands are free to pinch my nipples just as I feel I am about to come. There is this weird mental connection I have between the sensation in my clitoris and my nipples. Touching the nipple enhances the sensation in my clitoris. This sends me right over the edge.
—Babe (can reprise Raquel Welch's Space-Girl Dance)

Like private mascots for the breasts, nipples vary from the inverted nipple to the R. Crumb torpedo—on the same woman. Flashing, one babe (plaid shirt, red string-bikini bottom—with ruffles) observes:

> One nipple is an innie—the left boob, like the left brain, has forever been the poor cousin: shy, smaller. But it can be dead sexy when it pops out. And we all know boys like a challenge.

Sensitivity and preference, from breath to biting, spans an equally broad range. A bedtime story for you Bush Pilots from one babe (zebra wallpaper, velvet top hat):

> I have never thought of my boobs as magic. In fact, I always regarded them as rather unremarkable. Neither too large nor too small, not too round, not too pointy, not too high, not too low, just average. I can't say when my perception of them changed, as I can't recall the first time I discovered their magic powers. In all likelihood, I was by myself at the time, as clumsy fumbling with high-school boys didn't amount to much in the orgasm department. In fact, I probably didn't know that I had a special talent until I revealed my secret in a drunken session of shared confidences with a group of girlfriends. One friend told us about coming in the back of a taxicab when the seam of her jeans was aligned just so; another revealed that she never failed to climax while having her lower back massaged, regardless of the masseur. I shared the fact that I can have an orgasm based solely on nipple stimulation. The girls were amazed.

Oh how, Mistress, oh how can I do this and win my babe's everlasting love? BPs, you will learn all about groping her cosmic rack in Chapter 10. Wait for it.

Now, strap on your headlamps and let's head south.

THE PARTY IN OUR PANTS

With its showy costumes, big dance numbers and handlebar moustache, your anatomy is a lot like the Village People. Bush Pilots, we may not have your Macho Man or Fu Manchu, but we do have just as much disco—and devilishness—in our pants.

MONS

First, meet the mons pubis (not to be confused with the Viennese all-girl prog-rock band of the same name). And yes, you can call it "mons" for short. The mons is the mound of tingling flesh that sits on your babe's pubic bone, at the very top of her vulva, her lips parting beneath it. Bush Pilots, behold: The mons is not merely the folksy opening act for the hot headliner mere millimetres below. Do not overlook the erotic potential of the mons. How so, Mistress? The point where the lips and the mons meet is a crossroads called the front commissure. Bush Pilot Bonus: It covers the clitoris's internal shaft and suspensory ligament; both are heavy players in your babe's pleasure.

BPs, a long, long time ago, long before you were born, the mons was the grassy knoll of the body. Scandal! It was covered in a triangular shock of hair. Total scandal! Now, the mons pubis parades many a bush-do, ranked from least to most painful (for us, not you, honey), the beaver pelt to the Brazilian.

EXTRA CREDIT

THE BUSH-DO:
LESSER-KNOWN VARIETIES

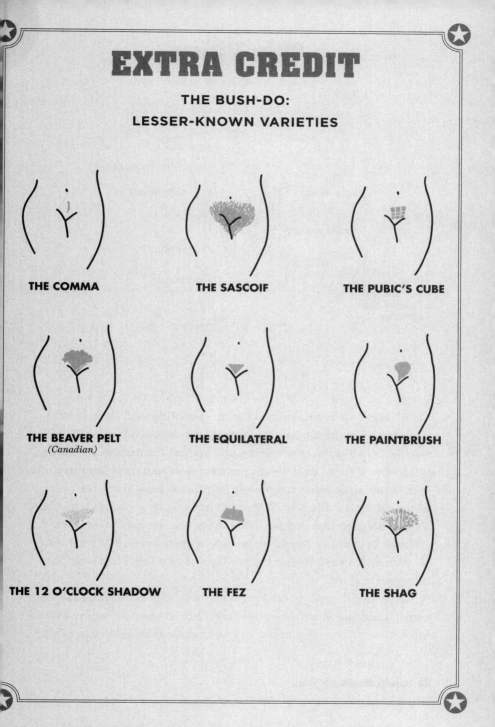

THE COMMA

THE SASCOIF

THE PUBIC'S CUBE

THE BEAVER PELT
(Canadian)

THE EQUILATERAL

THE PAINTBRUSH

THE 12 O'CLOCK SHADOW

THE FEZ

THE SHAG

The Vulva

AN AERIAL VIEW

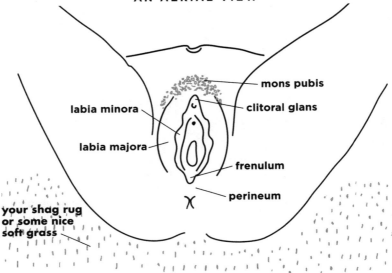

VULVA

Your exterior view: The vulva is the encapsulating term for your babe's nether regions. At its centre is the vaginal opening, bracketed from the inside out by the labia minora and majora, the folds of flesh often referred to as "lips." Bush Pilots, perhaps given your intemperate visits dive-bombing between your babe's thighs, you have overlooked some of the subtleties of her South Park. To remedy, be your babe's mirror. Pull off her high tops and her halter dress. Roll her panties down and, with the help of her hands, tip her knees open so her legs are a restful diamond. Thank her for the privilege of your front-row seat. Now, describe the show.

Note her shaggy, yet fetching outer lips. Note her Kojak-bald, yet comely inner lips. Bush Pilots, these are the most variable features in the land of the lady parts. Circumnavigating these luscious outcroppings, you will find black, blue, brown and pink. You will find smooth and wrinkled. You will find roses and recluses. Like your exuberant party favour, you will find no two alike. Their one commonality: hot-blooded. The lips swell and darken when turned on by your deft handling—the inner lips doubling and even tripling in size to grip your Gordie Howe.

THE GO-GO

The queen of the vulva sits at the northern intersection of your babe's lips. She is the clitoris. Unlike a lady's other hot spots—the breasts, the bush, the kit—the clitoris's singular purpose is sensation, its passage and proliferation. Translation: You want her on your side.

> The clit. This is my lightning rod, the entrance to a mass network of pleasure throughout my body.
> —Babe (Mexican harp, Chuck Norris posters)

> I'm a clit girl. I would love to climax by G-spot stimulation alone, but I haven't got there—yet.
> —Babe (swing set, evening gloves, netting over her eyes)

Bush Pilots, so gleeful with your hard-ons, perhaps you have drawn the hasty, yet grateful conclusion your babe's clitoris is as straightforward as its three syllables. A receptive nub of flesh, it flexes to your touch, following the same mechanics as any button—be it your stereo, your blow dryer, your Xbox.

Pilot error.

Contrary to the pink flamingo in your pants, your babe's nether regions have a catacomb effect, an extensive subterranean network, a vast interior life. Whoa, Mistress, you fret, are my lady's lady parts as complicated as my lady? Bush Pilot, I will answer your question by taking you through the clitoris step by step. In fact, we'll start with what you can actually see. Bush Pilot Bonus: The following exhibitionists account for the bulk of your babe's pleasure.

You have your head, and she has hers. Also bulbous, and when you charm it, reminiscent of a mini-boner. Salute the clitoral glans. Like an authoritative Veronica Lake, the glans stars as a femme fatale from under her satin hood. Beneath this thin tent is your babe's glistening bulb of blessedness; doorbell or doorknocker, like your Gun for Hire, her glans will be one of a kind.

The elastic band beneath your babe's glans, where the outer edges of her inner lips meet, is called the frenulum. In an act of sensual symmetry, it looks like the connective tissue beneath her pierced tongue and, you may (I stress, may) have noticed, it is one of her louder "ah" spots—as is the surrounding area, notably the aforementioned front commissure.

Your interior view: The clitoris, with incomparable genius and ambition, extends above the glans into a shaft. Full of thousands of blood vessels, the shaft will be hard to your touch. Provocateurs, blood vessels heighten blood supply to your babe's works; one word: engorgement. Bush Pilot Bonus: This tends to be mutual.

From there, picture a wishbone. Her shaft arcs into a set of legs that sit in their studded chaps astride the vaginal opening. These elongated gams run under your babe's inner lips and are replete with nerve endings, blood vessels and spongy tissue known as the bulbs of the vestibule; akin to orgasm couriers, these bulbs propel blood toward the glans. What does that mean for you?

> I like to be on top with my boyfriend on the bottom— pinned there for me to move, twist and grind at my own pace. Even if he starts to buck me up and down, I am the one ultimately in control. I can always lift up or pull off if I'm not quite "there" yet. And once I am, on top is the best place for me to be to stimulate my clitoris as hard or as softly as I like it.
> —Babe (could live in a lighthouse and be called Colette)

The Vulva

AN INTERIOR VIEW

with particular attention to the clitoris

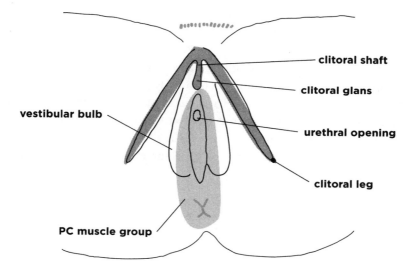

- clitoral shaft
- clitoral glans
- urethral opening
- clitoral leg
- vestibular bulb
- PC muscle group

Bush Pilots, now that you have a handle on your babe's circuitry (fist bump!), get this: Not only do her lady parts have reach, but, much like the head of your horn section, they are dense with erectile tissue that swells and hardens when played and blown. Given her architecture, your babe's clitoris is clearly the twin city to your tuba—though, with eight thousand nerve fibres, far more populated. Not to compete, but that is double your pleasure.

Now about the nomenclature: Because clitoris sounds like the cat, hairstyle and latest album by Nina Hagen, and because we reject a word so clinical it nearly neuters our lady parts, and because we love babes in black leather shorts who slither up and down poles to the thrum of a bass guitar, your babe's clitoris will heretofore be called go-go. It's a dance. It's a boot. It's a verb. It's an instruction. We repeat. Just in case you missed it the first time.

THE BUTTERFLY

Her vagina, your master.

Bush Pilots, the vagina is that sublime tunnel between a woman's legs you spent all of high school trying to ride. It's why you grew your hair over your eyes and learned how to play "Pour Some Sugar on Me"—the acoustic version. It's why you bought your Econoline van and faked that construction job. It's why you started smoking French cigarettes and stunt-reading *Within a Budding Grove*. And must I remind you of the beret? It is, when you think about it, why you have made most of your advancements and why you have told most of your untruths.

You know it feels good—so good. You know you would do anything for it. That is so rad, my BPs, but here's how. Your babe's vagina is not only a sleeve of humidity for your entertainment unit. It has other ecstatic properties.

I could stare at a beautiful vagina all day.

—Captain Goodscrew

First, the geography: Made of tissue and muscle, blood vessels and (far fewer than her go-go) nerve endings, your babe's vagina curves up and back to that bumper pad, the cervix—gate to the uterus—future flotation tank for your progeny, BP Jr. (Whoa, Mistress, you contest saucily, you just totally killed my buzz. I said future. Like the Grecian Formula future, Mistress? Yes, BP.)

Your babe's vaginal walls are the equivalent of velvet art, lined as they are with mucous membranes. One word: wetness. Excellent news to you heavily hung Bush Pilots with portraits of yourselves as centaurs hanging above your waterbeds: Your babe's vagina is three to five inches in length, but given its various visitors—fingers, fists, dildos, babies, your A-Rod—is cleverly expandable.

Now, consider the angle of your elite angler. Note well: The first third of your babe's vagina is the more responsive third. Why? It has more nerve endings. Its walls are textured, much like molten rock. Creased and corrugated, they love a good rubdown. It is also trap door to the illustrious G-spot.

Thereafter, the terrain of your babe's vagina changes. It grows increasingly even, and, with fewer nerve endings, less excitable. Bush Pilots, in mullet terms, one babe will love your friction at the front, while another will love your fullness at the back. Why? When your babe is turned on, two things happen: The first third of her vagina puffs up to make you a very happy boy in a room heaped with balloons. Understand this sensation in anatomical terms: Your babe's go-go—her head, her shaft, her legs—are all filling with blood, forming a tight collar around your tramp. Second, the inner two-thirds of your babe's vagina actually expand, the uterus pulled upward in a pre-orgasmic suspense. Hence, your babe's desire for something to hold on to—e.g., your Bush Pilot boner.

And what happens when your boner has left the building? Your babe's vaginal walls, like tired compatriots telling secrets, lean in on each other and review the screw.

That said, my spirited airmen, I am not suggesting you make penile-vaginal intercourse the flashy centrepiece of your sex life. This would be retro—retro as a Jell-O salad, permanent makeup and a faked orgasm. Babes need much more than your piston-like man parts (I'm not saying you!) before they will sing "My Moon My Man"—ergo, the rest of this book.

Bush Pilots, because, the word vagina has all the sexiness of an Austro-Hungarian autocrat with a ferret hanging from her epaulettes, your babe's vagina will heretofore be called the butterfly. Simple: It butters. It flies. And it's hard to catch.

THE G-SPOT

Famous as Greta Garbo—and sometimes, Bush Pilots, just as tricky to find—the G-spot, like any starlet recluse, has its own enduring allure.

Despite the frothy-mouthed insistences of the evangelicals, every woman has one. To find it, you must employ both art and science. Put on your lab coat. We'll start with the science.

DR. G

The G-spot—or, for those of you wearing a cravat, Gräfenberg—is named after Ernst Gräfenberg, a German gynecologist who, in the tradition of spotting storms and comets, had this body part named after himself—its "discoverer." Dr. G. became curious after collecting the anecdotal evidence of women throughout the 1940s and 1950s claiming their climaxes occurred from pressure deep within their butterflies. In an *International Journal of Sexology* (the centrefold is a picture of your great aunt wearing nothing but oven mitts) article published in 1950, "The Role of the Urethra in Female Orgasm," he posited another locus of pleasure, another "zone of erogenous feeling," this one "located along the suburethral surface of the anterior vaginal wall." He determined the go-go was not the only one shaking it on the dance floor.

In his explorations, Dr. Gräfenberg reminds you of this cardinal Bush Pilot truth:

To understand a woman's pleasure, you must first understand her anatomy.

Think of it as erogenous feng shui—lady shui—in appreciating the art of her placement, you will master the circulation of your energy.

EXTRA CREDIT

PUDENDAL VS. PELVIC

Bush Pilots, fast-forward to the well-versed vixens of this century. A carpenter-girlfriend describes the difference between her orgasms this way:

> Clitoral orgasms are like an old friend. A feeling I've known and loved for a really long time. They can still overwhelm me with intensity, but it's familiar and comforting. A G-spot orgasm takes me more by surprise . . . it's not as familiar . . . takes my breath away like something brand new.

And another:

> G-spot, or "inside," orgasms are definitely more intense. I feel their effect over my whole body a lot more than the outside, clitoral kind. Like you've pedalled your bike to the top of a really steep hill and then feel the exhilaration at the peak and also as you let yourself coast all the way down the other side. The smaller, outside kind just feel to me like smaller hills. I've cried after the big ones. The smaller ones also offer a release—sometimes just from boredom, or else to help fall asleep if I need to (for example, on a long flight for work if I'm having trouble getting comfortable and falling asleep, I just visit the bathroom for a solo mile-high club).

The tally: Some of your babe's orgasms are local, and others are three-dimensional. Your babe loves her clitoral orgasms the way she loves a pet or a boyfriend or a Wilco concert. Whereas her G-spot orgasms are like going to a sweat lodge for three days, drinking a potion, barfing and then seeing a deity astride an elephant—a deity that looks a lot like you. Who gives, BP, who gives.

Whoa, Mistress. Who gives? Yes, who gives. But, you talk back precociously, how can this be? Have I been booking the Sheraton when the Shangri-La is only inches away?

No, doofus. First, the distinction is not accurate. Just as there is no rock without roll, there is no vaginal stimulation without clitoral stimulation; in fact, some anatomists argue the G-spot may be the underside of your babe's go-go. To wit, naming your babe's orgasms—total moot point! So 1910! Leave it to the ladies! Second, ranking your babe's orgasms—economy suite versus seven-star—is also up to her, not you.

That said, in the interest of your higher (or, more precisely, lower) schooling, it is important you understand the following: In *The G-spot and Other Recent Discoveries about Human Sexuality*, Alice Kahn Ladas, Dr. John Perry and Beverly Whipple suggest there is, in fact, a distinction in sensation between clitoral (i.e., pudendal, i.e., minor-league) and G-spot (i.e., pelvic, i.e., major-league) orgasms, and that distinction is due to neurology. Let me explain.

There are two different nerve highways, one of which has a few more roadside attractions. Let's let *Good Vibrations* be our map. The pudendal nerve connects to the go-go and the PC muscle (a figure-eight of muscle between your babe's pubic and tail bones), while the pelvic nerve is connected to the "clitoral shaft, clitoral legs, G-spot, bladder, uterus, and deepest part of the PC muscle." The pelvic nerve also connects to the "internal organs and inner muscles." G-spot orgasms are often considered "blended" orgasms, a hybrid of "clitoral" and G-spot orgasms. Summation: They visit all of the locales listed above.

Now that you have this information, roll it up, stuff it in a Jameson's bottle and toss it in the ocean. That is an order. Bush Pilots, never qualify your babe's climaxes. It is, to use Freud's word, immature. A G-spot orgasm is not Penelope Cruz while a clitoral orgasm is her sister. You have not been downgraded, and neither has she. As orgasm sage Betty Dodson wisely states, "There's no such thing as the wrong kind of orgasm." Clear?

There's too much G-spot emphasis as it is. My preference is to not identify orgasms with body parts.
—Bush Pilot (piñata, aquarium, heart-shaped bed)

When I come, it's all over the map, depending on how I got there: a long or short session, manual or oral, toy or what our mama gave us—and my mood. My mood is huge. I would say my orgasm collection is in the hundreds, and each one is different from the next.
—Babe (ZZ Top eight-tracks, flower in her hair)

TURN ON YOUR GPS

Bush Pilots, now that you know what kind of pyrotechnics your babe's G-spot can perform, I am sure you and your Roman candle would like to find it. And you will. But before I can give you her coordinates, note: Scouts of nerve endings, your babe's G-spot has far fewer nerve endings than the glans of her go-go. All told, in the virtuous pursuit of your babe's explosive orgasm, her go-go is the flint to your firecracker.

All right. Locate the urethral opening, south of your babe's go-go and north of her butterfly. Its day job: transporting pee from her bladder out of her body. Hot. So hot.

Now picture your babe's interiors. The urethra runs, like a gorgeous, pacing, upstairs neighbour, for an inch and a half to two inches above your babe's vaginal canal. Tubular in shape, it is a kind of track lighting for her treasure trove. For those of you with no sense of direction, this places the urethra on your babe's ventral, or front, wall. The G-spot is the spongy tissue that surrounds it. It is home to the paraurethral glands, or juicer. Met with extensive attention (and I mean extensive), the G-spot will not only leave her New York apartment, but may exalt and perform that revered bedroom feat: ejaculation.

Bush Pilots, hold on to your flight missions. Uncovering your babe's G-spot is not as straightforward as simply landing on it. Rather, it is conditional on one thing: her arousal. Only then will this two-inch cushion packed with blood vessels make itself known to you. Otherwise, you are just circling in the dark. Here is Captain Goodscrew's approach:

> Clit rubbing usually works. I encourage the lady to rub herself. That will free up some hands. Once it's sufficiently juicy, I'll ask permission to put a few fingers up inside. It's best to put in two fingers and do a come-here motion. There's definitely a sweet spot in there. If a lady is

squirty, this can facilitate ejaculation. When the inside feels increasingly hard and is literally pushing out your fingers/dildo/cock/whatever, you know you're close to female ejac.

You will find your babe's G-spot about half a finger length in. Know that measurements are not reliable; touch is. The G-spot will be ridged and will vary in size from a dime to a walnut. For more wooing methods, you may, when I say so, consult Chapter 14.

PERINEUM

Continuing our sojourn south, Bush Pilots, pause at the oft-overlooked playground known as the perineum. Not simply a sling of skin between your babe's front and back doors, her perineum, like yours, is rife with nerve endings and blood vessels; in collusion with her go-go, it completes a cuff of pleasure that will respond to the push and pull of your package. As will . . .

THE KIT

Pleasure dome, pilgrimage, desired by most and reached only by some: the kit. You know where to find it, but do you know what it is made of? Bush Pilots, meet your babe's anus. The opening consists of two closely spaced muscle rings lovingly called sphincters, otherwise known as bouncers. They are less than a quarter of an inch apart and they will card you, frisk you, enforce the dress code and humiliate you in front of a crowd. Play by their rules, or get tossed.

The outer muscle is voluntary. Like your hand, it can clap, snap, hitchhike and flip you the bird. It can tense and relax at will. The inner sphincter cannot. It is involuntary. Like your heart, it responds to fear and anxiety. Do not scare it. That said, your babe can learn to tame it, teaching it to startle less and surrender more.

The Kit

INTERIOR VIEW

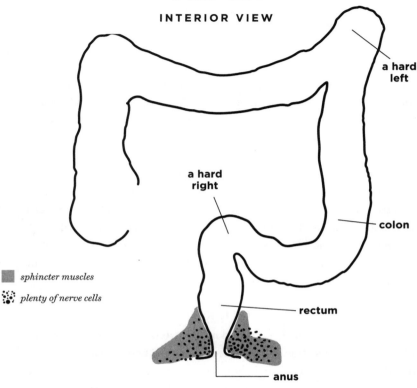

a hard
left

a hard
right

colon

sphincter muscles

plenty of nerve cells

rectum

anus

POOLANDER

Note well, neat freaks: The kit has been derided as the slums of the body. But is it, as small minds would believe, right next door to the dump? Not quite. Bush Pilots, your babe's anus is less than one inch in length, leading into her rectum, which is another five to nine inches in length, which leads to her colon, where her detritus lives in semi-squalor. Yet, despite its rambling layout, here is the dirt: After a rear romp, it is possible to find some caca on your man parts. Deal with it.

Oh. And what's this? A condom.

Much like our butterflies, the highest concentration of nerve endings in our kits is around the opening itself. Beyond the opening, your babe's kit is a narrow and winding road. The rectal walls are composed of delicate tissues—think Japanese paper and antique lace. This fragility, combined with the curvature of the canal, makes it susceptible to tearing. Be careful, or be kicked off the course. This is sex in slow motion. Also, please note: Her kit is not her butterfly. Her kit does not have the same kind of lubrication. This is why, Bush Pilots, you must be well basted. Have your survival kit on hand, replete with your favourite thick water-based lube. We all know the true delight that lies in a succulent bird.

The sum of her bum: The kit is the Polynesian Island of the body—mythologized, lusted after and yet defamed by taboo. Bush Pilots, this isolationism is entirely misguided. When it comes to your babe's anatomy, you must think inclusively. Her kit, like her butterfly, her G-spot and that omniscient wishbone, her go-go, is a crucial part of her whole. Not only is it next door to all of her Tahitis, it's part of the shared musculature known as your babe's pelvic floor—or, perhaps more pointedly, her dance floor. It contracts when she comes; give it its due. You will find further instruction in your Booty Camp, Chapter 16.

Bush Pilots, this nearly concludes your spin through your babe's pelvic network, flush with fifteen thousand nerve endings. I know! So many! You're stoked. You're shadowboxing. You're doing air lunges. You're spelling B-O-N-A-N-Z-A with your limbs. It's not easy. You're sweating. You recover. You high-five everything in your apartment and make the whoops of a cheerleader. Nice round-off, and whoa, was that a human pyramid of one? Hold up: Don't rip your robe off yet. You still have one last locale to view.

At the top of her tower, under her headset, she times the takeoffs. She clears the landings. She patrols the skies. She identifies violations of airspace. Her radar misses nothing. She can command that your Norseman be sent back to base—with blue balls. She can shoot you down. Meet your babe's air traffic controller. Meet . . .

HER BRAIN

Aside from your babe's Joan Holloway breasts, her Joan Holloway kit, her Joan Holloway pout, her Joan Holloway mane and her Joan Holloway slink, your babe's brain was clearly her main attraction. You see it at work constantly: at the breakfast table, speeding through the *New York Times* crossword puzzle while you toss out irreverent and ill-fitting suggestions; calculating the mortgage while you hover adorably; weighing Kant versus Hegel while you listen intently to her cleavage; replaying the pass she dropped in overtime while you imagine her naked on a pony.

But Bush Pilots, what you may not know is this: Like your brain (represent!), your babe's brain continues to function when you are busy under your bison throw, screwing to the three-four time of the Scorpions' "Rock You Like a Hurricane." The question: Is her brain working for, or against you? And do you have a say in the matter—the grey matter, that is?

THE WIRE

You see, Bush Pilots, while you will find your babe's cerebellum firmly located above her plunging neckline and under her crop of rivulet-like red hair, you will also find it roaming the rest of her lush countryside, either kicking up or striking out her sensual life. Despite your ability to make her beer bottle levitate and to surreptitiously recite the Spanish alphabet while giving her head, your babe's brain, not your tricks, is the kingpin here. If it is not convinced of your skill and loyalty, it will take you out.

Think of it as a very buff and stern Stringer Bell, sitting in a locked room on the top floor of a strip club, deciding how much sensation goes where when. Stringer is counting the money. Stringer is wearing the reading glasses. Stringer is ordering the hits. Stringer is handing out the promotions. It may be all G-strings and pasties and "Use Me" below, but upstairs, if Stringer thinks you're a snitch, he will, after he finishes his Campari, make you disappear. So how, Bush Pilots, can you coax your babe out of her brain and into her Joan Holloway body? Or more to the point, how can you recruit her brain, make it boss and make you family?

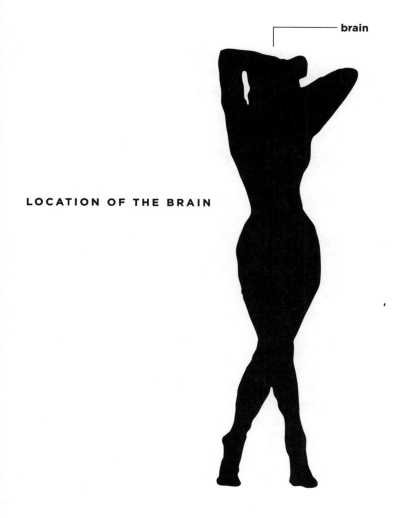

brain

LOCATION OF THE BRAIN

EXTRA CREDIT

AIR TRAFFIC CONTROL
TO BUSH PILOT

The following comments and scenarios mid-flight, however honeyed and propitious, will short-circuit your babe's pleasure:

"My mother can't wait to meet you."

"She's in the next room."

"She uses a hearing trumpet."

"And can see through walls."

"Whoever comes first is the winner!"

Bush Pilots, stress, anxiety, exhaustion, her heavy cargo and the stopwatch dangling from your neck will kill your babe's mood much in the way Bengay and a pantsuit will kill yours.

BRAIN WASHING

The bad news: Research about women's desire is inconclusive. Simply put, Boy Scouts, your tent-pitching is much easier to measure. What does that mean for you and your well-mannered boners?

The good news: There is nothing innate in the female brain to account for the divide we expect in the expression of desire. Your babe is not stuck with some less excitable gadgetry. Her brain is just as influential as your hardware; it can even be rewired with her own tools.

The result: Those compulsive naysayers that swarm her subconscious—panic, fear, worry, the grocery list—are supplanted by fresh (and I mean fresh) neurons.

THE OTHER F-WORD

Just as you picture yourself mounting The Body in her angel wings backstage at the Victoria's Secret show, your babe's desire (the hunger!) can also be cultivated. It can be courted; alongside the other things that make your babe tingle, it can be left offerings at the door—e.g., handcuffs, a cat mask, and Samuel L. Jackson. The operative word here is fantasy.

Bush Pilots, when you have earned it—which is, to clarify, not yet, Juniors—we will prowl fantasy's most salacious corners in Chapter 6. But in the meantime, because I am your bedroom de Bergerac, here it is: Your babe's fantasies are incendiary, even when you are not in them.

All right, all right. Unlock the bathroom door. Stop playing "Big in Japan" on your flute and put down your babe's Lemon Drop. I know, Bush Pilots, I know. You feel defeated. You feel extraneous. You feel like a stand-in. Here you are, drinking protein shakes and lifting dead weights with your tongue and then bringing that bit of fitness to her lady parts. And here she is, in her mind, licking cheap liquor off Mickey Rourke circa *Rumble Fish*. You are doing all of the work and getting none of the kudos. Great job, Motorcycle Boy, great job. Bush Pilots, I hear your sarcastic clapping.

So your babe's brain is duplicitous and weird. Trust me: You want it to be.

THIS IS HER BRAIN ON SEX

One babe (under the strobe lights of a biker bar) describes her sex brain as:

> My own personal movie in which my husband and/or multiple partners take part.

Another babe (who deserves a pet wolf) confesses:

> What turns me on most are my fantasies that happen at the same time as I'm having sex. There is usually a forest, and we are in the eighteenth or nineteenth century, and we are a gathering of men and women on horses stopping somewhere remote to hold a picnic. Naturally, I wear a voluminous skirt.
>
> I'll be eating and talking elegantly, removing my kid gloves finger by finger, while all kinds of dirty things are taking place under my skirt. A whole person could have snuck underneath it, and my kit is being invaded with all manner of instruments (candlesticks, the handle of my dandy companion's pocketknife, etc.).
>
> This is where sex in real time brings me out to a place where I can balance both fiction and fact. As I straddle my partner with his cock hard in front of me, he puts his fingers into my kit and I get this simultaneous sensation of having my mouth filled. Then I get flashes of the horses outside mounting one another by moonlight, and now my cunt is desirous, and it has this urgent longing to be filled too.

Um, what does this mean for me, Mistress? Must I hire horny steeds and be a "dandy companion"? No, my darlings, you must simply ensure your babe's fantasies (however demented, however Spartan) have the space to course through her mind—and, successively, her lady parts. Yes, Bush Pilots, your searing boner, your man musk and your football pants are all persuasive in the desire department—thank you for those—but your real hard sell: your babe's brain. Whether your doing or hers, it must be set off too.

We all learned ABC-early that our brains respond to repetition. Our brains respond to repetition. As with building any muscle, your babe repeats the exercise of her own pleasure. This takes practice. This takes time. This takes props. And, thankfully, this takes you.

CHAPTER 2

THE MAN PARTS

THE BOY NEXT DOOR

Just when she thinks she will die of boredom, a moving truck pulls up next door. Tara pops the bubble gum in her mouth, kicks the cat aside and saunters out to the front yard wearing nothing but her leotard, a worn copy of *Tiger Beat* in her hands. She wants a lollipop. She wants a Fanta. She wants a kiss. She wants a later curfew and an older boyfriend. She wants Don Johnson to love her. The movers are burly and less than handsome, and the furniture signals old people. Disappointment. Just then, from the passenger seat, he descends. He should have his own smoke machine. He looks at her. Tara wants to rush him like a screaming fan. Tara wants his autograph on her neck. Tara wants him naked and oiled. Instead, she turns around, snaps the elastic on her leotard and disappears into the backyard.

For the next week, Tara lies on her diving board, slathered with sun cream, bouncing lazily. She imagines him lying hard on top of her, and then not hard, and then hard and then not hard and then hard and then she rolls over and drops into the water. What is he doing in there? She has not seen him for days. Lunges? Kung fu? Arithmetic? Baking? Masturbating furiously in a fisherman's hat to the image of her lithe poolside repose?

Tara steals the telescope off the balcony, kills the lights, paints her face and places the lens against her bedroom window. It swings across his house. She tries to steady it. Fast. She hears the *Miami Vice* soundtrack in her head. She admits to herself she would be a terrible spy. She has a brother. She has a father. They vote Liberal. She has seen a penis. But she wants to see his. The lens climbs, quivering in her neophyte hands. It reaches his attic bedroom. Airplane curtains parted, there he is: full frontal. She swallows her gum. His lips are moving. "Your turn."

THE PARTY IN YOUR PANTS

Bush Pilots, you want to get busy. You want to put on "Fever"—the Peggy Lee version—and watch your babe strip at the foot of your bed and then be stunned when she stands there wearing nothing but a crystal merkin. And then you want to remove that merkin and apply all of your new-found anatomical intelligence to what lies beneath it.

Almost, my darlings, almost.

Why, oh why, not now, Mistress?

I know you will scoff. I know you will leer. And I know you will perform that lowest circus trick, the "whatevs" for men: the crotch grab. But the truth is, Bush Pilots, how can you expect a Captain

Goodscrew performance when you are not fully cognizant of your ace? Time to meet your man parts. Whoa, you protest winsomely, I know those parts. I visit those parts. Often. I have pet names for those parts. Those parts love me.

Yes.

But they could love you more.

NIPPLES (YES, YOURS)

Bush Pilots, are you in touch your twin peaks? Does asking you that prompt you to make a Freddie Mercury joke? If so, drop your clubs and lift your blouse. Your nipples were first declared an erogenous zone in the year 1937 by Theodore van de Velde, a Dutch gynecologist. So catch up, Bush Pilots. You have just as many nerve endings in your nipples as your babe does; as such, they are just as responsive to stimuli—e.g., tongues, teeth and clamps.

Still wary? You're not alone. One BP comments on his man-nips, "I've never liked it on myself. Chest kissing, okay, but not nipples." And another: "The only sensation is like a mild shock. So it's not really that pleasurable."

And heed this Bush Pilot Forum:

> BP #1: So, anyone like getting tweaked?
> BP #2: Wow, not what I expected you to ask. Not sure if I'd say that's any fun. Not better off for it.
> BP #3: Dude, that's painful. Like my shins. They hurt, don't touch them. Hot point. Ow. Shit.
> BP #4: Dude, come on.

But just when you were going to hang a PRIVATE PROPERTY sign over your man-nips, a babe (who could go by Fantasia) comes along with this boner-worthy rebuff:

> I was quite surprised to discover sensitive nipples in a certain man. It's definitely a role reversal, getting a guy off by flicking your tongue over his nipples. He writhed and I had to pin him down and he let me.

Another babe describes how her Bush Pilot liked to have his nipples "sucked on languorously." And yet another finds this middle, common ground:

> I've done it (nipple play) in conjunction with other manoeuvres, usually on the way down the body. And sometimes I've gotten "I actually enjoyed that" afterward. But it's never been a main thing or an asked-for thing. But if they have expressed a like of it, I will repeat.

BPs, as scouts of nerve endings, no sensation should be denied. (Bust out your man-nips!) I'm just saying.

YOUR PENIS

Hey, you! Otherwise known as your life partner and your life's work, your penis is that friendly—hey, you!—if unruly—hey!—fellow you pack into your Pilot pants every morning. As you have observed, he likes to be stroked, slapped, sucked and sent on frequent tropical vacations to that sweltering oasis, the butterfly. Bush Pilots, I am sure you will both agree: He is one game appendage.

PEPPERS

And yet, aside from his general felicity and obvious enthusiasm, Bush Pilots, your penis has other, more earnest aspects. Dare I say, gravitas.

It would be unfair to think of him solely as the bald good-time guy at the party with the wrap-around beer funnel, amiably yet erratically throwing confetti at other, bewildered party guests and willing to dance to anything. He is, despite your babe's nicknaming, not Seann William Scott. He is more Hamlet in a shaft of light than that guy.

Little does she know the pressure that rides on his sloped shoulders—and can you even call those shoulders? He is supposed to look different than he does. He is supposed to be bigger, longer, wider, not crooked, and circumcised—oh, now not circumcised . . . excuse me, I can't keep up. He is supposed to get hard when his babe whistles "Sharp Dressed Man." Does she know how difficult that is? And then, when he is hard, he is supposed to stay that way like some kind of single-celled organism for an indefinite period. All the while suavely locating these folkloric domains, supposedly pulsing unanswered throughout his babe's body in a high-stakes game of advanced penile hide and seek.

You know, he is not horny all of the time. Is that not manly enough, that admission? Should he get a monster truck, and kick in his plasma television set with his chainsaw boot and then hunt illegally? Some nights, he wouldn't mind a little private lie-down against the warmth of his own unspeaking thigh. In the comfort of his track pants. Curling up. Or maybe reclining undisturbed on the downstairs couch in nothing but a grey jockstrap. Is that not cool? Is that not hot? Some quiet, reflective penile time. To read. True, he reads. Wittgenstein. Just think, if left alone long enough, what roles he may have played, what books he might have written, what operas he might have composed. Laurence Olivier. That one's obvious. All of his roles apply. Charlton Heston, too. *Planet of the Apes, Ben-Hur, The Ten Commandments.* The book? *The Old Man and the Sea,* clearly. Or *Ulysses.* Or *The Three Musketeers.* The opera? It would have to be *Electra.*

Oh, and in the meantime, he is supposed to make his babe come, like, seventeen times until she leaves the really nice hotel room he has paid for with all the money he has earned not working too hard at something artful yet cunning.

WE'RE SO MADE FOR EACH OTHER

Bush Pilots, hush now. You see, while your babe does, at least once in her life, want to come seventeen times (in a really nice hotel room)— to tell you otherwise would be New Age and lying—she does not want you to be a slave to pressure, patterns or expectations. Why? They will wreck the sex. Do you see how much we have in common? There's more.

Outwardly, your penis is made up of a shaft; its cone head is the glans. On the uncircumcised Bush Pilot, the glans is tented by that peek-a-boo player, the foreskin. Densely populated with nerve endings, the glans is your cover of your babe's go-go—though, as I have mentioned, and will mention again with more affection than gloating, significantly pared down.

The elastic band beneath your glans is called the frenulum; much like the ligature that anchors your babe's go-go, you will (I stress, will) have noticed, your frenulum is one of your louder "ah" spots—as is the surrounding area, notably the crown-like ridge that forms the base of your glans.

Not to be confused with the wet-eyed wax museum of an actor, your raphe is the seam that runs from the tip of your foreskin, along the bottom of your shaft, down the centre of your pool boys, all the way to your kit. Bush Pilots, walk the line and find another Johnny cache of nerve endings.

The Penis

AN AERIAL VIEW OF YOUR ROCKIN' SHAFT

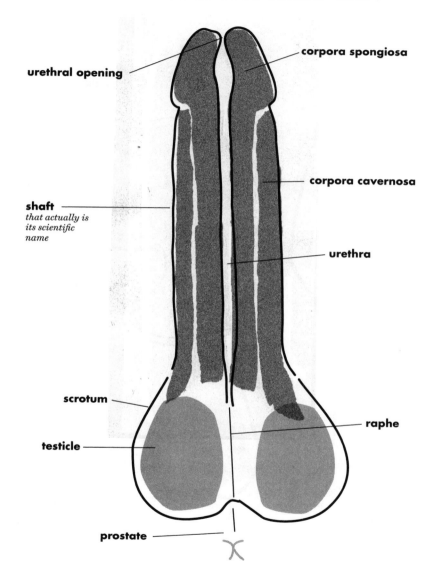

urethral opening

corpora spongiosa

corpora cavernosa

shaft
*that actually is
its scientific
name*

urethra

scrotum

raphe

testicle

prostate

Man Parts

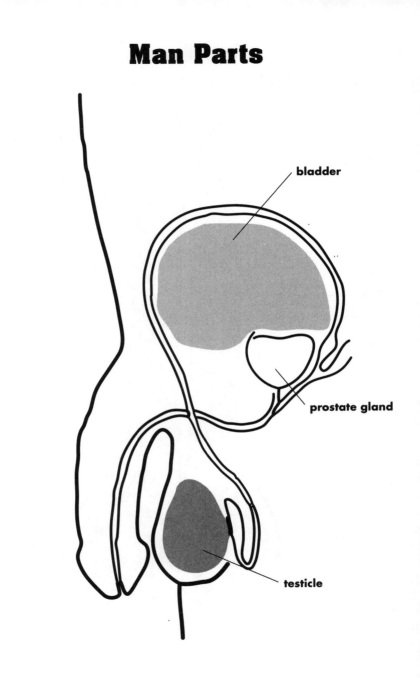

bladder

prostate gland

testicle

YOUR LOVELY BALLS

Forget snooker. Forget bowling. Forget bingo. Bush Pilots, your favourite balls to fondle are those unevenly hung, fast-dropping glands called your testicles. Because of their noble work manufacturing your swimmers and pumping out your testosterone, these sensitive princes are protected by that elderly bag known as your scrotum.

Unlike the consumptive, cloak-wearing royals it protects, your scrotum likes to play. Homely yet scrappy, it can be pulled, licked, pressed, constricted, tickled, cupped, slung into any manner of ring and sung to by yourself and others (try anything by Journey). But rest assured, when duty calls and your future kings are sunk in frigid—or hot—waters, your muscular scrotum will lift your testicles up toward the safe house of your body.

About your nuts, one babe (a flirt and a ruffian) writes:

> Women just think penis. It's actually penis plus balls. They are equal to each other. That's the secret equation. Cupping is vital. There can never be enough cupping.

(Yes, you may read that quote aloud to your babe in her hot pants, and then shrug as if to say, "Who knew?")

ALL ABOUT YOUR BONER

Boys, would you believe your dark and handsome boner is even taller than he looks? By half? Did you just buy a Hummer? And call it the Shady Mobile? And are you freestyling to "My Name Is"? All right, Bush Pilots. Hold on to your flight missions.

Let's take it inside. Like your babe's go-go, your penis extends into your body and then splits in a wishbone shape. Its ends latch onto the base of your pubic bone. That's all fascinating, Mistress, but (you inquire suggestively) can we bring it back to my totally rocking shaft? How is it that, you ask—truly confounded now—my totally rocking shaft is harder than my totally rocking pecs and traps when I don't even crush it at the gym?

Bush Pilots, your penis has two internal chambers that run its length and account for most of your totally rocking girth. Think of them as twin power lines; rather than electricity, the corpora cavernosa deliver your boners. Parallel cylinders composed of spongy tissue, each bull's-eyed by its own major artery, they, when aroused (which is so much of the time!) are engorged with blood and, to your undiminished awe and delight, harden and grow.

Below these magnanimous double currents, along the bottom of your penis, lies a third, smaller, power line: your urethra. Surrounded by the corpora spongiosa, which also make up the merry glans of your penis, your urethra starts at your bladder, barrels through your prostate gland and ends in the spout for your signature (swimmers plus prostate plus seminal brew) and your pee, the urethral opening. Hot. So hot.

A word on the word penis. Penis. Does it make you think of a vinyl nurse's outfit pornographically filled out and coming toward you to the beat of "Dirty Deeds Done Dirt Cheap"? Penis. Does it make you think of having a threesome with Megan Fox and who cares who else on the back of your Zamboni? Me neither. Bush Pilots, your penis will heretofore be called a promiscuity of euphemisms, most of which are the names of rap moguls or sports personalities. Congratulations, stud. Or should I say, Terrell.

DUDE, WHERE'S MY ASS?

Attention, Bush Pilots: nerve endings. Just below your bladder, at the very root of your penis, your urethra is gift-wrapped by the prostate gland. Gift-wrapped, you say, Mistress? By wanton elves in skin-tight red dresses with bells for trim who sit on my knee and whisper their wishes in my ear with a Brazilian accent? Yes.

I know your prostate gland makes you think of Fletch in his hospital gown singing "Moon River," but Bush Pilots, the equivalent to our

G-spot, your prostate gland is a second source of your swimmers—and, more important, home to the infamous P-spot. Most Bush Pilots discover this erogenous zone late in adulthood when they finally loosen up, imitate The Dude, start surfing and try butt plugs. With the revelation of their P-spot akin to stumbling upon a second Big Lebowski, they really wish they had found it earlier.

The P-spot can be massaged externally or, for more intense and direct stimulation, internally. Roger that, Bush Pilots: To get into this very private, roped-off club (you always thought was gay), you must go in through the out door. It is time to bare your backyard. It is time to look . . .

BEHIND DOOR NUMBER TWO

Let's admit it: This is your sexual hinterland, your unchartered territory. Of all the players in your nether regions, this is your shy choirboy. But when a finger or tongue brushes by your back gate, you are secretly startled by the sensations ignited throughout your totally rocking body. You don't know whether to shift toward them or away from them. They are so new. They are so prohibited. If you ask for more, will your babe think you're into window dressings and small dogs in purses?

No, knucklehead.

As the people of *The Good Vibrations Guide to Sex* say, "sexual orientation is not defined by how you fuck, but who you fuck." So, Bush Pilots, drop your sloppy joe inhibitions. Your backyard is packed with erogenous possibility and is home to such luminaries as the aforementioned P-spot and the million-dollar point.

> In the beginning, we'll call her Shona, Shona would touch lightly around my ass during a blowjob. I was far from receptive at first, but she is a persistent woman. I finally did allow her to put a finger inside me and I was surprised by the way it felt.
> —Bush Pilot (contractor with his own business, three lovers in friendly rotation)

Treasure Map

SOME TABOO LOCATIONS THAT YOU SHOULD TOTALLY GO TO

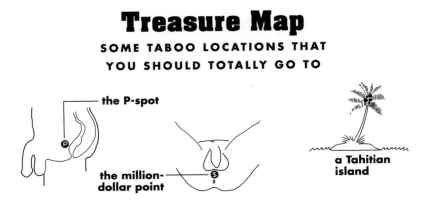

the P-spot

the million-dollar point

a Tahitian island

THE P-SPOT

Bush Pilots, in Chapter 1, with headlamps on and compasses primed, you so assiduously studied your babe's bum. Guess what? Kit for kit, yours is a match. Let's review. Approximately one inch in length, your anus, like hers, is the front foyer for your rectum—which, you will recall, is a vast recreation centre measuring five to nine inches in length.

That firm bit of infamy: The P-spot, formerly known as Puff Daddy, now Diddy, brother to your Notorious B.I.G., and answer to your favourite fly girl, the G-spot, is two to three inches inside your rectum. Latitude and longitude: behind your pubic bone and below your bladder. Like a studded collar, it wraps itself around the thin neck of your urethra. Bush Pilot Bonus: This heat-packing gland lies along those excitable pelvic (rather than pudendal) nerve pathways between your brain and your Busta Rhymes, spelling your name with a sparkler: BUSH PILOT. YO.

While you may treat it as a loner locked up and scratching the walls in solitary, appreciate your prostate's central positioning. It is actually a kingpin. Among other allies, it has your sphincter and perineum muscles in its thick, flexing Rolodex. In other words, when it says come, you just might.

Intrigued? As you do when soliciting your babe's Luscious G, stroke toward your stomach. To the touch, your P-spot will feel firm and walnut (or, as you age, Ping Pong ball) sized. Bush Pilot Bonus: Reaching your P-spot can be a contortion. Instead of throwing out your back again, let your paramour's fingers, and her deft handling of a well-lubricated toy, do the trick (see Chapter 3).

THE MILLION-DOLLAR POINT

There is more.

Like the pornographic film starring Desiree Cousteau, *Inside Desiree Cousteau*, the name says it all: the million-dollar point. Bush Pilots, with your Magnum P.I., you knew you had beach access and an ocean view. But who knew your back forty was prime real estate too? You will find your million-dollar point where that diamond in the rough, your perineum, meets your anus. A milestone, your million-dollar point has as many nerve endings as your mouth—think ice cubes, think nipples, think ice cubes on nipples.

How to be a millionaire? Explore the area the sexperts call your "taint" (pronunciation: "taint") with varied levels of pressure. In the Bush Pilot's appropriation of Scout's Honour, begin with three fingers—yours or your babe's—placed firmly across. Or have your babe nudge her knee up against your million-dollar point while she gives you transcendent head. You may also employ the buzz of a vibrator, or, if frightened of electrics, the tease of your babe's spider fingers. Your instruction: Play in your million-dollar point, and in playing, identify your preferences. Bush Pilot Bonus: You can only get richer.

Bush Pilots, your kit, like your babe's, is a keen part of your orgasm. It shares in your engorgement and your contractions when you come. To ignore it would be like laying down a drum solo with no crash cymbal. Curious? So are we.

A SHORT NOTE ON SIZE:
SHAFT! CAN YOU DIG IT?

Bush Pilots, it could be preceded by the *Monday Night Football* theme song and followed by Beethoven's *Fifth Symphony*. It is the bar-raising moment of every first encounter, for you and for your babe: the unveiling of your tackle. It is the black velvet pulled from the trophy, the ump's final call, your full disclosure. Together, topless as wrestlers, your babe speculates, between tumbles, leg drops, superkicks and—whoa—moonsaults, just what lies beneath those Heartbreak Kid tights. Those paint-splattered Carhartts. Those oil-streaked coveralls. Just what kind of heat are you packing, Bush Pilot? Peewee or panther? What is it going to be?

THE LEGEND OF BIGFOOT

Despite the statisticians' compulsive attempts to arrive at a median number, there is no definitive answer as to the length of the average Bush Pilot's member. (Hey, you!) I know, BPs, you wonder: Where does Peppers fit in? (Hey!) From Kinsey to the Bulge Report, your boner measured like a balance beam parallel to the floor, figures fluctuate between four and a half and seven inches. Bush Pilot Bonus: Many of you will think you are too small, when really, my darlings, you are not; most likely, your monkey is in the middle. Double Bush Pilot Bonus: The biggest human penis on record is thirteen and a half inches (erect), wears metallic pants . . . and lives with his mother.

Before you bring a tape measure to your Hulk Hogan, let's regress, steal the Drambuie from your parents' liquor cabinet, and take a ride on the rumour mill. Luminaries purported to reside in the House of Dong include: Milton Berle, apparently not just equine of face; Jimi Hendrix, who, according to Cynthia P. Caster, did in fact break the plaster cast; and—note well, Bush Pilots—in a turn that demonstrates the futility of assumptions, the brothers Cassidy. Whoa, Mistress, you respond gamely, who knew among those velour-shirted pop geeks were actual birds of prey? Yes, Bush Pilots, this does give new meaning to the Partridge Family. Gold star!

The "who knew" factor is something babes have been trying to decode for centuries. Do you have a penis that deserves its own postal code, or its own pincushion? Either way, Captain Goodscrew laments, and then (observe closely, boys) galvanizes himself:

> After overhearing the conversations women have amongst themselves, I was determined not to be one of their anecdotes. They disseminate information about dick size, hardness, skill set, who else the man has slept with and bad breath.

PARDON THE INTERRUPTION

Babe 1: After some time, the guy actually stopped fucking me and looked down and said, "Es tu endormi?!" (Translation: Are you asleep?!) He was outraged. Well, jeez, my friend, if you're gonna pump me like a spare tire, whaddaya 'spect?

Babe 2: Like the Energizer Bunny, but faster.

Babe 3: Like a toothpaste tube, but travel size. But smaller.

Babe 4: Rough, awkward, non-feeling, in Halloween costumes on top of a building—after which I ran for my life.

Babe 5: Quick and dirty. Take both of those literally—while tree-planting.

Babe 6: Getting flopped around like a fish out of water. Very sweet fellow, though. Sadly, that did it.

Like hushed but way hotter gangsters, babes convene in underground hideouts, holding up salt shakers and ketchup bottles—and matchsticks—as illustrative props. Like spies, but way less discreet, babes trade secrets. Like dimwits, but way smarter, babes dole out nicknames for your Mr. Daydream from the 1970s Mr. Men series:

Mr. Tall, Mr. Skinny, Mr. Perfect, Mr. Slow, Mr. Worry, Mr. Rush, Mr. Lazy, Mr. Quiet, Mr. Rude, Mr. Clumsy, Mr. Forgetful and, of course, Mr. Small. It is now, Bush Pilots, that I must deliver the difficult and contentious truth from my cabal (incoming!): If you are one extreme or the other, your size matters. Instruction: Talk about it. You are baring your hot parts. Why don't you and your babe try to bare your self-consciousness too? Heed this testament:

> Too small was not an impossible impasse. As one of the owners put it, it's the size of the fight of the dog, not the size of the dog in the fight. And thinking back, my two petites harnessed other talents with more passion, and perhaps more creativity. The big dick can breed laziness.
> —Babe (BMX, sequin dress)

DAVID VS. GOLIATH

For the Time Bandits and the Tom Thumbs of the hot dog crowd, I would love to pour you a glass of Quik, throw my arm around you before a roaring fire and tell you: It is all in how you play the game. But that would be a partial truth and a false comfort.

That said, consider the following: If you were in a lineup with other primates, you would no doubt be picked out, for you are lengthier and thicker than even a gorilla. Also, if you had lived in ancient Greece, you would have been plucked from the general unwashed to pose for painters and sculptors who saw the smaller sword as desirable. Or, my Bush Pilots, most tellingly, examine Michelangelo's *David*. Not exactly overwhelming in his proportions, and yet, whom did he slay? None other than that frothing goon, Goliath.

My suggestions for you, Little Leaguers: Remember, your shortstop is not the sum of your parts. Never overlook the blaze of glory that is the talented tongue and the nimble hand.

Note the placement of CAPS:

One of the best I can remember was this guy who was a wine dealer. He was quite cute, and we met to talk about importing wine. Things got a little hot and heavy and we ended up at my place. It was quite sensual. We started touching and feeling and I realized he was not so well endowed. Seriously. He had the smallest penis on the planet—not a third of an inch. I tried to play with it, but even hard, it was almost nonexistent. I could tell he was shy and embarrassed by it, and he kept telling me to lie back while he pleasured me. MAN. I guess, due to the lack of man stick, this MAN knew how to use the tongue. He licked his way down my bod and then did some type of magic down in the nether regions!! It was obvious that he has learned and overcompensated. He made me scream, and it was excellent. When we went in for the sex part, I seriously didn't know if he was in me at all (I didn't feel a thing), but God love the man!

Alongside your other very worthy, highly specialized offerings, make friends with your tiny Elvis. Include him in the party. Recall: Most of the butterfly's nerve endings are in the first third, which roughly translates into the first two inches of the vaginal canal or less. Exhibit A: One babe cites "a tryst with an on-the-small-side" Bush Pilot as "multi-orgasmic, so it just kind of reinforced my belief that bigger is not necessarily better."

WHO DAT?

On that note, for those of you nine-inch Nelsons wearing your bicycle shorts to the bar, stop strutting. You could choke your babe with that thing. Or hurt her—or hurt yourself.

I had one experience on a night out with a very large, handsome man who, as it later turned out, had a shockingly large occupant. I knew there was no way it was going to work. It was terrifying. Contrary to what most men think, a too-giant penis is actually far worse than a tiny one. So there was a lot of foreplay that ended with terror for me (and alas, no consummation) and serious blue balls for him.

—Babe (most likely to cartwheel and come at the same time)

My advice to you, XXX-Large Bush Pilots: Lube up and slow down. Also appreciate: Most babes prefer girth to length. Why? Rather than a long wand, it is the flare of width that puts pressure on her go-go, which—as you undoubtedly recall—presides over her pleasure. So, Bush Pilots, the long and the short of it: unless we are size queens . . .

A big Johnson can't buy our love, but a Magic Johnson can.

MY, WHAT A PHAT DENALI YOU HAVE

Bush Pilots, you look and look so furtively and try not to appear dodgy or like a perv; you even got the tinted windows and those huge shades, but try as you might, conclusions about other Bush Pilots (who did the "Bump N' Grind" with your babe) cannot be drawn in the shower, on the field, in the boardroom or from the gold detail on his high-tops.

The aforementioned factors—as well as what an (ex) Bush Pilot bench-presses, his height, his weight, his race and his freakish piano-playing digits—also do not correlate to his cup. There are no predictor kits and no quick conversions here, BPs; just as when your Fall Guy is flaccid, there is no way to determine what he will be like when he is Lee Majors–hard. Grower or shower? Only your babe, sitting in your office after hours, wearing nothing but a trench coat and heels, can answer that.

THROW DOWN YOUR CRUTCHES!

For some Bush Pilots, size is an obsession rivalling any spiritual quest; essentially, they are looking to put the Big Guy, not in their prayers, but in their Pilot pants. This has inspired a quackish industry of enhancement, which, like any promised miracle spun by preachers, medicine men and mad inventors, comes in some unbelievable forms.

First, do no harm; that's one of the tenets of the healthcare system.

—Dr. Stubbs

SUPERSIZE ME

Surgery to lengthen your Thin White Duke is most famously performed in this country by, I kid you not, Dr. Stubbs, who learned his trade in China from, I kid you not, Dr. Long. When asked just how many centimetres he could add, certified plastic surgeon Stubbs answered (from under his long white beard and star-covered cape), "The average gain is 3.2 centimetres, but the most I've ever gotten is six centimetres. For a guy who has got a four-inch penis, this is a phenomenal improvement." He then added, "Some guys lost because they didn't follow the aftercare." These operations cost thousands of dollars, and, should you land near the knife of a charlatan, they can leave you with a noduled, scarred, and horizontal hard-on. In the cautionary age of (R.I.P.) Michael Jackson (I love you), I would urge you, if reading this book in the waiting room of a cosmetic surgery clinic: Beware the huckster in the white suit. Study the consent form closely. My darling Bush Pilots, not unlike your precious brain, you have only the one.

EXTRA CREDIT

YOUR BABE DOES NOT WANT TO SEE YOU:

☞ Edward Scissorhands-ing your pubes into a Faux Cock.

☞ downing two Aspirin before going for your Brozilian.

☞ dangling her glass paperweight from your Hans.

☞ jelqing your Franz.

☞ pantless and lisping, "D.I.Y. surgery."

☞ pantless and lisping.

☞ going on a grapefruit diet.

☞ in clamps.

☞ in a water wing.

☞ giddily scrolling through the testimonials on GetBigDong.com.

☞ angrily making a soup of red ginseng and tiger claws.

☞ I repeat, tiger claws.

☞ popping "pills" that only make you fart more.

☞ explaining penile athletics to your trainer.

☞ never nude.

☞ worry so much.

THIS SORT OF THING IS MY BAG, BABY

BPs, one of the more common and Austin Powers–worthy props in the battle for the bulge is the penis pump. Remember when you were twelve and living in the suburbs and you had the bungalow to yourself and, while thinking about Cheryl Tiegs, you eyed the vacuum cleaner and decided to plug it in and put your pubescent pecker in its hungry hose? The penis pump is the adult take on this early experiment. Placing your penis in a cylinder, you pump the air out. The pressure inflates your blood flow and, in turn, your size.

Please note: The effect is as temporary as donning an ascot and badger teeth and saying things like, "Danger is my middle name." Second, if buying a pump, drop your bagpipes and don't be cheap. Third, as important as having a spotter at the gym, always use a thick, water-based lube while pumping—both on the interior of the cylinder and on your International Man of Mystery. And fourth, please, no more than fifteen minutes at a time or risk bruising your Boy Scout.

DO YOU HAVE ANY
ARTIFICIAL PLATES OR LIMBS?

Remember the bassist from *This Is Spinal Tap*? He of the formidable moustache and shag haircut? He of the produce section packed into his pants, getting busted by the loud R2D2-like drone of a metal detector at airport security? Bush Pilots, do not let that be you. Consider the aptly named Derek Smalls a cautionary tale to you all, and keep your cucumbers where they belong: in the bottom drawer of your fridge.

THE SUM OF YOUR PARTS

At the end of the day, with its downturned face and low-slung balls, your penis really is a sad and funny-looking bloke. A tragicomic organ, he is the Charlie Chaplin of the body. That said, boys, give your Tramp the attention he deserves; put away your ruler and give him a hand, a ring, a vibrating sleeve, or the flick of your paramour's tongue. Bush Pilots, the only way to cultivate a true sense of largeness is, of course, through the one thing that cannot be sold: love.

(You can drink now. No. Not eight beers.)

CHAPTER 3
TOOLS OF THE TRADE

SLIDING INTO HOME

Hugo, a pork bellies trader in a mid-weight suit, is sitting in his car, wipers on high, listening to the suicide strain of The Smiths, wondering if the planet is indeed sliding into the ocean. Hugo cannot face his doom. He is due for another blind date.

Grabbing his trench coat, he walks, hunched, into the bar, looking for a "petite redhead." He knows what that means. And yet, there she is, exactly as promised. Hugo is dumbstruck. It's Gigi. Twenty years ago, Hugo and Gigi rolled around in his neighbourhood ravine until Gigi had to catch the bus to meet her curfew. They have not seen each other since. Looking at her now, Hugo considers whether she has been the source of his soulful disease. Motorcycle boots, a smock-topped dress from the fifties, Gigi strides over to him. "Let's go," she says, her voice just as gravelly as it was then, "to the ravine."

Twenty minutes later, with her dress gathered up around her waist, mud streaking her legs and arms, Gigi unzips Hugo's fly. Before she touches him, she does something he has never seen before. The equivalent of pausing for prayer, Gigi pulls a bottle from her purse and rubs a cream into her hands. Too stunned to inquire, Hugo surrenders to the most astronomically perfect handjob ever known to man. Looking into the cosmos, in love with everything—the squirrels, the owls, the drunks roving nearby—Hugo asks, "What was that?" But Gigi is gone. Hugo wants to call out to her. He has one last question. Not about whether they are two halves of one entity split apart by a cruel universe, but about the bottle. What was in the bottle?

LUBE

Bush Pilots, you want to get busy. You want to put on your medley— "Father Figure," "When Doves Cry," "Jump," "Save a Prayer" and "The Final Countdown"—and strip at the end of your babe's bed. Mostly in jest. You've hung some chili pepper lights and put on devil horns. You're wearing your tearaway goalie pants and you've got your Sher-Wood goalie stick for a pole. You've practised some stripper moves and feel fairly confident about your back hook, your crucifix and your sun wheel. You tear away, and whoa, what's this: your New Jersey Devils tearaway goalie shorts. Pleather. Your babe quickly slips a bill into them. She wants to remove them. Immediately. For a few reasons, including applying all of your new-found anatomical intelligence to what lies beneath them.

Almost, my darlings, almost.

Why, oh why, not now, Mistress?

Bush Pilots, there is sex, and then there is better sex. The differential? Lube, toys and, of course, safety.

We'll start with the lube—not the lube you used in those heady days of humping your bathtub, your CHiPs pillow and your stuffed bear. Not the Crisco, the Vaseline or your mother's hand lotion, but lube designed by aerospace engineers to mimic the sultriness of saliva and those more southerly secretions, making for just the right combination of freedom and friction. Lube is booming. And you, my John Bakers, my Frank Poncherellos, my Pilots of the Bush, are missing something if you don't boom right along with it.

DISPEL THE LUBRICATION MYTH

We make the assumption that natural lubrication is directly proportionate to desire. Untrue. Your prowess notwithstanding, many factors can modify your babe's wetness: hormonal changes linked to pregnancy, breastfeeding, menopause, a hysterectomy, The Pill. Moreover, the hooch you had with dinner and the herb you smoked after, cold medications and antidepressants—not to mention those bonneted killjoys, stress and shame—can also disturb her dew. Furthermore, the toy department, with its seemingly innocent offerings like Randy, Bandit and Buck, can, like soft straws, suck up her juice.

If you have condom sex, you must use lube. Even the juiciest pussy gets dry after fucking for thirty minutes. I bring a little kit with condoms and lube everywhere I go. Everywhere! Nothing is more tragic than not having condoms when a fucking opportunity presents itself.

—Captain Goodscrew

Tool of Seduction

THE BUSH PILOT'S SURVIVAL KIT

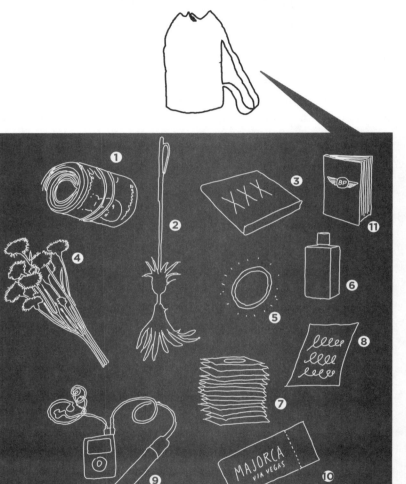

1. cab fare 2. quiver crop (with feathers) 3. *Behind the Green Door* on DVD
4. flowers (Centaurus cyranus) 5. cock ring (shiny) 6. fancy lube 7. condoms (lots)
8. her address 9. vibrator and iPod (playing Cat Power's "Jukebox") 10. plane ticket
(out of town) 11. *How to Be a Bush Pilot: A Field Guide to Getting Luckier*
12. Your mojo (not pictured)

LET'S GET CLINICAL

Bush Pilots, look at lubrication from an anatomical perspective. Your babe's butterfly is not a far-reaching sprinkler system. Her lady nectar cannot completely hose down her go-go. To boot, as you studied in Chapter 1, your babe's back door is not her butterfly; it needs ample buttering, as it churns no butter of its own. Also, do not overlook your affable, flashlight-swinging security guard, latex; he too is thirsty. The bottom line: Whatever your babe's state (or yours), store-bought lube bolsters your love play.

That's all fascinating, Mistress, but tell me again, does lube mean I'm lame? No, Bush Pilots, using lube does not mean you have failed at foreplay and should start calling yourself Pathos and do knife tricks in restaurants. The opposite is true. Take Captain Goodscrew's expertise. Now pretend it is your own. It is the Bush Pilot who does not bring his lube "Everywhere!" who loses. Lube tells your babe you know what you are doing. Its absence? Novice.

> Sometimes, just the presence of some slickness applied suddenly gets things going for real, almost immediately. Not to fool me into thinking it's my own wetness—I know the difference. But the simple suggestion of wetness is often enough to trigger the mainline.
> —Babe (a black belt and a burlesque performer)

Bush Pilots, there is an abundance of choice in the lube laboratoire. When buying, narrow your choices by taking into account content and purpose. Ask yourself: Where am I heading? What is the forecast? Will there be butt plugs? Beads? Fisting? Humidity? Water play? Or, oh wait, am I flying solo?

ALLERGEN ALERT

Hear the sirens? Bush Pilots, before you pour, examine the ingredients. If you or your babe has any skin sensitivities, test the lube on the inside of her wrist before her wishing well. Wait twenty-four hours before using it in sexual congress. (Sucks, I know.) Look out for the following: glycerin (sweet and suspected, though not proven, to cause yeast and bladder infections) and parabens (a preservative that can cause an allergic reaction).

Sticky Note: As if the name were not prohibitive enough, please avoid that outdated spermicide, nonoxyl-9. It will irritate your babe's butterfly and the tender membranes that line her kit. Bush Pilots, not only is it a detergent, but it tastes like one too.

OIL

Like our political candidates, lube comes in three distinct forms: oil-, water- and silicone-based. If, as I suspect, you are planning on doing anything with your babe, from stroking to screwing, you must absolutely avoid door number one. Oil-based lubes (à la Vaseline) wreck latex; they will destroy her diaphragm, your Japanese condoms and Glyde dental dams. Incompatible with safer sex, oil-based lubes are hard to find.

Not for the lady, and not for the latex

Another significant drawback: Oil-based lubes are difficult to wash out of her butterfly and, like cheap graffiti on her walls, can linger for days, leading to a proliferation of bacteria (and your subsequent banishment from the neighbourhood).

As such, oil-based lube is for your palm tree only. Handjob or hand solo, look for ingredients like vitamin E, aloe and shea butter. Try the classic Albolene cream, the smooth and never-sticky petroleum-based

Stroke It, or Boy Butter, which even comes (just like you) with an "EZ Pump."

<u>WATER</u>

Water-based lubes account for the vast majority of what you will find on the shelves of your local sex shop and drug store. Why? Most important, they are safe with all precautionary accoutrements—dams, finger cots, gloves and rubbers. Bush Pilot Bonus: They are close to flavourless, least likely to stain your sheets and will not, unlike those oil barons listed above, overstay their welcome and pollute her environment. The best water-based lubes are (drum roll, please):

Probe. The classic, Probe is distinguished by its stringy consistency and its short list of ingredients. It is an excellent paraben-free option.

Hathor Aphrodisia. Neither sticky nor fragrant, this lube is composed of pure ingredients including two aphrodisiacs: horny goat weed (which, sadly, BPs, you cannot roll up and smoke) and Siberian ginseng.

Astroglide. Mister Popular, Astroglide was designed by a former NASA scientist who was clearly abiding by NASA's motto: "For the benefit of all." Its thin consistency makes it a non-intrusive accompaniment to any sex play. Suburban Bush Pilot in Dad Jeans Bonus: You can buy it at Walmart. Just ask the lady in the blue vest. Double Bonus: Now available in a glycerin- and paraben-free formulation.

Liquid Silk. It lives up to its name, but is slightly bitter in taste. Also note (for you fine-print types): Liquid Silk is technically a hybrid; it has enough silicone in it to make it last, but not enough to sabotage your silicone toys.

Ruby Sunrise Lubricant. Handing out C-notes to strangers for kicks? This water-based gel has a most promising, if leading, tagline: Clitoris Climax Cream. Bush Pilots, aside from your opportunity to wow her with alliteration, this gel is, like your babe, honey-flavoured. The rub: It is not a magic potion; without your informed application, the climax stays in the bottle.

Despite their versatility, the drawback of water-based lubes is that, while they enhance, they also evaporate and must be reapplied. The solution? Water begets water. Operating from that generous principle, reignite your babe's wet spots with saliva or a squirt from any other water conduit (aside from your Supercannon II—unless, of course, that's her thing).

SILICONE

Silicone-based lubes, by contrast, have infinite slide and, in turn, are the fastest-growing option on the market. I know, bearded, back-to-the-land Bush Pilots, silicone is the filthiest of all the S-words. I know. But in this case, you need not be put off by that slur against the skin. Why? These nectars are completely non-toxic. Another boon: You can put on your flippers and screw in the pond on your off-the-grid property. Silicone-based lubes will last in a lake, the shallow end of any stranger's kidney-shaped pool and the Maid of the Mist. Slightly pricier, they are just the way we want you: sleek without being greasy.

The best silicone-based lubes are (guitar solo, please):

Eros. Just don't say it aloud when pouring it onto your man-paws. Safe for your sheath and for her body electric, and excellent for slip and endurance, Eros can be used for any part of your love play. The hitch? It requires more cash, more cleanup and—note well, Bush Pilots—silicone lubes cannot be used in conjunction with silicone toys.

You don't want to take the heat for damaging your babe's beloved Big D.

Sliquid Organics Silk. This lube is half-water and half-silicone. Glycerin- and paraben-free, it has both the slip and the staying power.

Pink. The invention of a group of ex-Marines who were, when thirsting in the desert, left only with the option of gun oil. These ex-Marines then made a product called Gun Oil (in name only) and served it up in bullet-shaped bottles. How gauche! Deal-breaker Alert: These will shoot down your babe's tingles and make for her sit-in rather than your bed-in. Instruction: Choose an identical product, the peace-signing Pink. With added vitamin E and aloe vera for durability, Pink goes the distance.

FOR YOUR ASS ONLY

Bush Pilots, when it comes to the much slower-paced backdoor play, choose a lube that is thick and long-lasting. Avoid anything specifically marketed for anal play, as these dullards are often full of analgesics and numb the sensations that you or your babe want to engage and, if necessary, temper. Leave the freezing to her rich dentist.

SEX WAX: THE BEST FOR YOUR KIT

For good slip and no stain:

Maximus. From the makers of Liquid Silk, Maximus will not chew up your dildos, prostate toys, cotton sheets or condoms. Its gel-like consistency, designed specifically for anal play, will cling to your sensitive, slow-loving kit. Bummer: The complaint department says a slightly bitter taste.

Slippery Stuff. Like Maximus, Slippery Stuff is substantial but silken, enduring but easily showered off. Unlike Maximus, Slippery Stuff is nearly tasteless and odourless. N.B.B.P.: Both of these water-based lubes are glycerin free, though they have parabens.

Astroglide Gel. Perfect for a hump-a-thon, this stuff sticks. From the makers of the interplanetary Astroglide, the gel is its thicker cousin (every family has one) and is sold in drugstores. Downer: Does contain glycerin and parabens.

Expecting Company?

TRY THIS HANDY LUBE COMPATIBILITY CROSS-CHECK

type	compatible with	not compatible with	operating conditions
oil	**your unputdownable man parts**	**her lady parts, your latex**	**your private love for your unputdownable man parts**
water-based	**latex, her lady parts, your man parts, sex toys**	**allergies to parabens and glycerins (if applicable)**	**versatile, especially when close to a water source (like say a hotel pool)**
thicker water-based	**latex, her lady parts, your man parts, your sex toys, her kit, your kit (you name it)**	**allergies to parabens and glycerins (if applicable)**	**same as above**
silicone	**latex, her lady parts, your man parts**	**silicone sex toys, your sheets, allergies to parabens and glycerin (if applicable)**	**hump-a-thon**
Nonoxyl-9	**shuffleboard**	**her lady parts, your man parts**	**any activity that might lead to the application of "Vanishing Scent" Bengay**

EXTRA CREDIT

KICKING IT OLD SCHOOL

BPs, there is foreplay. And then there is afterplay. You often miss that part because you are sleeping cherubically or are perhaps unconscious; sometimes, it's hard to tell.

Post-screw, lead your babe down your narrow hallway, past your punching bag and the stacks of your dad's old *Playboy*s. Bring candles. Do not set anything on fire. Enter your bathroom, which you scrubbed clean in anticipation of your babe's arrival and yearned-for disrobing. Fill your claw-foot tub. With hot water. This is called a bath.

A Bathtub

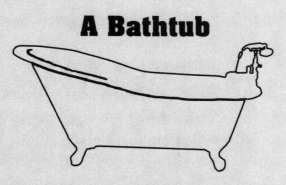

USE IT

Submerge. Wash your babe (Y.B.) with soap and water. Let her wash you. Steam your windows, and then, when you get out of the tub, write your initials on the steamed window. Encase in a heart shape. The lesson: No one is too cool for old school.

B.P. + Y.B.

SO CLOSE I CAN TASTE IT

Preference, the desire to mask the taste of latex or to add-on to your oral may lead you to flavoured lubes. Suggestions from the Bush Pilot Taste-Test Lab: O'My's all-natural Cappucino and Melon (sugar-free, water-based) or Good Clean Love's Mint. If you are trying to conceive, do not use any of the lubes mentioned above, as they will, like a science-fiction plague, slow and kill your swimmers. Instead, look into Pre-Seed. And if you are a Bush Pilot forager in the woods, weave your own clothing from your beard and know the year only from the angle of the sun, I have not forgotten about you. You can always try egg whites or aloe—or the first organic, vegan lube of the lot: Capotain's Strawberry Frenzie. Send up a smoke signal, and I will get it to you.

The only rule: Find what works for you and your babe. The fun, of course, is in the trying. So get messy. Get slick. And, for the sake of the ace screw, find out what's in the bottle—before it's too late.

VIBRATOR-R-RS: BEST FRIEND OR WORST ENEMY?

Sideman or stiff competition? My Bush Pilots, like our stereos, our cell phones and everything else that can be plugged in or run on batteries, the vibrator is evolving at lightning speed. As sophisticated pleasure scouts, you must keep up with it. If not, you will be left behind in the unforgiving dust of a flat planet circled by the sun. Like gravity, like guitar licks, the vibrator is not going away. It is in our purse. It is in our pants. So why not yours too? My advice: Join the modern age. Show your babe her friends are your friends too.

You will not be electrocuted, abandoned or replaced.

Bush Pilots, our vibrators cannot flirt, pour wine or spoon us. Thank you for that. They are simply a tool for pleasure, not solely for your babe's skilful use but for yours as well. Your babe's vibrator is distinguished from her dildo in that (listen closely now) it vibrates. Depending on its properties, a vibrator can be used for both penetration and for titillating her go-go. Another advantage: Hands, tongues and, I know it is outlandish to say, but even your beloved centre fielder can tire. Vibrators cannot. As such, they are often the spiritual homeland to many first orgasms—reached in a matter of seconds.

The pleasures of youth will throb within you.

("You" being your girlfriend.)

The history: Invented in the Victorian age to cure "hysteria," the vibrator was quickly freed from the medical world and adopted by the masses. Marketed in women's catalogues, the corsets of yore didn't need much convincing to become "glow getters." A century later, the consumer is that much more savvy. Gone are the days of the groaning, dwarf-sized, peach-coloured dong. To meet the mojo of today, manufacturers have had to step it up. Vibrators are being designed by aerospace engineers and sold as objets at Fred Segal to the likes of that peerless pussycat, Kate Moss. Babes know what they want and are not afraid to ask for it: beauty, quality and a "don't stop" button. Sound familiar?

It makes you fairly tingle with the joy of living.

("You" being your girlfriend.)

FLIPPER JR.

While we are, um, on it, let's immediately dispel the vibrator-only-for-masturbation myth. Certainly, alongside the court documents and the tape recorder, babes are packing Flipper Jr. in their carry-ons for that deposition in Buffalo, but, Bush Pilots, if you had a night alone at the Super 8 in Buffalo, wouldn't you pack him too? That said, while this is a common scenario (especially for legal aides), vibrators are by no means an exclusive activity. They are not, as commonly thought, a private lap dance behind the beaded curtain, far from the general unwashed that is you.

Nor are they a crutch, a cane or a prosthetic for your babe's unyielding anatomy. No. To the contrary, vibrators are simpletons in every way. In fact, unlike your babe, her vibrator is less than discerning; suggestible creatures with suggestive names, vibrators do not care who operates them, for how long or how fast. They do not even care where they go. They have no curfews, no morals, no history and no hang-ups. Most important, they do not care how your babe comes. So, Bush Pilots, why should you?

They don't add pressure. They take it away.

—Bush Pilot (Airstream RV, pirate ancestors)

THE TOUR DE VIBRATOR

Vibrators come in infinite shapes, colours and materials, ranging in price from eight dollars to ("For Posh, Love Becks") a million pounds. Two rules, Bush Pilots: Don't go cheap and do buy extra batteries. Also consider: plug-in or portable; internal, external or dual stimulation; dirty talk (yes, there is a creepy toy called Talking Head) or stealth-quiet; high intensity or low; silicone or cyberskin; and, for the wealthy collector, waterproof, gold, steel or diamond-encrusted.

PLUG-IN

Hitachi's Magic Wand with Accessories. The Wand is the most popular vibrator on the market for external stimulation—and it is, just short of doves flying out of your sleeves, magic. Sure, its size can be intimidating. It does dwarf your drill, and it must be said, your other power tools. But, reminiscent of a 1970s microphone, this toy will make your babe hit the high notes. Made famous by female masturbation guru Betty Dodson, its strong purr can be the "tipping point," or flipping point, for many pre-orgasmic women. And paired with attachments, this is an excellent choice for the G-spot novice. Bush Pilot Bonus: Look for use of the Magic Wand—among other toys and tricks—in Tristan Taormino's directorial effort, the very worthwhile *Expert Guide to the G-Spot*.

G-Spotter or G-Plus Attachments. Depending on your babe's preference, try the harder vinyl G-Spotter Attachment or the more supple, hypoallergenic and phthalate-free G-Plus Attachment, or "Gee Whiz." Phthl-what, Mistress? Phthalates, aside from being impossible to pronounce, are chemicals many people are putting a question mark beside called cancer. Still found in some plastics, they are—like the piano tie—slowly being phased out.

BATTERY–POWERED

Bush Pilots, the following vibrators are not plug-in but battery pow-ered. While they can be stored in your argyle sock and used in first class, they are also less durable than the plug-in vibrators. Note well: Remove batteries between flights.

The Pocket Rocket. Like the iconic Wand, the Pocket Rocket is a powerhouse of pleasure. But, true to its name, it is the size of your thumb—better for overnights at your in-laws should there be any confusion near the karaoke machine.

Bswish Bgee. Fit for your maiden voyage, the water-proof Bgee is small in size, bright in colour, seamless plastic and phthalate free. Ideal for your underwater fantasy—slide the Bgee into your wet suit next time you go deep-sea diving.

Ohmibod G-Spot Vibe. One letter away from what she will be saying when you turn it on. Gearheads, you can plug this into your iPod, your MP3 and even your Walkman. Bush Pilot Bonus: It delivers vibrations to the beat of your playlist; you can even pump up the volume. But. Please. Bush. Pilots. No. Erik. Satie. And. No. Philip. Glass.

Orchid G-Spot Vibrator. Its angle and bulge put pressure precisely where your babe wants it—and it is made of plastic, giving it, and your babe, the firmness required. Too much? The Orchid now comes in a "deluxe" edition. The difference: An added bump to its tip provides texture and length, and cyberskin sleeves pad the plastic.

DUAL STIMULATION
(FOR HER—AND FOR HER)

Always turn Japanese.

Rabbit Pearl (external battery pack) and Rabbit Habit (wireless). That's right, BPs, these top-of-the-line Japanese vibrators buzz both your babe's go-go and, as if that were not enough, her G-spot. They are pliable. They are available in phthalate-free elastomer rubber. They are vibrator royalty. All hail. For the Cirque du Soleil of vibrators, try their light-show cousin, the Vibratex Butterfly. Sticky Note: Run for thirty minutes at a time, and please, Bush Pilots, have extra batteries on hand. If you

have forgotten what I have just said, immediately purchase the following:

Fun Factory Delight Rechargeable Vibrator. Now you
see the S-curve, now you see your babe come. Handle
this. It strokes Lady Go-Go. It stirs Big G. It even has its
own case wherein it recharges itself. Yes, it costs. But so
does running to the corner store for AA batteries.

Clarification

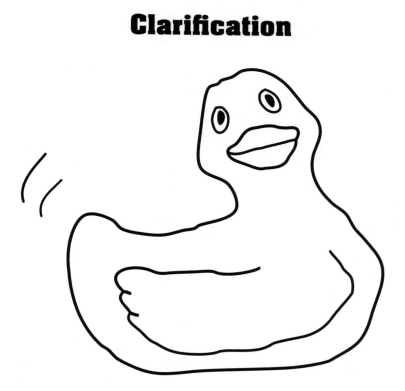

as a matter of fact, this is her vibrator

Sticky Note: Like us, these playthings are porous. Between sessions, use a mild soap and hot water to clean. Air dry. Stay away from bleach, rubbing alcohol and dish soap—unless you are playing with silicone toys. Your silicone dildos can withstand boiling water and even, lazy pants, a run through your dishwasher. Your vibrators, on the other hand, cannot be put in the dishwasher, nor can they be immersed in boiling water. Why, buzzkill? Because you will damage—and silence—your babe's favourite motor. Solution: You may use tongs as you would with cobs of corn, and keep the vibrator's motor clear of the vicious, boiling water, or return to the second and third sentences of this paragraph. And on this note, darlings, please wash your toys before using them for the first time. It saddens me to have to tell you that. Copy? Copy, Mistress.

Also note that, if you are ringing the bell at both your babe's front and back doors, fresh condoms must be used between visits. Preferably, toys are designated for one or the other.

UM, WHERE DO I FIT IN?

Feeling vulnerable? Threatened? Endangered? At risk of extinction? Speed-dialling the World Wildlife Fund to place protective measures around your condor? Bush Pilots, your babe's vibrator, along with all the smooth moves you will study in Parts Two, Three and Four, can be your foreplay, not your floor routine. Or, save your heavy hitter for when he counts, and use these vibrators as a seventh-inning stretch during a long night of passion. Remember, the vibrator is only the rhythm section. You still get all the solos.

INCOMPLETE!

Bush Pilots, there is the Rose Bowl, the Sugar Bowl, the Cotton Bowl and there is the Bush Bowl. Try as you both might, the vast—and I mean vast—majority of babes do not come from the penetration of your Brett Favre alone. This is the truth, and this is where the vibrator, pulled from your well-stocked survival kit, makes its record-holding entrance on to the field. Less bouncer and more backup band, the vibrator is there to help you, not upstage you. Being frightened of it is like being frightened of a loot bag—or your babe's orgasm extravaganza.

If you still consider yourself some inviolable Don Juan or a naturalist born from a Russian novel who just cannot believe in the buzz, I urge you, prehistoric Bush Pilots, to surprise yourself. If your babe hasn't already initiated you, introduce the idea to her. Your M.O.: finding new paths to her pleasure—and, after that (I repeat, after that), yours. Bush Pilot Bonus: Nimbus, Le Tigre and the rest of their vibrating ilk swing both ways.

EXTRA CREDIT

TO-DO LIST

☞ Put on your smoking jacket.

☞ From your settee, watch your babe masturbate with her toy.

☞ Think "When in Rome," and masturbate too.

☞ As part of your extended foreplay, skirt your babe's body with her toy.

☞ Buzz the junction where her thighs meet her kit.

☞ Tease the junction.

☞ Apply water-based lube to the toy and move it up to her go-go.

☞ Gently place her toy against her go-go until she possibly comes.

☞ Proceed with your panther-like congress.

☞ Place your babe on top and watch as she uses the toy.

☞ And possibly comes and comes again.

☞ Take a break from your panther-like congress.

☞ Watch as your babe uses the toy persistently against her G-spot.

☞ And possibly gushes.

☞ Return to your panther-like congress.

☞ Possibly come. Possibly together.

☞ Send the toy a thank-you note:

HEY,
THANKS
MAN!

B.P.

Dear Quiver,
On behalf of my babe and
I, thank you for a most
memorable evening.
We so enjoyed meeting you and
very much look forward to our
next visit.
Again, thank you for your
warmth and hospitality.
We were most touched by it.

Fondly,
B.P.

plain

fancy

EXTRA CREDIT

NOT-TO-DO LIST

- ☞ Use her vibrator grudgingly against her ankles and say, "You like it like that?"
- ☞ Move it up—deliberately skipping her lady parts—to her stomach and repeat, "You like it like that?"
- ☞ Continue up to her hairline—deliberately skipping her breasts—and simply offer, "Perm?"
- ☞ Use it on yourself while giving her the hand.
- ☞ Use it on yourself while laughing like Vincent Price.
- ☞ Plug it in and say, "Desperate times. I get it."
- ☞ Let your dog use it as a chew toy—accident!
- ☞ Drain the batteries—total accident!
- ☞ Set it on fire—total, total accident!
- ☞ Yank it away when she says, "I'm going to come."
- ☞ And then sulk, "What about my orgasm?"

The lesson, boys: Whether making love from behind or from above, simply make room for the toy. Consider your return: a first orgasm, a first set of multiple orgasms and, lest we forget the flood, your babe's first experience with female ejaculation.

MAN TOYS

> There is the stigma about being gay if you like anal stimulation, which is crazy because it is my beautiful wife making me feel this way. She often tells me to put a plug in when she is in that mood. It's very stimulating to lie on the couch and play with each other as foreplay. She'll play with the plug, moving it around, rubbing the prostate. She could make me come just like that. It gets her very aroused.
>
> —Bush Pilot (swagger, tarantula collection)

I know, I know. Sometimes, stranded between your babe's Turbo Glider and Night Rider, Little Dolly and Rosebud, you can feel a little left out of the toy department. Do not despair BPs, there are many small wonders out there designed with you and your man parts—especially your hindquarters—in mind. Whoa, Mistress, you back-talk companionably, my hindquarters? Your hindquarters, BP. No offence, Mistress, but I think I'll speed-read this part and then flip ahead to Chapter 16 while mind-humping Halle Berry.

Pilot error.

I see you are unsure, my BPs, my Beeps (represent!). You and your dead-bolted back door have hang-ups. When it comes to your kit, you have prejudices and you have assumptions. Secretly, in that unevolved part of your brain, damaged during those brief months spent in a condemned fraternity house doing whippets and sleeping in a dentist's chair, you think: Back-door sex is for lonesome, sad and hunky cowboys. Sure, the performances in *Brokeback Mountain* were brave and moving, but they could have been career-killers! No wonder Jake Gyllenhaal did *Prince of Persia: The Sands of Time*! Did you see his insane buffness? Did you see his Bret "The Hitman" Hart hair?

I INTERRUPT YOUR PROGRAMMING

Dorkus, when your babe throws down a killer solo on your kit, you will not cease to be the flatulent stallion, stingray and stud we all know you are. Your favourite song will still be 50 Cent's "Candy Shop." You will still be able to beat most mortals at pool. You will still love nothing more than a nipple held between your teeth, the floss of a thong plucked high between your fingertips. You will still be unabashedly straight and aspire to little more than a good burp, fart, headbang, man-joke and screw. Bush Pilot Bonus: Perhaps in visiting your kit, you will also remedy that stilted Neanderthal part of your cerebellum sophomore year's nitrous-oxide experiment nearly sucked up. How?

HIT THE BUZZER

Hold up. Before you do, recall Chapter 2? How could I forget, Mistress? The cupping, the currents, Charlton Heston. Remember stroking your P-spot toward your stomach? I do. Wait . . . I don't. Bush Pilot, please use gloved and lubed fingers—yours or your babe's—before you break out the less intelligent and less pliable toys listed below. Interlude. Now, meet . . .

Pandora. A perfect prostate toy for the initiate BP. This curved bit of silicone, with a handle, not only vibrates at multiple speeds against your "male G-spot," but with its compactness, will, like the spy gadget you have always dreamed of, fit into your tuxedo pocket between your little black book and her bikini bottoms.

Rude Boy. Throw your hands in the air, or on your Rock-steady, and have your million-dollar point and P-spot massaged by this strategically curved silicone vibrator designed just for you. Suggested soundtrack: The English Beat's 1983 album *Special Beat Service*.

SHAMELESS PLUG

Aneros Helix. Named like seersucker-clad aristocrats cruising Monaco, Eupho, Maximus and their baby brother Helix are, to look at, a cross between modern sculpture and Mars Attacks! With its "patented, anatomical design"—an angled head to hit your P-spot and uplifted external tab to press against your perineum—the Aneros Helix makes for a thoroughly unique and much celebrated prostate massage delivered not by the strength of store-bought batteries but by the strength of your PC muscles. Note: Eupho and Maximus are for the more seasoned pubococcygeal player only.

Pure Plug. Now for something completely different. The Pure Plug is sleek, silver, shaped like an angled lollipop and could be left out on the living-room table as an objet d'art. Made of medical-grade steel, the Pure Plug comes in a box fit for an engagement ring, lies heavy in the hand, is easily insertable and topped by a spherical protrusion tipped to press against your P-spot. Imagine walking around with a weighty secret that comes in sizes S to XL.

Sticky Note: Any man toy that goes near your man-cheeks must be well lubricated (e.g., Maximus, Slippery Stuff or Astroglide Gel).

N.B.B.P.: These man toys are used by BPs who could easily audition for the next Bond film. Like you, they know their Scotch. They have made love in a boardroom, a hostel, a stadium, a funeral parlour, a theme park and a canoe. They have pulled down thigh-high stockings and lifted up a kilt. They have felt like a king in the sack and, on one flushed occasion, even kissed their biceps. Their curiosity is as piqued as ever. And yours, BP? Open to anything? Now, that's manly.

Man Toys: A Decoder

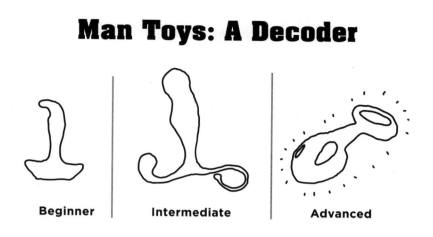

Beginner | **Intermediate** | **Advanced**

COCK RINGS

Bush Pilots, you know when you have the kind of orgasm that is more like a backdraft? And, after regaining consciousness, you have to look in the mirror to confirm you still have hair? And, upon seeing you don't, you say "my God" and discover you've gone from a tenor to a baritone? For some Bush Pilots, it is the cock ring that does that. It is the cock ring around his Love Unlimited Orchestra that leaves him hairless and singing "You're the First, the Last, My Everything."

YOUR INSTRUCTION MANUAL

Yes, it appears a tricky number, but simply slip the cock ring onto the base of your Bellagio—behind and herewith—including your bellhops (non-adjustable cock rings go on when soft; adjustable ones, when hard). The cock ring will form a tight cuff. The physics? Constriction slows blood flow, preserving and parlaying your boner (and maybe even adding girth to your Goldfinger—maybe). Good for her. Good for you? Bush Pilots, just as you tie a string around your finger, the cock ring creates a comparable warmth and pressure—and reminds you: It's your babe's birthday.

NUMBNUTS

Heed: Lords, if you stay in the ring too long, you risk numbness, bruising and, at worst, the Gollum of erections; a slave surpassing his natural life span, a Slinker made monstrous in his obsession. It can only be corrected in the emergency room—with metal cutters—and can lead to internal scarring, as well as damage to nerves and blood vessels. Why risk it?

DAMAGE CONTROL

- ☞ This is a thirty-minute workout only.
- ☞ Remove after workout and before post-coital zombie state sets in.
- ☞ Start with the readily removable rawhide, that adjustable classic: leather with snaps or Velcro for easy catch and release (watch your man-curls).
- ☞ One size does not fit all.

HOW DID IT COME TO THIS?

Bush Pilots, in the timeless pursuit of fullness and staying power, the cock ring made its first appearance on the cock in China around 1200 A.D. in the form of the naturally elastic goat eyelid—with the gentle tease of eyelashes—for him and for her. Some four hundred years later, cock rings were carved from ivory in the shape of dragons, the dragon tongue positioned strategically to lick a lady's go-go. Another four hundred years later, we have a storehouse of options, which fall into two very different camps: adjustable and non-adjustable. Now, look at your lap and have a think on that.

HOG TIE

First, for you DIY types, please do not lift your kilt and convince your lass into a "look what I made!" simulacrum in the form of hair elastics, skipping ropes and parcel string. You will injure your Ploughman Poet. Instead, if you are a beginner in the ring, go to your local sex shop and look for the forgiving—and adjustable:

- leather
- silicone
- elastomer
- cyberskin

Flexible, even sentimental, these materials, like a marriage vow, promise to grow with you. Unlike a marriage vow, they are easy to be released from.

Only once you are more experienced in the ring may you (if you wish) make the aesthete's choice and move into the beautiful, though firm, non-negotiating and non-adjustable:

- metal (the weighty nickel and steel)
- rubber (if you have a latex allergy, look for nitrile)
- wood

Sticky Note: Regarding the metal cock ring, boys, this must be put on, balls first (one at a time now), when flaccid. If discomfort ensues, immediately talk down your boner by dunking your donut into an ice bath.

THE VIBE

But, Bush Pilots, larger layman and longer lay aside, let us get back to why we are really here: your babe. So why not choose a cock ring made of phthalate-free elastomer rubber with spikes, studs or nibs? Or take it one battery-powered step further.

Mini Double Dolphin. Stretchy and soft, this cock ring will hug your tree while shaking it. Removable bullets above and below you vibrate at multiple speeds, buzzing your tackle and her tickler.

Incredible Stretch Vibe. Embellished with nibs, this cock ring has a single vibrating ring to be pointed in the direction of your babe's choice. Bush Pilot Bonus: Can be used in the bathtub. (Get one!)

Lelo Bo. For the high-rolling Bush Pilot, this gentleman's ring could sit beside your Swiss Army watch, vintage jackknife, shaving brush and half-smoked cigar. It is handsome. It is Swedish. It is your sex toy for the afterlife.

BLING FOR YOUR BOY SCOUT

Bush Pilot, while your babe's pleasure is indubitably your M.O., she does not have to be the only one benefiting from the toy department. If you are a rap mogul, or his Shawty, look for "C-rings" made of jade, pearls and hammered silver. N.B.B.P.: Given their materials, these gems are for experienced C-ringers only.

IT'S A BIRD . . .
IT'S A PLANE . . . IT'S MY BONER

Adding girth (maybe) and endurance, the cock ring transforms your boner into its superhero version. And hark, Man of Steel, when you're at the top of your game, there is only one thing you can do: Play it. Safe.

SAFETY FIRST

I've fucked a grandma, a high school teacher, a stripper, seventeen lesbians, a virgin, a Dutch shoe designer, and a flamenco dancer. Always bag it.

—Captain Goodscrew

Bush Pilots, if you think rolling a condom onto your mullet-ed rocker is a vibe killer, throw this book alongside your ex-wife's clothes and furniture in the uncontrolled burn devouring the ancient forest behind your trailer.

Or, consider your good fortune—and your babe's. She is no longer mixing crocodile dung with honey and placing that hair-of-the-dog drink in her Peloponnisos; nor is she combining willow seeds with cedar gum, alum, myrrh, asafetida (in the Worcestershire sauce you put on your fried eggs this morning) and, most punishing, white pepper to stave off pregnancy. Nor are you King Minos, counselled to slip the bladder of a goat over your grazer or, alternately, into your babe's pasture. Hair-raising? What about this? In the 1828 *Gray's Supplement to the Pharmacopoeia*, the "intestines of sheep . . . soaked in water for several hours . . . macerated . . . then exposed to the burning brimstone . . ." (But still, Broseph, condoms are such a total hassle!)

SAFER SEX AND FREE LOVE

Despite the 1930 invention of latex rubber, it was not until the 1960s that the studious, spectacle-wearing Safer Sex and her topless, folk-singing sister, Free Love, were born. Especially taken by that vibrato nightingale, Free Love, our parents and grandparents, with their middle parts and amulets, had sex with nameless vagrants in farmer's fields. They got diseases—and shotgun weddings (I'm not saying you!). Fifty years later, have we wisened up?

Allegory: Jarome Iginla wears a mouth guard, gloves, protective padding and a helmet; do you think this lessens his feel for the game? When you think to yourself, Just this once, here, Bush Pilots, is your debilitating cross-check, your concussion, the diagnosis you have to utter to every future paramour: chlamydia, genital herpes, gonorrhea, hepatitis A, B and C, HPV, pubic lice, syphilis, scabies and AIDS. Therefore, Bush Pilots, when high-sticking, you must suit up.

But, Mistress, how do I broach this with a prospective babe? From the cockpit, here is Captain Goodscrew's approach to your safe landing:

You must have the awkward conversation about STIs.

(Bush Pilots, STI is the abbreviation formerly known as STD, which a long, long time ago simply went by the scarier VD. It stands for sexually transmitted infections.)

> This is best done when it's obvious that some kind of fooling around is imminent. I usually say something like, "I'm pretty militant about wearing condoms and I check myself at the clinic twice a year. How about you?" I will ask about their experience. If they have an STI, they may not know about it. Many folks with STIs have a handle on it and will let you know if they're actively flaring up.

And in the interests of your own suaveness, he adds:

> I practised putting on condoms and jerking off with condoms. You gotta wear them so you may as well get good at working with them.

The last motivational speaker on the subject of your safety:

> It is incredibly sexy if a guy takes the power of instigating safer sex with condoms as his standard. There is nothing more annoying than a guy begging for unprotected sex. It is disrespectful and surprisingly still happens a lot. It is much more sexy if the guy insists before you do.
> —Babe (most likely to have David Bowie buy her a drink)

Word.

THE RUBBER ROUNDUP

Bush Pilots, listed below are the best condoms on the market, which you will carry at all times—not in your wallets, wet suits or beer coolers, but in your Bush Pilot survival kit at room temperature and, most important, at arm's length. Bush Pilot Bonus: For added sensation, spill a drop of your favourite water-based or silicone-based lube in the reservoir tip (only!) of your—as Casanova called his (rumoured to be linen)—English overcoat. Remember, BPs, unless specified, your oil-based lubes have no place here.

Kimono Microthin. For sheer pleasure, made of natural rubber latex, this winged Japanese dragon is, as the name suggests, the king of the ultra-thin condoms. Glove thyself and do as the king of the ring did before you: "Float like a butterfly, sting like a bee."

Kimono Maxx. These are lubricated, latex and larger; a good choice for you lovers of UFO-for-a-hat size queen, Lady Gaga.

Crown Skinless Skin and the snugger **Beyond Seven.** Another couple of Japanese exports, these perpetual bestsellers are the Caspers of condoms; friendly ghosts, why not choose these silk stockings for your Slinky?

Crown Skinless Skin Studded and **Beyond Seven Studded.** The same as above, only Lance Armstrong and Tom Brady are in them, adding texture.

LifeStyles Natural Feeling. The Canadian Tire of condoms, this one is reliable, durable, made in North America and can almost be bought with Canadian Tire money. With its stretched-to-sultry latex, Natural Feeling is updated to be the thinner, less merely functional version of its former incarnations.

LifeStyles True-Fit. The same as above, but with a soundtrack by Deepak Chopra for added contouring. If you have a latex allergy, look for the non-latex **LifeStyles Skyn** or **Durex Avanti Bare.** N.B.B.P.: These are made with polyisoprene—thinner than latex and not compatible with oil-based lubes.

Reality Female Condom. Whoa, Mistress. Female condom? Yes, my Pilots of Bushness, female condom. Your primer, your dignity: The female condom looks like a loose tube with a closed end—a.k.a. sheath. Your babe locates the closed end. She pinches it with her thumb and forefinger and inserts this end into her butterfly or kit. With her pointer finger inside it, she then pushes the female condom up as deep as it will go. Made of polyurethane, it is safe with oil-based lubes and can be lubricated on both the inside and the outside. Score. Your job: Your babe guides your rhythm and blues to go inside the condom. When it sounds off so very many minutes later, the bottom end is twisted and pulled from your lady friend's hot parts. Attention: The condom, like uncomfortable stockings, is not twisted during tortoise-like coitus. Also, the open end stays outside the butterfly; if it bolts, hasten your retreat and take it from the top. Bush Pilot Bonus: The female condom can be put into play up to eight hours before sex—i.e., it does not need your salty dog standing at attention.

Bush Pilots, the condom is the most important tool in your survival kit. As such, here is a step-by-step to the "condom procedure" with Captain Goodscrew:

This is the part most men fuck up. Don't even bother thinking about penetrative sex until you're both all relaxed and connected and hard. Getting a condom out of a package when your hands are all lubey and cunty is problematic. Take it out and place it somewhere accessible. Also, double-check the condom is right side up, which can be hard to see in the dark. Putting it on backward sucks. Make sure you wipe off any lube on your dick before putting on the condom. That'll just make it slip off. Roll it down as far as it'll go. There's always a bit at the bottom that it won't cover. Now, during the fuck, I check it about every three to six minutes to make sure the condom isn't slipping off. All you have to do is feel the rolly bit at the base of your cock.

Every three to six minutes. That's an affirmative.

EXTRA CREDIT

TROUBLESHOOTING

- Bush Pilots, if it's been a while, it's been a while for your condoms too; please check the expiry date. (Worry less about yours.)
- I know you are hungry but please do not open the packet with your teeth or any sharp objects forbidden by airlines.
- Do you feel protected when you think about lambs? Me neither. No lambskin, please, as viruses—like wolves—will eat through it.
- Make sure your helmet is on correctly. It should be unfurling from the inside—as opposed to the outside—of the ring.

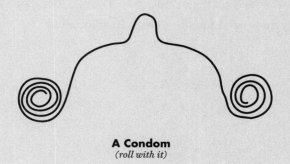

A Condom
(roll with it)

- If you are Bush Pilot Uncut, pull back your foreskin before you place your helmet on it.
- When rolling it onto your Rocky Balboa, hold the tip. This will prevent air bubbles—and breakage—as you race victorious up her steps singing "Gonna Fly Now."
- After you fly, to avoid slippage, grip the base of the condom before you pump your arms and begin your retreat.
- Sorry, Stuart, condoms are not reusable.

THE DOCTOR IS IN

DENTAL DAM

No, it is not the work of that other tail-slapper, the beaver. Yes, it is that same square sheet of latex your dentist puts in your mouth when he asks you, "So what did you think of *Memento*?" Thicker than your condoms, the dental dam forms a barrier between your tongue and your babe's fiery bush and buttocks. Um, but Mistress, how does it stay there? One of you prudently holds it in place. Bush Pilots, you can achieve the same effect by cutting a condom in half—and losing the tip—to exact a square shape.

GLOVES AND FINGER COTS

What kind of coverage do you need? Will this be a one- or three-finger salute? Choose accordingly, and when donning, as with your dams, please check for holes. Note: Mood rings and fake nails are hazardous here—and everywhere. Latex allergy? Look for nitrile at your local sex shop.

THE PREACHER IS IN

ABSTINENCE

By far the most effective safer-sex method available. The hitch: Only if you hunt moose, race snowmobiles and want to be a teenage father is this a truly viable option.

BPs, you have made it. That's the end of Part One: Understanding the Instruments. Congratulations! High five and a high kick, BP. Right back at you, Mistress. You so diligently studied the lady parts and the man parts, the toys that make them buzz, the lube that makes them slide and the props that keep them safer during panther-like congress. You know it, Mistress. I do, BP. You may sew the following badges onto the crotch of your Pilot pants: the She's My Lady Not My Stereo badge; the I Know

What a Merkin Is badge; the Oh, Yes, There's My Ass badge; and the Certified Safer Lover badge. You're ready for Part Two: Turn On.

Now, don't forget your survival kit. Where we're going, you're going to need it.

PART TWO
Turn On

FLIGHT MISSION:
BUSH PILOTS,
MAKE RADIO CONTACT.
REQUEST CLEARANCE
FOR TAKEOFF.

A HUDDLE WITH
CAPTAIN GOODSCREW

Captain Dylan I. Goodscrew

BUSH PILOTS, YOU'RE ON YOUR FIRST DATE and your babe is explaining the way the U.S. electoral college works while smoking you at Scrabble. You lick your teeth. She sets down the letters of a word you do not recognize. You wink lethargically. She says, "Your turn." Reading her subtext, you unzip your flight suit just so. She says, "Do you have the number for a cab?" You shake your head and reply suggestively, "What's a cab?" She responds, "A taxi." And you think, This is some flirtatious banter. So you retort, "But the game is not over." She says, "I'll just walk. Good night." "Good night," you offer allusively, but with an emphasis on good. And as she's leaving, you think, She is clearly vibe-ing me. So, with coolness and exactitude, you dim the lights with your remote, and then, with your other remote, close the blinds, and then, with your other remote, turn on Jay-Z's "Show Me What You Got" real low, and then, with yet another remote, kick-start the fireplace.

A good move?

Not quite, my darlings. Let's break it down: BPs, you love to screw. We love to screw. What a happy ending! But sometimes, in our race to get there, we miss a whole story in between: seduction. I know, the word makes you think of a sparse moustache, matching comb-over and chest tuft—or maybe just Yanni. But it is time to take this prologue to your Screwtopia seriously.

Like foreplay, but with no hands, seduction makes for the especially portentous boner and mini-boner. You wonder as you graciously dump the box into bowls equally: Is Bits & Bites dinner, and, after eating them, will she take her shirt off? You ponder, upon discovering your date's giraffe collection, should I mount her in an exaggeratedly gangly manner and then make giraffe sounds, whatever those might be? Is revving my engine "flirtation"? How to pick up Mistress, oh how, and when I do, what then?

From the flight deck, Captain D. I. Goodscrew:

What has worked for me is to have no expectations. Seducing a lady is a skill set like drywalling or playing oboe. Flattery is crucial. Be hilarious. Men can get away with being less handsome if we're funny. The last thing a lady wants to feel is obligated to fuck.

No expectations. That's an affirmative. Drywalling or playing oboe. That's also an affirmative.

Where to start? In this, Part Two: Turn On, we will cover the slow, suspenseful roll down the runway: flirtation, aphrodisiacs, fantasy and talking dirty. Bush Pilots, there is a lot you and your babe can do while waiting for clearance.

Break.

CHAPTER 4
FLIRTATION

NOTE FROM THE FIELD:
ACROSS THE CROWDED ROOM

There she is. Across the crowded room. Her bosom is full, like a woman who runs an orphanage. She wears an angora sweater that puffs at the shoulders, those tight horseback-riding pants and high-heeled boots. It's a strange outfit, but in it, George sees that she is peculiar and majestic. She could be named Rhapsodia. How did she end up here, in this scrum of the slicked and batted down? These balding heads, diamonds and stock portfolios? She must run. Run from this minimalist condo, back to the overgrown forest that sprung her. And yet, there she sits, sprawled on the granite floor, like a child on a rainy day, crocheting. Crocheting something long. It is probably a sock for an octopus. She probably has an octopus friend. The polished oxfords and pumps step over her. No one speaks to her.

It is as though no one sees her. Except George. She looks at him.

Oh God. Her eyes are magenta. This is not poetry. And sorrowful. Sorrowful as a room filled with broken plates, opera rising scratched from a gramophone in one corner and an injured kitten dancing in the other. It lasts less than one second, and in that second, George feels love. She looks away. George does not move. She looks back. This time, the eye lock is longer. Still an inky dream, he knows in this moment that she will be the mother of his children. She dips her head and lets it fall slightly to the side. She smiles to herself and twines one strand of hair around her fingers. George puffs his chest, sets his jaw and makes his way toward her. It is a swagger. The swagger of a man with a holster. The swagger of a man who has finally, after crossing the dust and sand and dirt of this animal kingdom, found his mate.

FLIRT OR DIE

Flirting: the other F-word, and just as crucial to our civilization. Flirting is why peacocks have tails and stags have antlers. It is why doctors have stethoscopes and your babe gets discounts. It is why you get laid. Without it, we would all be living in the black-and-white melancholia of a Bergman movie. So, Bush Pilots, get with it. Flirting is not the innocent game that it purports to be. It is our prologue to mating. It is evolution's Gong Show.

With our arched brows, swaybacks and small talk, we, your babes, are not being breezy and forward. While we may appear, in the words of Samuel Johnson, "a pert young hussey," our motives are profound, if primordial. We are combing the world for the taller, richer, older father to our brood, and you, my twinkle in the eye, my witty repartee, are being auditioned. This is serious business—show business. So, Bush Pilots, play your part. Learn how to read the signs. And learn how to send them. Or face extinction.

STAYING ALIVE

First, stick to your league. Are you Sly or Frank Stallone? No one wants to see the flyweight fight the heavyweight. No one wants to see you get creamed. History has shown this caveat does not apply if you are a rock star, movie star, royalty, billionaire, decorated athlete or Cyrano de Bergerac. Women love proficiency (and a microphone). Exhibit A: The Cars' Wayfarer-wearing Ric Ocasek and France's father to the jolie laide, Serge Gainsbourg. Exhibit B: Paulina Porizkova, Jane Birkin and Brigitte Bardot.

But Mistress, you say, I cannot sing, paint or act! I could never have written "Far from Over"! Do not fret, Bush Pilots. The examples presented above remind us: Flirtation, and success therein, is not about writing a chart-topping number, nor is it entirely about matching beauty for beauty, face for face. If this were the case, we would live in a Noah's Ark world—a sad and boring proliferation of like meeting like. Happily, the pools you wish to hop into are not that shallow.

THE WHO

Be a realist. For instance, you wear bow ties, collect beetles and bawl at credit card commercials. Is it wise to approach the girl in the black unitard cracking her knuckles and doing squats, preparing to break a board with her head while the crowd chants "Cujo"? Ask yourself: What would I say to her? Perhaps she is better suited to the oaf in the corner, doing chin-ups in his grey sweatsuit and counting them incorrectly. Then ask yourself: What am I doing here in this underground gym full of murderers? Why am I trying to pick up in prison? Bush Pilots, know thyself, and know thy setting. When prospecting for gold in a gold mine, your return is that much greater.

THE WHERE

Second, turn up the heat at the bar, the arena, the house party and in the classroom. Turn it down in front of your girlfriend, your brother-in-law and your boss. Consider your company and consider your location: Baghdad or Buenos Aires? Denver or Dubai? Boardroom or billiard hall? Hot tub or hospital ward? Calibrate, Bush Pilots, calibrate—or risk being the smarmy guy with the headset and attaché case who clears the room like a McFart.

THE WHAT

Third, consider flirting an act unto itself. Like seals, sharks and elephants, we do not want to be hunted. We want to be charmed. We want to know you can operate a power tool, build a tree fort for the neighbourhood children and spend hours under the hood of your pickup truck before surfing at sunset. We want to know you can wear a tuxedo with bare feet, have a rescued hound called Dixie, a record collection and stacks of books you have read, underlined, annotated and can recite from. We want to know you have a secret dance routine to Chaka Khan's "I Feel for You." We want to know you are interesting. So please, leave it at that. Give us a glimpse. Stop short of the come-on and the pickup. Trust me. Be salt. Be pepper, Bush Pilots. Just enough. And not too much.

DON'T FENCE HER IN

For those of you spritzing yourselves with Silent Seduction Pheromone Cologne and packing a pair of edible underwear in your Pilot pants pocket, let me break down the above: No lines. No dirty jokes. No staring at the tatas. (We're so on to you!) No fawning. Nothing about your exes. Nothing about your plumbing. No "I'm bringing sexy back." No "So when do I get my pass to Pussyville?" We want courtship, not creepiness. Not confessions. Of utmost importance: Respect her personal space. Do not cross the line from stud to stalker. And please, no close-talking.

The opposite of these flirting faux pas is that gallant knight in shining, indestructible armour known as chivalry. Like a strong jawline and a Belgian beer, chivalry has never gone out of style. Bush Pilot Bonus: This persuasive quality is readily available to all men—even those of you currently watching *Talladega Nights: The Ballad of Ricky Bobby* while snorting spaghetti in a cut-off football jersey.

Try the following: Attend to her comfort. Ask the waiter to turn on the ceiling fan, to close the window, to fill her glass, to call a cab, to turn down the music. Do retrieve her coat, open the door for her and walk her home. Do steal the flowers at the lavish event and present her with the laughably extravagant bouquet. Do not get caught. Key: Know when to cut out. Always leave on a high note. Be memorable without asking for memories—such as your Lancelot storming her Camelot. (Patience, young sir, patience.)

EASY DOES IT

Children flirt. Wolves flirt. Monkeys flirt. Fruit flies, pigeons and rodents flirt. How hard can flirting be, you ask. Not hard at all. In fact, it should be effortless. George Clooney–Clark Gable–Marcello Mastroianni effortless. Oh, you say, wet eyes cast downward.

BE THYSELF

Do not despair, Bush Pilots. Burlesque performer CoCo La Crème, teacher of Flirtation 101, says the trick is to "be yourself." No need for "the personal sell." How to achieve this? Stay true to the Bush Pilot's ever-present goal: making her feel good. Ask her about her: What is she reading right now? Does she like the Champagne? Where did she find that feather hanging from her ear? Listen. Pretend she is the only woman walking the earth (in a loincloth with a cat on a leash singing the Stones' "Satisfaction" really slowly). Allow the exchange of information to be reciprocal. Let her up the ante.

THE FUNNIES

Your humour is our striptease. Never underestimate funny; aside from the act itself, there is no better shortcut to intimacy. Bush Pilots, note well: Let her laugh first, and let her laugh harder.

Alongside humour, women love two things: confidence and mystery. We love a man who knows how to walk into a room as if it were a saloon and he were the law. We love a man who looks like he could commit a crime. We love a man who looks like he could solve a crime. You mean I have to be Dirty Harry? Only if it's convincing.

LOVE THYSELF

Bush Pilots, what is it in you that people are drawn to like hapless metal shavings? Make a (CLASSIFIED: TOP SECRET) list titled "My Magnetism." Memorize. Believe. And then burn. Do not be anything other than what you are. Drop that leather cowboy hat and lasso. Stop hoisting your biceps like balloons. If you present a distortion or untruth, you will be presented with one in return. As CoCo La Crème wisely warns; for men who posture, "If they are not being themselves, they are not going to find someone who is right for them." Cujo, anyone?

HIT THE PLAYING FIELD

Practise, Bush Pilots. As often as you try to duplicate Jon Bonham's solo on "Moby Dick," go out and flirt. Cultivate your social self; the more you converse, the more conversational you will become, and the less intimidated you will be by this form of engagement.

If you have been living in an attic, drawing nonsensical epics if you have, until today, mistaken yourself for a chicken having k raised in a coop, begin with the empirical. Observe your surroundings and circumstances. Observe her clothing and carriage. Offer a compliment. Sharpen your instincts and your ability to improvise. Monitor: Are her responses long or short? Is her disclosure reciprocal or reductive? Is she speaking to you or the man beside you?

THE LADY WHISPERER

Bush Pilots, to underline the primacy of physiology in the delivery and reception of flirting, know your babe is attuned, not to your knowledge of Bauhaus and Boogaard, but to the pitch and pace of your voice. Good news for Billy Joel, bad news for Peter Brady.

At a loss for words? Not to worry. At this preliminary point, we take style over content. According to the Social Issues Research Centre's *Guide to Flirting* (CLASSIFIED: TOP SECRET. Read it. Know it. Shred it.), body language is much more compelling than what is said. This is true for both of us, and why we have eyes to make wide, hips to sway and lips to lick. In fact, our preference for your moves over your material is primeval; it has been traced back to the Age of Silence, when we were savages with whalebones holding up our hair. Many millennia later, just how far have we come?

BPs, I know how you love the hard facts, so here are the numbers to illustrate how first impressions are formed—and that, opposable thumbs or bust, we really are pre-verbal Neanderthals after all:

"Appearance and body language".........55%

"Style of speech" 38%

"What you actually say"................................ 7%

CHEAT SHEET:
SHE'S JUST NOT THAT INTO YOU

Read her face and read her physical signals. Ask yourself:

- ☞ Are her arms open or crossed?
- ☞ Are her motions mirroring mine?
- ☞ Are her stilettos pointing toward me, or the door?
- ☞ Is she staring at me with menace, or longing?
- ☞ Is she smiling, or saying, "Security,"?
- ☞ Is she nodding, tilting her head and throwing her hair back in a gesture reminiscent of shampoo adverts?
- ☞ Is she coy (i.e., lids lowered, gaze averted, chin tucked)?
- ☞ Or is she curt?
- ☞ Red light or green?

Remember, Bush Pilots: Despite your efforts, she directs the traffic.

Longing

More longing
(close-up view)

EXTRA CREDIT

THIS IS NOT A MATING CALL

- ☞ Yo
- ☞ Hey
- ☞ Dang
- ☞ Ouch
- ☞ Mm
- ☞ Mm-mm-mm
- ☞ Hey-yo-dang-mm
- ☞ Dang-mm-yo-hey-ouch
- ☞ Ouch-dang-yo
- ☞ Sup
- ☞ Sup-yo-dang
- ☞ Mm-dang-sup
- ☞ Hey-yo-mm-sup-dang
- ☞ Dang-dang-mm-sup-yo
- ☞ Mm-mm-sup-sup-yo-yo-dang

THE ART OF THE GESTURE

If you get the go-ahead, how do you follow up? Employ the art of the gesture. One bookish girlfriend whose cat-eye glasses say "Let's do it in the Fiction section" recalls that she and her now husband graduated into "full-scale flirting" when he sent her a bouquet of "weird flowers that looked like Dr. Seuss characters" by email. Its spell? It had "zing."

Flirting is in the details. It is in the inscribed book in the mailbox, the fortune cookie on the desk, a handful of fiddleheads, a contemporary art magazine, a note and some lilac cuttings, a Woodhands song on her answering machine, a ticket to a heavy metal concert, your pantomime of *Nacho Libre*, a pair of flamenco heels left on her windowsill with a lucky penny in the left shoe. Your token reflects her preferences, her curiosities, her quirks; this is, of course, very promising whilst measuring you as a potential bedmate (N.B.B.P.: ongoing.).

To brush up, watch the ghetto blaster–wielding John Cusack in *Say Anything*. Let him be your mascot, Bush Pilots. Let him be your master.

WE CHOOSE YOU

You know the script: the look, the conversation, the kiss, the deed, the diner breakfast. But I beg you: Heed the subtext. Listen in on this Bush Pilot forum:

BP #1: You've got to be at the right place at the right time.

BP #2: Being attractive and somehow mysterious.

BP #3: With nine other dudes trying to disrobe her.

BP #1: The logistics are huge.

BP #3: If men just shut up, they'd get laid more.

BP #1: Women really are running the show.

BP #2: And they don't know it.

BP #1: Neither do we.

So tune in, swivel, stretch and preen. Let your every pore say, "My sperm is healthy, and with my hulking pectorals, big brow and strong nose, I will protect you and our starlings from predators." After all, Bush Pilots, the world is just one big crowded room, and the future of humankind is at stake. No pressure.

CHAPTER 5
APHRODISIACS

NOTE FROM THE FIELD:
DESSERT?

Lev meets her at the laundromat. Her name is Sally. They are both in their bathing suits. All of their other clothes are dirty. They laugh about that. They fold their laundry together and put it in their baskets and, without deciding to, they walk to a park. They talk for a long time. Lev makes jokes about Spumante Bambino, lays down some cardboard and breaks out a backspin. Sally pulls out a pike freeze. They talk more—mostly about Billy Dee Williams. Finally, he is sure she is sure he is smart (he knows, sometimes, with all that grinning, it's hard to tell). Then they get some wine and talk more—this time, on the front steps of her apartment building. They stand up and say good night. They kiss. Still carrying their baskets. Still in their bathing suits. The kiss is so good Lev pictures them atop a wedding cake. Then Sally invites him in for dinner. He knows what that means.

Climbing the stairs to her attic apartment, Lev checks his bathing-suit pocket. Condom still there. Roar. Sally unlocks the door and immediately goes to the kitchen. Lev wonders how long she is going to keep up this charade. And then Sally opens her fridge and starts doing incredible things to fish and vegetables with knives, saucepans and shakers. Three hours later, dishes washed, Sally and Lev, still in their bathing suits, lie on her kitchen floor, pretending the ceiling lights are stars. Outside, they can hear the traffic, a summer rain starting. Sally gets up and retrieves a pint of strawberries. Sidling in, she pulls back the stem, inches one into his mouth, and then says the only word Lev ever needed to hear: "Dessert?"

WHAT A FEELING

Remember Alex from *Flashdance*? Of course you don't. Nineteen eighty-three. Welder by day, dirty dancer by night. Legwarmer-wearing harlot with ballerina dreams. She sits across from her boss in an upscale seafood joint, tackling that difficult screamer of a crustacean: lobster. He asks one simple question: "How's the lobster?" Apparently, it is so good she must suck it off, remove her bra from beneath her off-the-shoulder shirt and then press her socked foot up against his foreman. N.B.B.P.: This could be you.

GET YOUR HEAD IN THE GAME

Named for Aphrodite, the Greek goddess of love, aphrodisiacs are, like their titular origins, accompanied by a vast mythology. The great debate being waged: Is there an attendant science to these tinctures, these fruits and spices, these animal parts that are said to heighten our desires? Or is their effect purely a placebo?

Despite the keen cultural curiosity in aphrodisiacs, the hard science is weak. Why, Mistress, oh why must it be weak? Like the weather, apparently, the libido is difficult to measure. What those meteorologists of the man parts and the lady parts do know is this: When it comes to sex, the brain is crucial; if your babe's brain is convinced, her body will likely follow. Think of it this way: Her brain is the bright umbrella of a tour guide; her body and her lady parts line up behind it. In this case, the sights are culinary.

For the last five thousand years, Bush Pilots and babes the world over have been feeding on flamingo tongues, ram's testicles, and rhinoceros horn to make their screwing that much more potent. BPs, it is time to repurpose this epicurean practice of aphrodisiacs and the properties they purport to bear. After all, your babe's belief will get you most of the way there—there being naked. I.e., simultaneously, Mistress? Gold star, BP!

To begin, set the stage. Will it be a bacchanalian night in your bedroom? Or will you picnic on your rooftop, feasting under woollen blankets, redefining the slow-food movement by insisting every course be devoured before you get horizontal, the entire affair a slow burn? Bush Pilots, land your setting. It could be your tree fort, an empty bandstand, your fire escape, a teepee in a blueberry field or the front seat of your Impala.

Just to clarify . . .

EXTRA CREDIT

THESE ARE NOT APHRODISIACS

- ☞ In-N-Out Burgers
- ☞ Mike and Ikes
- ☞ Miller High Life
- ☞ Anything microwavable
- ☞ PowerBars
- ☞ Gu
- ☞ Jerky
- ☞ Toast
- ☞ Ketchup
- ☞ Ketchup on toast with a side of Gu, washed down with a Miller High Life, chased by an In-N-Out Burger and a PowerBar for good measure, with Mike and Ikes for dessert—who knew those little bastards were microwavable?

IMPORTANT NOTE:
not an aphrodisiac

A Mike and Ike (microwaved)

CHEAT SHEET:
SET THE MOOD (WITHOUT LOOKING LIKE A DROOLING JERK WHO HAS NOT BEEN KISSED SINCE GRADE NINE)

If you choose your domicile, your babe will open your medicine cabinet and, no matter how cool she is, judge you by its contents. The following could land you on the No-Fly List[1]:

- ☞ Your Preparation H Cooling Gel
- ☞ Your jock-itch powder[2]
- ☞ Your strip club matches
- ☞ Your handwritten beatitudes
- ☞ Your Sun-In

Your babe will also soundlessly open your bedroom door and, no matter how cool she is, judge you by its contents. The following could land you on the No-Fly List:

- ☞ Bong. Dismantle.
- ☞ Tiki lights. Hide.
- ☞ "Loving Lamb." Deflate and stuff under mattress with skin magazines.
- ☞ Unmade bed. Clean sheets and make bed.

---

[1] No-Fly List *adjective-verb noun* (noh:flylist) Short for "No, Flyboy, you've just been blacklisted" and loosely translated as "ew"; the sudden and irreversible onset of "ew"; causes of "ew" vary, but have included such things as white sport socks pulled up to the knee, a mock turtleneck worn in a logging camp, a minstrel vest donned without irony, a fanny pack, man-highlights, a barbershop quartet, a sponge painting and a Hanson tape.

[2] We know. It happens. You get an H-roid. You get a J-itch. We can dig it. We have medicine cabinets too. We concur: the human body is one tricky outfit. Give it some time, my BPs, and then you are clear to reshelve.

N.B.B.P.: A sleeping bag is not a duvet (pronunciation: "du-vay"). Update your Star Wars sheets (pronunciation: "sh-ee-ts"). And if you do not have any "sh-ee-ts," cancel "dinner" and hire a life coach.

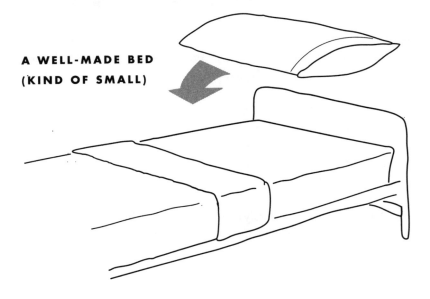

A WELL-MADE BED (KIND OF SMALL)

IS GATORADE AN APHRODISIAC?

Now that you have attended to your housekeeping, it is time to perfect your menu, for this, my darling Bush Pilots, is the passport into your babe's pants.

No clue? Pick up the sumptuously shot, intelligently sourced and tested *The New InterCourses: An Aphrodisiac Cookbook* (CLASSIFIED: TOP SECRET) written by Martha Hopkins and Randall Lockridge. Deal-Breaker Alert: Between the soup and salad courses, whilst draping smoked salmon across the steep incline of your Babette's nipples, do not borrow the pun "intercourses"—or you'll risk instantly devolving from lady killer to mood killer.

TAKE ONE FROM *TOM JONES*

Still at a loss? Dust off your extensive collection of classic literature and use it as fodder for your feast. What are you talking about, Mistress, and what is "classic literature" exactly? BPs, if you cannot find your copy of Henry Fielding's *Tom Jones*, watch the 1963 film adaptation starring that bandaged scamp, Albert Finney. Soundtrack: mandolin. Dishware: pewter. Gauze-wrapping: optional. To re-enact: Survey the Georgian eat-off between the incorrigible Jones and the top-heavy Sophia Western involving endless platters of meat, fruit and the very effective splitting of a wishbone.

HOW TO PUT OUT A CANDLE
WITH YOUR FINGERS

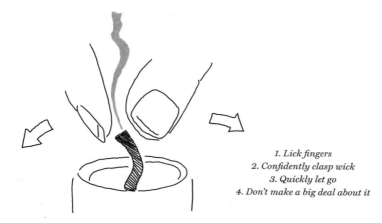

1. Lick fingers
2. Confidently clasp wick
3. Quickly let go
4. Don't make a big deal about it

Bush Pilots, an ongoing note: Always look to your lusty forefathers. The *Tom Jones* seduction scene culminates in this smooth move: Finney, finally alone with his ravenous paramour, extinguishes a candle between his fingers—an old trick, and surely one worth reviving. Hey, why do you think the tight-panted, oft-screwed crooner renamed himself Tom Jones? Study the album cover for *The Best of Tom Jones*. Look at that Welsh tan. Look at that needlessly bared, yet persuasively shined-up chest. Could he pull that off if his name were still Thomas Woodward? He knew history would give him a leg up. Or two.

A good menu is like watching a good sex show. You become the passion you see, the passion you eat.

SHUCK ME

When curating your menu, BPs, think: scent, flavour, texture, temperature and aesthetic value. Another quality to look for: rarity—e.g., Japanese puffer fish, truffles and tiny vials of saffron covertly handed to you by Mennonite farmers. But the queen of elite food, the Cleopatra of the kitchen, remains those salty fish eggs: caviar. A suitable, if lavish, appetizer for your delectable night, it is described in Isabelle Allende's *Aphrodite: A Memoir of the Senses* as "one of the most expensive aphrodisiacs in the world." She adds, "I can think of a thousand pornographic ways to serve it." Bush Pilots, quote the above to your Babette—and consider it a dare.

Mounting panic? She'll be there in ten minutes? For starters, know you're already halfway there. You did not order in. You did not get takeout. You did the grocery shopping. And you did the cooking. Congratulations, caveman. To celebrate, I suggest a glass of Champagne and fresh oysters upon her arrival. Why these silvery, spherical delights? They play with the "law of similarity"; essentially, like your large automobile, wall-mounted stereo speakers and spurs, they possess the power of suggestion.

How so, Mistress? Oysters mimic the lady parts and, in so doing, tease our senses. Moreover, they are eaten with our hands and require our heads to fall back for their consumption, baring the necks you might nosh on later. For an arousing demonstration, revisit the aforementioned *Tom Jones*; that provocateur Sophia Western understands there is edibility to this act alone.

GO AHEAD AND
Eat an Oyster

the oyster

the shell
(do not eat)

Just swallow it (don't chew)

Wine, lots of wine, is the best aphrodisiac, notwithstanding the inherent risks of overindulgence. And a date that begins with oysters is likely to end well, for reasons that may be more suggestive than physiological. I don't, strictly speaking, believe any particular thing you eat will make you more susceptible to another's overtures, but it's hard to imagine any seduction that didn't involve sharing a meal of some kind, even if it's by fridge light afterward.

—Bush Pilot (gastronome, a night in jail)

RED RED WINE

After your oyster-Champagne beginning, bring out a good bottle of red. The colour alone (the bedrooms of bawdy houses, blushing, engorgement) is invitation. Moreover, the aroma is believed to replicate human pheromones, those come-hither signals we, on par with moths, sea urchins and boar, emit.

Bush Pilots, have you ever noticed how the brief descriptors for wine are actually apt stand-ins for personal ads? What might yours say? Are you dark and robust, or light-bodied and fruity? Do you have hints of boysenberry and currant, or are you a heavy conflagration of leather and tobacco? What kind of legs do you have? What kind of bouquet? Deal-Maker Alert: When describing, err on the side of the sublime monologues delivered by Paul Giamatti in Sideways. Then maybe you, too, if balding, portly, faintly lisping, and yet tragically smart and so attractive because of it, will be presented with the chance to make out with a buxom blonde on her front porch. Or be Buster Keaton: Say nothing at all, and with your "Great Stone Face," let the libations speak for themselves.

DON'T PICKLE YOUR PECKER

Warning: Alcohol can be the ineffective telephone booth; you may think you're Superman, but we don't. Heed the hauntingly portentous lyrics of UB40's "Red Red Wine" before you find yourself weeping them into a fire extinguisher while wearing nothing but ski goggles and a judo belt. BPs, while wine might free you from your hang-ups, beware: Too much will also free you from your grace, pride, wit, charm, body functions and, most injuriously, your well-intentioned lust.

FIRST COURSE

Serve a salad of peppery arugula—also tellingly known as rocket. Cited in the Cambridge History of World Food, arugula has been used since the first century to unlace corsets and watch them fall like handkerchiefs to the earthen floor. Sweeten your greens with a honeyed vinaigrette. Why? Filled with vitamin B, honey stimulates the production of testosterone, a key ingredient in charging the libido. Additions: avocado, for the voluptuous way it meets your babe's tongue, and any number of nuts (hint) and seeds (hint). I recommend pine nuts. They are rich in zinc, a mineral that, unlike cranking "Dick in a Box" while building a shed wasted on Jagerbombs, pumps your potency.

BIG MACKING

Your main course should be centred around the pluckiest anatomies of our horniest wildlife—namely, rabbits, goats and bulls. The Neanderthal, yet irresistible logic? Once consumed, their virility is contagious. Deal-Breaker Alert: If your babe is wearing hemp pants, likes Kate Bush and thinks yogurt is murder, redirect and stick to the produce department. Code word: farmer's market.

Tool of Seduction
YOUR GROCERY LIST

N.B.B.P.: The following are fruits (pronunciation: frr-oots) and vegetables (pronunciation: vej-e-tah-bulls):

- ☞ bananas (bright yellow, in bunches and must be peeled before eating)
- ☞ figs (a fruit shaped like your pool boys but even more sad in color)
- ☞ peaches (stop winking)
- ☞ berries (Ice-Breaker Alert: If you sense nervousness— quivering hands, a brow slick with sweat, a sour perfume emanating from your pits—try a spontaneous display of "Berry Face." Instructions: Place two berries beneath your upper lip and present your babe with your version of *Planet of the Apes*. Graduate to grapes.)
- ☞ carrots (carrot sticks, but bigger)

- asparagus (left long and uncut)
- celery stalks (eaten raw, these contain androsterone, a spin-off of your main man, testosterone)
- cucumbers (their scent has been recorded to increase circulation—translation: more blood flow to your boners and our butterflies)
- garlic (go easy, fart-slacks)
- ginseng (also known as "man root"—and I mean also)
- artichokes
- fennel (ask someone in an apron for help)
- turnips
- avocado (hanging in pairs, they are alternately titled "the testicle tree" by the Aztecs—but don't mention that)

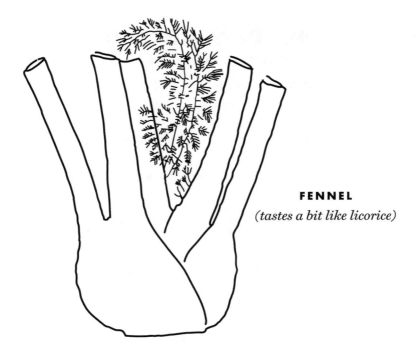

FENNEL
(tastes a bit like licorice)

BODY HEAT

Whichever of these creatures you can find at your local butcher or fish-monger—mussels, shrimp, squid and scallops being the most fabled—the secret to your dish will be in the spicing. With it comes a hit of instant exoticism. For those of you who wear suspenders, suck on ani-seed and read while walking, find a copy of Michael Ondaatje's poem "The Cinnamon Peeler." Tape it to your kitchen cupboards while you cook. As if written by a steely-eyed romantic who can stop his heartbeat and face down a charging bull while rolling a cigarette, its bravado challenges you: Spice imprints her skin. Leave your mark.

While spicing stimulates smell and taste, its heat (think chilis and curries) works internally to quicken our pulses and stir our nerve endings. This stampede to the senses causes us to sweat and potentially (Bush Pilot Bonus) disrobe. Imagine: We are flushed; our hearts beat faster. What does this physiological response slyly evoke? Clue: It is usually accompanied by the breathy utterance of the word yes.

Naughty-inducing notables: mustard, licorice, vanilla bean, coriander, cardamom, garlic, sage, sweet basil or, if it fits, nutmeg and ginger root, the aroma of which ups circulation, providing a boost to the lady parts and the man parts.

Sticky Note: BPs, when spicing, please follow your recipe: Amount and placement are paramount—i.e., do not improvise and add, just for kicks, a dash of vanilla bean to the scallops; the wrong combination will make your babe mini-barf.

LIKE HUMMER FOR CHOCOLATE?

For dessert, there is only one option: dark chocolate. Heat and serve with bananas, plump berries, peaches, papaya, pineapple, mango and split figs—fruit that, in its architecture, reprises a more private set of structures. Aside from the invocation of anatomies, there is also: juice. Bush Pilot Bonus: rare opportunity to break out your parents fondue set. Après-ski theme: optional. If going in this direction, see earlier note regarding the mock turtleneck and the No-Fly List.

Beyond the folkloric properties of chocolate, there are chemicals at work. Chocolate contains the stimulant phenylethylamine, or PEA—not to be confused with that Boy Scout badge, PDA. Called by Theresa Crenshaw, author of *The Alchemy of Love and Lust*, the "molecule of love" (aside, of course, from your natural man-musk of wood shavings), PEA mimics the feeling you had when you first saw your babe at the Flaming Lips concert in her nightgown dancing on a picnic table; its effect is akin to an endorphin high—the rush after you sprint, bask in the Riviera sun or smoke opium with The Beatles. In effect, chocolate mimics—if not, some argue (I don't), surpasses— foreplay. Whoa, Mistress, just what kind of chocolate are these compadres eating, and more to the point, just what kind of foreplay are they busting out? I mean, there is grinds and then there is grinds, if you catch my man-drift, Mistress. Caught it, BP.

Gold star!

More, you say? We do, Mistress, oh yes we do. Before I say yes, I must issue this Deal-Breaker Alert: BPs, you know that feeling you get after you go to a French restaurant and you eat raclette and then foie gras and then, after more wine, you eat some other things that are brown but also textured, like congealed butter, and then you get home and all you can do is cup your bloated gut with your paw while your babe cups hers with her paw and you lie down on your bed and listen to each other's stomachs gurgle and laugh, but then it ceases to be funny? Do not overeat. Your blood will rush to digest your dinner rather than to fire up your parts. One sensualist, speaking from experience, advises:

> The best aphrodisiac meal is not all the heavy things, but lettuce soup and a sparse salad so that you will have plenty of energy and an empty stomach to fill with the night's pleasures (not the culinary kind).

With that in mind, if you wish to indulge à la Caligula, you may, sparingly, add sweet cream to the mix. But, please, not sprayed from a can like Silly String—and absolutely no sugar near her sugar shack. Also, please vet any allergies ahead of time.

> A friend of mine, with her boyfriend, concocted an aphrodisiac dinner followed by "her" as dessert. Apparently it involved a lot of whipped cream. It didn't end well. Needless to say, it's how her partner found out he was lactose intolerant.
> —Babe (curvaceous glee in a cowhide skirt)

COFFEE IS FOR CLOSERS

One final note: If you and your babe are coffee drinkers, make two shots of espresso. According to Chris Kilham, author of *Hot Plants: Nature's Proven Boosters for Men and Women*, coffee, like strobe lights to the central nervous system, "excites nerves all over the body, including the ones involved in sex."

NATURE'S ALL-YOU-CAN-EAT BUFFET

By now, all cutlery and dishes should be banished—or broken. Nothing tastes better than your babe's skin. Consider this: Roman orgygoers used to eat their sea urchins, scorpion fish and honeycomb with their fingers. The food was served by slaves who would wash guests' feet upon arrival and their hands—with perfumed water—between the seven courses. Hands were dried by the slaves' long hair. Licked animal bones were thrown alongside togas (and inhibitions) to the floor. I'm just saying.

Bush Pilots, you have fed your Babettes. Now, feed yourself. You have worked hard. And you still have a long night ahead.

EXTRA CREDIT

THIS IS ALSO NOT A MATING CALL

☞ camo
☞ the rain poncho
☞ the jogging on the spot
☞ those pants that unzip at the knee to become shorts
☞ demonstrating the pants-shorts feature on your pants-shorts
☞ shorts
☞ stretching in a non-athletic environment
☞ the sudden accent upon the context-less mention of: Cuba (koo-bah), Texas (te-rjh-as), or blowjob (blow-rjh-ob)
☞ any pet that has been "artfully" shaved
☞ any "artful" shaving
☞ lighting a More
☞ use of the term *in crowd*
☞ totes (the bag, not the word)
☞ the singlet
☞ snapping—even at the best of times

CHAPTER 6
FANTASY

NOTE FROM THE FIELD:
AFTER-SCHOOL SPECIAL

Jonathan. Come to my office.

The syllables are hard, the voice is low, her accent all of eastern Europe. Professor Hasek, the medievalist. Her mouth is a splendid and fleshy shock of red. Aside from mummifying her cat, this is Professor Hasek's reigning mystery: that mouth, lipsticked to perfection, home of the exhausted command; she should be surrounded by maps on pigskin, mosquito netting and the enemy. She stands square in front of the blackboard, hair pulled into a bun, heavy glasses frames on her face. She is waiting for you. You have been doing your best Marlon Brando all semester—seduction from the last row. You are The Wild One. It is your time. You can finally ask her, "Whattaya got?"

You follow her through the marble halls, her stilettos the only percussion. Up three flights of stairs to Room 328. Her office: papers piled high, overstuffed bookshelves, a suit of armour. She leans back against her desk. The sun hits her from behind, spotlighting the shape of her breasts. She lights a Gauloise and hands it to you. You smoke in the tradition of the aloof prowler. You reach into your bag and pull out peach juice and Prosecco. *Jonathan. I don't have glasses.* You motion for her foot. Professor Hasek lifts her leg in a slow ballet. You pull her black stiletto free. She laughs a husky *ha.* You *ha* back, mix Bellinis, pass the stiletto back and forth, feel the onset of afternoon drunkenness—mortal levitation—and defend your reading of Ovid's *The Art of Love.* The stiletto is emptied. She looks at you from under heavy lids and places your hand inside her blouse. Her nipple is hard, perfectly crystallized; her heart pounds beneath. *Jonathan. It will happen only once.*

SMILES, EVERYONE, SMILES

Bush Pilots, with the irrepressible truth only kitsch can deliver, Mr. Roarke reminded you every Saturday night, as you sat with your knees bent beneath the afghan blanket—one hand in the popcorn, the other on your Private Benjamin—that fantasy is a universal language. You speak it. We do too. Remember playing "pretend"? Remember storming castles and saving princesses, being a superhero with a tea towel for a cape and a stick for a sword? Well, this is the adult version.

When we fantasize, we roam a world of infinite possibility and permission. We are sexy. We are satisfied. We are cuffed sluts and lusty saints—ourselves, wildly or mildly exaggerated. We are pirouetting in pointe shoes across the back of a dwarf while being fed escargots by your monocle-wearing uncle. We are a stripper in a seedy nightclub, a call girl to the governor of New York, a delinquent who needs straightening out. We are bad, bad, bad. And you?

While we dream in naughtiness, you dream in numbers. You are being fellated by triplets, baby-oiled by miniskirted nurses and taken back to *One Million Years B.C.* by Raquel Welch, cavewoman. You are James Bond getting laid by the likes of Honey Ryder, who has just emerged from the froth of the ocean in her white bikini, a knife affixed to its belt, two seashells in hand, singing "Under the Mango Tree"—to your Dr. Yes.

As if.

ERASERHEAD

While fantasy is our imagined life, it is also our denied life. Fantasies will not come true—nor do we necessarily want them to. While they excite us, fantasies, in equal measure, disturb; they are macabre, the stuff of the King of Creepy, David Lynch. We dig through our lopsided thoughts for their origins. You worry: Where did this slippery pile-up in the shower with my hockey team come from? Like an unsure compass needle, is my sexual orientation starting to tremble? Why am I getting a hickey from Howie Cosell and not the hot, grinning cheerleaders sucking on Sno Cones behind him? Why is Mike Tyson, in his silk robe, dancing like an inchworm at the end of my bed? And why am I wearing his blood-spattered shorts?

Bush Pilots, your existential angst has no place here. Do not banish, deadbolt or suppress your sensual wanderings. We, your co-stars, are just as weird, aberrant and taboo, our brains a bundle of perverse concoctions. Fantasy, as the cowboys say, is big sky country. Anything goes. We wake confused after a torrid night with a litter of rabid hounds, foot soldiers, tulips, aliens, Republicans. Sick. And sicker: We wake aroused by, according to Nancy Friday's *My Secret Garden:*

Women's Sexual Fantasies, the "very common" rape fantasy. Do we want the violence to materialize? Of course not.

What about the more beautiful fantasies, the more kinky fantasies? You ask: Does my babe really want to be mounted by a tiger in the middle of the Rose Bowl? Does she really want her hunchbacked financial adviser to spank her over his knee, the sweat-streaked bronco rider to ride her, the teenage gas-station attendants to hose her down, the crooked-toothed philosopher to lick her toes and place apple slices between them, Gabriel Byrne to call her a "naughty little girl" when she spills her milk—on purpose? Yes. And no. Desire is one thing; desire suspended is quite another. Does she want to satiate the ache, or does she want the ache? My reconnaissance tells me she wants the ache.

> I had a crush on the coffee shop guy. I'd go in. We'd flirt. He'd check out my ass. I'd pretend not to notice. Once, he checked me out so hard it bugged me, but still, he became my fantasy guy. Sometimes he was really moody, and I liked that. I'd get off thinking about him tying me up with his bike chain, or imagine bumping into him on the street and bringing him back to my apartment and then having some insane afternoon with him, or him just showing up at my place and us fucking. Anyway, we finally got together. He had bad breath (he had no sense of smell, it turns out) and just wanted to fuck me with no preamble. And his skin felt rough against mine. And his body was not the way I thought it would be. It was all just weird and not good. Oh, then I found out he had a girlfriend the whole time.
>
> —Babe (tasselled leather jacket, chipped nail polish)

REALITY CHECK

✓ "Bad breath."

✓ "No preamble."

✓ "Skin felt rough."

✓ "Girlfriend the whole time."

Another babe (posed nude with a stag) writes:

My long-term boyfriend once blindfolded me, then suddenly shoved a dildo up my pussy. It freaked me out. It was Valentine's. We had all kinds of fantasy conversations about things we wanted. This was his surprise present to me. He was trying to be all subversive and sexy, but honestly, I felt pretty violated, and it took me some time to recover. The dildo was hard and could have been plastic fruit stolen from some old lady's straw hat.

REALITY CHECK

✓ "Pretty violated."

✓ "Plastic fruit."

✓ "Old lady's straw hat."

RAID THE PROP DEPARTMENT

So, how do you, BPs, unsurpassed purveyors of pleasure, bridge the gap between your babe's fantasies and their fulfilment? In portions. Rather than their actualization, rather than being a literalist, think of fantasy in terms of accoutrements and totems. No one wants the Robert Bateman rendition of their subconscious. Instead, employ the theatre of fantasy. Bring home a garter belt. Leave a short kilt on the bed, a pint of cherries, fresh oysters, a tarot card. Don a blindfold, a saddle. Allow the part to suggest the whole. Be the minimalist. Leave room for mystery. Leave room for longing. N.B.B.P.: The erotic element is the unattainable one. Full disclosure is for fools. A flint-eyed friend with every bad habit describes the ideal fantasy as "the one you come close to, but can never touch." Take his cue.

How? Have a conversation. Enter the sweaty confessional together. Unlike our jobs, our families and our high school yearbooks, sex allows us to be something other than what we are. Ask your babe: What does it for you? Is it being watched from the chaise longue in your bedroom while you touch yourself under your uniform? Is it being stripped and then having your wrists tied to your desk with your stockings by your boss, who looks so much like Clive Owen, but angrier and a bit more beaten up and with a Welsh rather than British accent? Is it hospital equipment? Shall I call you Marguerite? Visit her outer reaches, just on this side of shame, and visit your own.

WHAT ARE YOU THINKING?

While I urge you, Bush Pilots, toward unrepentant transparency in your trysts, there are some things your Honey Ryder may not want to be told (the one about her cousin, the pink bunnies and the change table, for starters). Like any sideshow, fantasy not only invites, but begs for a select audience. Be mindful in your telling. Gauge appropriately; is she easily frightened, repulsed, offended? Is this one best left unsaid? Might it be enough to simply seduce yourself? Like any ballplayer's bizarre superstitions—the chicken claw in his sock, the lucky coin in his cup—you do not need to betray your trade secrets on game day. So you are "Hot for Teacher." So you want it harder. So you're being pile-driven by your pet. Let your sublime erection say it all.

The flipside: Do not press your babe to narrate what is suddenly turning her on. Do not interrupt her make-belief. She may prefer it to be a sullied bundle on the tip of her tongue, in the vault of her mind. The important point here is:

In the throes of fantasy—
however demented and
dangerous it may be—
her grey matter is turning red.

Bush Pilot Bonus: So is yours. As such, who needs confession—and who needs consummation? It is the sexiness quotient that counts. Like putting The Brothers Johnson on the turntable, fantasy is preparatory and it is provocation. Whether articulated or not, fantasy brings you both one inch closer to coming.

STRANGERS IN THE NIGHT

Sometimes it is the unspoken, the unpredictable, that thrills. Create a scenario together—and take it outside. Enact that most, according to Daniel Goleman of the *New York Times*, "prosaic" of fantasies: screwing someone other than your partner (say, Beyoncé, Bar Refaeli or the bartendress). Decide to meet each other in a restaurant, a park, a crowded club. Be strangers. What happens when you see each other for the first time? Does she approach you? What does she say? And more important, what does she offer? What is her name? Do you end up on a hill overlooking the city at the end of the night with a bottle between you, inventing entire lives, or in a filthy public washroom with your pants around your ankles? Script it just enough to be safe, and always allow for surprise. One friend who never fully does up his shirt comes at it from this angle: "The sexual mind, the sexual dharma, which demands playfulness, demands creativity, hates the unspontaneous."

DREAM ON

We love tension—the tension just before a first kiss, a first touch, a first screw. One babe even takes it so far as to admit she "prefers sexual tension to sex." Fantasy is the ultimate expression of tension; the kiss, the word, the screw never happens. It remains a petrified, unalterable moment in time. When it does not, it ceases to be fantasy and becomes life, usually with the attendant dose of disappointment: Raquel Welch is spoiled, Gabriel Byrne is clumsy, Tyson cannot dance to save his life. Working in this seedy strip club was not what I had in mind. Nor is the governor of New York.

> I did intentionally keep lots of guys at the sexually tense but unrealized position since I sensed acting on any attraction would have ruined everything.
> —Babe (cites Zanzibar as her birthplace)

> I had a huge crush for a couple of years—there was a lot of innuendo and a lot of flirting. Finally, we got it on, and it was horrible. The sex was awful and the whole scenario was awful. He kept saying that we were due for another try, but everything was horrid after we got it on. I was so shocked. Finally, after years, I made the crush a reality, and it was the worst sex I ever had. Stiff and not sensual—so not what I imagined.
> —Babe (claims Gypsy blood)

> There was this six-foot-four Czech guy whom I admired from afar while diving in Indonesia. He was with a beautiful dark-haired woman who turned out to be his best friend (whom I sort of fell in love with), so when I found myself in his room overlooking the ocean, it was not far off from fantasy. Anyway, for all of his brooding hand-

someness, he was the equivalent of a limp handshake in bed. It was shocking. I didn't believe it, so I went back for more. I remember seeing that housekeeping had made up his bed, strewn with rose petals and other beautiful, fragrant flowers, the kind that screams honeymoon! Or wild passionate sex! Or basically anything but what was going on between those sheets.

—Babe (rode the back of a whale)

TIM, TIM, TIM

Or, Bush Pilots, take the cautionary tale that is Tim. An Antarctic explorer of excellent square jaw and fit torso, Tim finds himself in a hotel room with four Swedes. They are luscious hellions, and he is their prey. Lucky bastard, you say, clinking your glasses and corroding with jealousy. Not so, says Tim. He recounts: "I got confused, so I decided to just focus on one. The others got mad . . . they all left." The fallout: Tim is alone with his Liberty Valance—another hero shaking his head, wondering what went wrong.

What if Tim were alone in his hotel-room shower and the Swedes were still at the Black Jack table? I wager that would not have been so confusing. As one art dealer friend decodes: "With fantasy, you are in control. Where else does this happen in your life? Rewind, replay, replace, change, alter, and savour. You are head of casting, choreographer, lighting man, best boy, director, the works."

The lesson? With fantasy suspended, you, BPs, are freed from the flaws and consequences of entanglement, left to muse on what could be rather than living with the fallout of what is. There is no regret. There is no reckoning.

One babe (the rustle of silk stockings) epitomizes the debate when asked if she's had strap-on sex with her Bush Pilot:

I wish! It's a big, unfulfilled fantasy of mine. But would I lose respect for him?

REALITY CHECK

✓ "Unfulfilled."

✓ "Lose respect for him."

Think of it this way: What would the world look like if all our fantasies did come true? It would be an Elvis universe populated by insatiable drones covered in chicken fat, poutine and body fluids. It would be a Sunset Strip of aimless, well-meaning fluffers. Everyone would be naked under their trench coats. There would be no country music. No Romantic poetry. No cage matches. Pamela Anderson would be messily shaving her legs in your kitchen sink, looking drunk and tired. Porn stars would be out of work and hitchhiking with small knapsacks. The *Penthouse* centrefold would be eating hickory sticks on your couch and no longer airbrushed. Mona Lisa would be laughing.

Now you tell me: What's hotter? That, or this: A scribe friend recalls a fantasy that, buried in a time capsule, twenty years later, endures.

> I had this huge crush on a teacher when I was seventeen, in high school. She was about twenty-four or twenty-five, I think. We used to get talking about pretty serious things. She gave me the key to her apartment, and I fed her rabbits when she was away (except the time I forgot and she almost cried when I told her). I had an "individual study" creative writing course with her—just her and me. Once, as writing "inspiration," we went outside and made a snowman. She was wearing a short skirt and the snowman building involved some bending over! And then, the climax . . . I was walking out of her classroom and she was walking in. We found ourselves on opposite sides of one of those school doors that have the long, vertical rectangular window on them. And we just spontaneously both walked up to that window and kissed on the lips, with the glass in between. Then, we both turned around and walked away like

it didn't happen. Nothing else happened after that, though I sometimes imagined having sex with her in the back room of journalism class when I'd go there on the weekends and would be all alone. I Google her sometimes. She's now teaching in Kansas.

Bush Pilots, pleasure begins in our brains. Exhibit A: You Rollerblade (so well!) past a woman at a street corner waiting for the light to turn green. She is wearing a sundress. What could be under the sundress? You—skilfully—consider the possibilities. You—again, skilfully—decide on nothing. Exhibit B: Later that night, your babe stands on your doorstep with her old-school headphones on, listening to "Girls, Girls, Girls." Walking over to your place, she pictures herself a groupie at the whim of Vince Neil, a nameless hurdle in the sexual obstacle course he is running in some hotel room in Dallas. The point: When you start to get busy, the business is hot. Jostling around in your cerebellum is a woman on a street corner in a sundress with nothing underneath—and jostling around in your babe's? Having her pink spandex fan-pants ripped off by one rock-hard Vince Neil.

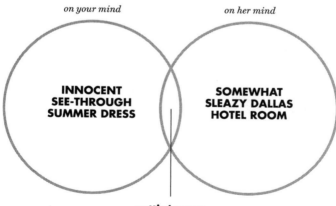

Fantasy is the match to the fire, not the fire itself. Your job? Make space for it. Prompt it. Answer to it without smothering it. One Bush Pilot, a modern Casanova with a thing for pout-mouthed medievalists, considers fantasy a crucial step in advancing his sexual prowess. He calls it "batting practice, foul shooting, meditation: the stuff of greats." But does he want them to come true? "Never." Do we? Same.

EXTRA CREDIT

THE UNMENTIONABLES:
A SELECT LEXICON OF LINGERIE

Bush Pilots, do you fantasize about your babe sliding down a stripper pole in your bedroom, wearing nothing but that underwear Marisa Tomei wears in *The Wrestler*, which are not really underwear but go in a T-formation up her bum and might be named after a kitchen implement, but you are not sure which one? I thought so.

Because you are my peep show and I am your Pole Fairy, here is a guide to the magical closet of lingerie, that sartorial Narnia you dream of. Guess what? We do too.

TYPES OF LINGERIE

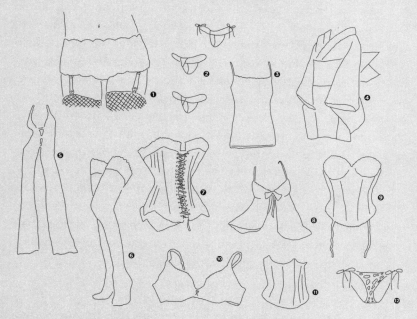

1. *Garter* 2. *G-string, T-string and thong* 3. *Camisole* 4. *Kimono* 5. *Negligee* 6. *Stay-ups*
7. *Corset* 8. *Babydoll* 9. *Bustier* 10. *Bra* 11. *French cinch(er)* 12. *Jungle love*

To be worn with a hair toss:

Baby Doll. Where Roman Polanski meets *Valley of the Dolls* in sleepwear. This abbreviated nightgown has an empire waist, which means that, like you, it hugs her breasts and flares beneath them. Short, sometimes sheer, and sometimes with matching panties, the Baby Doll works equally well with a pacifier, French cigarette or spatula over the hot stove when heavily pregnant in a dirt-floored cabin. Inspiration: Watch another one of Tennessee Williams's iconic, lustful housewives: the dirty, drawling, soda-sucking, junior Monroe Carroll Baker (backed by a music-box soundtrack) in the 1956 film (you guessed it) *Baby Doll*.

Bra. That helpful number nudging her breasts closer to her neckline, the bra was your first mention in the unmentionables—beneath her angora V-neck, in your front hall closet, squirming on top of the Cougar boots, smelling like bootlegged liquor, Frankie Goes to Hollywood taunting you from the record player. It varies from the breast-flattening *Boys Don't Cry* (But Will When They See This Bra) sports bra to the torpedo-shaped cones favoured by June Cleaver. Identify your preference and purchase accordingly. Deal-Maker Alert: Consider taking your babe along for the ride. She will be ushered into a curtained room and fitted by a bossy doyenne with a measuring tape for a scarf. Have fun with this unabashedly sexist *Pygmalion* scenario; be the wealthy Richard Gere to her streetwalking-yet-classy-on-the-inside Pretty Woman. Peruse the extensive buffet de bra. Fastening in the front or back? Underwire for contour, or simple strawberry-printed cotton? Black, white or red? For inspiration, despite her considerable, if not fatal, missteps since, revisit that lace-wearing, armpit-drying tramp Madonna in *Desperately Seeking Susan*.

Corset. Fearsomely sexy, the corset still reigns as queen of the undergarments. With the boning in her bodice, she lifts your babe's breasts and cinches her waist. The most democratic of all fetish garments, the corset can be found in many a material, from lace to leather to latex, for your breathy submissive or your sculpted domme, your Elizabethan royal or your bar wench, your bride or your punk. Bush Pilot Bonus: Bush and bottom are bared. Deal-Maker Alert: Consider the aforementioned shopping excursion; take your babe, blindfolded, to a corset maker—in San Francisco or Madrid—for her very own, made to measure. If she prefers less press, choose the waist-only version, called (not to be confused with that belle du jour of the same name) the French cinch. Or instead, buy the extended strapless bra known as a bustier. Made famous by Swedish goddess Anita Ekberg in Fellini's *La Dolce Vita*, in which she, after (I swear) carrying a tiny white kitten—at times, on her head—through the streets of Rome, happens upon the Fontana di Trevi and ducks under its falling waters, only to be joined by Marcello Mastroianni, who went (I swear) to get a glass of milk for the kitten.

Camisole. Her version of your Fruit of the Loom undershirt, the camisole is the silk number she wears beneath her blouse. Reminiscent of *Working Girl* (and most other Harrison Ford movies), her breasts swing freely beneath it and her nipples are teased to tautness by its fabric. Can also be worn with jean shorts and combat boots by the babe who cannot help but laugh at the word blouse. (No-Fly List Alert: Never say "cami.") Alternatively, let your babe steal your Fruit of the Loom undershirt to reprise Kim Basinger's cross-dressing in *9 1/2 Weeks*—or to evoke those naughty mid-nineties Calvin Klein bus billboards wherein androgynous teenagers, already exhausted by their own beauty, lean against prop ladders.

Garter Belt. The classic garment that, in a feat of blazing practicality, manages both to facilitate the wearing of stockings and be a belt. Huh, Mistress? The part around her waist is the garter belt, and the straps that run down her thighs are the garters. Consult the 1969 film *Women in Love*, adapted from that perverse scribe D.H. Lawrence's novel of the same name, starring the inimitable King of Hearts' Alan Bates and the garter belt–wearing "Ursula," Jennie Linden.

G-string. G-string and her sleeker sister T-string comprise the fiery and prolific daughters of thong (not to be mistaken for the tool hanging from your barbecue). The wedgies of the undergarment world, these lucky hussies ride the crack of your babe's kit. If you are not familiar with these microscopic offerings, drop this book and your itchy monk's robes right now. Get thee to thy nearest strip club (or convenience store parking lot), for this undiscerning triumvirate is everywhere and loves to be seen. When peeking out above her jeans, the T-bar is the drive-thru of lingerie: long lineups, low prices and the implicit promise of faster service. When not peeking out above her jeans, the T-bar is French lace, part of a set—and the reason your boss doesn't have a panty line.

Kimono. Think of the starved romantic, the incessant diary-keeping Anaïs Nin. Think of the French high schooler in Marguerite Duras's *The Lover*. Think too of Nagisa Oshima's *In the Realm of the Senses*. The mistress and her master make love ferociously. They never eat. They barely lift themselves to drink sake. They are so consumed with each other's bodies that one peripheral geisha remarks upon the master's virility. You will too. Anxious they will be discovered, the mistress and her master abscond to a love den. They are insatiable fugitives, swearing that to reach total pleasure you must go almost to the end. For fear of ever being apart, the mistress pulls the sash from her kimono and strangles her master while they make love. He is euphoric. They perform the act again, and this time he urges her not to stop. And then he dies. And then she cuts off his penis. And then she goes crazy and walks the streets of Tokyo with a knife in one hand and her bloody prize in the other. The moral of the story: Get her a kimono, but don't ask her to strangle you with it.

Negligee. The Tom Collins of the lingerie bar, the negligee, or peignoir, is a long, often sheer robe best worn over a matching nightgown with high-heeled slippers in a penthouse apartment, sitting at the vanity whilst brushing hair, cigarette smouldering in the ashtray, wearing dark lipstick to bed and going by the name Bette Davis.

Stay-ups. We know how you love to tamper with images of our virtue; stop trying so hard and let the stay-up do it for you. No garters needed; silicone and special rubber act as an adhesive, gripping her inner thighs before you can—and doing what you cannot: staying up. Foot resting on the kitchen table, in her Parisian apartment with her pet rooster on the balcony, lazily eating a pastry, your babe rolls them on—and up—before slipping into her kilt, flight-attendant uniform, graduation gown, angel wings or horn-rimmed glasses.

String Bikini. Another classic undergarment, this covers her front and back with two very diminutive triangles. With its sides cutting high and its waist sitting low, in the wild, wild world of panties, the string bikini is one skimpy little number. While it may not growl, it can be purchased in a print that does: The leopard, the cheetah and even the tiger can spread themselves like a rug before her fire. Present with irony. I suggest baring the cashmere on your chest and singing The Time's "Jungle Love," as opposed to—note well—The Steve Miller Band's song of the same name.

Tap pant. Knickers that like to play but, disappointingly, cannot tap dance, though you of the spats and cane may, upon seeing them, do your own shuffle and brush. Reminiscent of those waistline-flouncing, cloche hat–wearing rebels, the flappers, the tap pant is the 1930s prototype for our much less subtle "hot pant." Choose silk or cotton toile for your babe who bakes shortcake from scratch, knows the difference between eyelash and chantilly lace—and has never heard the term cyberspace. Ruffles optional. Bush Pilot Bonus: When presenting these to your pin-up, cite the surprisingly practical-minded President whisperer, Marilyn as The Girl in 1955's *The Seven-Year Itch*: "You know when it gets hot like this, you know what I do? I keep my undies in the icebox."

Teddy. Camisole + tap pant = the enthusiastic teddy!

Your pajamas. For the spendthrift and Hef, these never fail. Please, at the very least, buy silk.

CHAPTER 7
TALKING DIRTY

NOTE FROM THE FIELD:
MARY, MARY, QUITE CONTRARY

Talk dirty to me, James thinks to himself, and immediately banishes the thought. Her name is Mary. Or Good Mary to him. She is all wistful glances, French braids, sonatas and volunteer work. She sits three pews in front of him. She should have birds trilling on her shoulders. Now, to James's astonishment, after several shy conversations at the samovar, he is on his knees and face to face with her panties—identical to a pair he watched a nun buy the day before. Good Mary in her good panties, and James is in her seashell-themed bedroom. This is a surprise.

He lifts her frame in a pose reminiscent of the Pietà and lays her down on the hard bed. She glistens in the sunlight. James unbuttons his Sunday pants. *Save me*. He trips over a rescued pet and lowers himself to her, taking in her willing lips, supporting her arched spine. She is more sensual than he expected. But there is an element of suffering to it, and this seems appropriate. Good Mary's breathing turns to moans. Vocal, James thinks to himself. She might scream, or maybe she'll sing. Either would be nice.

On the brink of communion, her moans take the form of words. "Pardon?" he says, throat clearing, incredulously. She repeats her request. James stares at her. Good Mary becomes Fast Mary becomes Commander Mary before his eyes. Her usual soprano is now grainy and fatal. Her words are clear. They hang in the air, orphaned, expectant. He winces, he stutters. He looks to the heavens, really seeing them for the first time. She says again: "Talk dirty to me."

DON'T LET HER WISH BE YOUR DEATH WISH

Bush Pilots, you have spent your lives seducing women. You can quote Yeats and discuss the Bible as erotic literature. You speak Cantonese and some holiday Spanish (e.g., "Screwito?"). You flirt in your sleep. You have faced many tests, all of them administered by your paramours, but none as steep as this one. Talk dirty to me. Four words strung together in such a way as to spell sudden death for you, the articulate man. They are the black ice in your bedroom, the dark horse in your stable, the deer in your headlights. But, Bush Pilots, they don't have to be. Let's talk. Let's talk dirty.

KNOW YOUR AUDIENCE

Your babe's invitation is extended. Her instructions are succinct. Before you utter one suggestive word, ask yourself: Just how dirty can I be here? Do some quick cultural reconnaissance. Is your Mary inclined toward Márquez or Metallica, Pasternak or Poison, Emily Post or Eminem? When you fart like—in your words—an injured sea lion, does she find it funny or cruel? When you break out your Bob, does she break out her Doug? Or is she too busy with her embroidery? When she watches *Heroes*, does she mean to? What does she like to listen to: children singing or Lady Gaga? Calibrate, Bush Pilots, calibrate.

Dirt-o-Meter

DROPPING THE F-BOMB

To swear or not to swear? That is the question. The activity may be X-rated, but it does not mean the talk can be too. Don't roll your dirty dice and expect to win big from your wager. For some women, having their nether regions repurposed as an expletive is a fatal mistake, especially in those early, defining stages of a carnal courtship.

In her stunned eyes, you of the "beeps" quickly devolve from Cyrano to Psycho, cowboy to Cro-Magnon. Don't find yourself tumescent and stranded on her fire escape, foaming Irish Spring from the mouth like a rabid incubus. Make sure your babe is game before you turn her lady parts into profanities. How? The shortest route: Ask her.

That said, we of the bush know just how hard it is for you of the bushwhacking to ask for directions. Note your babe's verbal tendencies. These indicate the rules, conscious or unconscious, by which she lives. Beware the following telltale chestnuts: phooey, fudge and, most damning (oops), fiddle. These are the Brutus to your foul-mouthed Caesar. Of course, we recognize that once a woman is locked in a voluptuous stronghold, rules may be broken—but, until given further permission, let her habits be your goalposts. Aim between them.

THE VERB GIRL VS. THE ADJECTIVE GIRL

Now that you have established your rating, you are ready to move into your material. Which camp does she belong to? Does she want to know what you are planning on doing to her? Or does she want to be described by you? In other words, is she a verb girl or an adjective girl? Or, is she, like most babes, both? But how, Mistress, oh how can I tell?

You can't, my darling BPs, unless you pull your panicked boner over and ask her for directions. No way, Mistress, you object, only losers do that; I am, like Jimmy Page in his white suit with his double-necked Gibson, too mythical a lay to ask you of the bushes for guidance through your thickets. I'd rather be totally augered yet appear coolly in charge.

All right, Hammer of the Gods. Then, your surest bet is to start out adjective and finish verb. Start descriptively. Comment on your babe's hair, her skin, her smell, her chain-mail bra and how she really works it with that medieval spear. Follow up with your follow-through: the promise of a legendary screw broken down into details. Just how will you ravish her nipples, the slope of her neck? Just what will your hot rod do to her lady parts? Again, know her preferences and adjust delivery and content accordingly.

A man telling you everything he wants to do to you before he does it is amazing. This can be totally simple and slow. It does not have to promise sexual prowess. For example: "First I'm going to take this button and undo it. Slowly." (Adjectives are a bonus.) If the guy looks at the button and then looks you in the eye as he grasps the button on your blouse and unbuttons it just after he says he will, it is incredibly sexy because the temptation is so close in time to the reward. The build is so fun and titillating. He has the power to tell you a story and what will happen next, and I love instigators, so I have a real weakness when it occasionally happens. Also, if he changes up the pacing with anticipation, there is nothing better than snaps on a shirt that you can rip off in one go. Or Velcro. They need to make more of this.
—Babe (orchids, Westerns, mosh pits)

Velcro. Affirmative.

NO COMMENT

Stage fright? Like a good detective, begin with the facts. Get on the case. Inquire after her sensations. Questions can be your starter fluid. Try the gruff classic: "Do you like it like that? Or do you like it like this?" Note your decibel. We want hi-fi at low volume. Never turn it up to eleven. Take your time; you are not auctioning us off. And as a general rule, heed the words of Mark Twain: "Eschew surplusage." Keep the sentences short. Oh, and no comments on your own prowess. No "Danny Boy." No clinical terminology like urethral sponge. No purring and no prompt notes. That said . . .

SHOW NO FEAR

Bush Pilots, do not hesitate. One no-mercy-men-for-breakfast friend put it this way: "There's nothing worse than the half-assed dirty talker." Without conviction, you are an unsure Dom, a crying man crawling out of a birthday cake. Only the believer is believable.

But, my usually smooth male friend retorts,

> When they ask you to talk dirty, there is a huge self-consciousness on my part; I feel ridiculous. My lines feel formal and stilted. "Oh. Ah. Baby." You can just hear the question mark on the end.

My response?

Unleash your alter ego.
Find a suit that fits.

As what, oh Mistress, what shall I be? Spicoli? Aaron Neville? King Richard III? All of the New Kids on the Block, but especially Donnie?

Pilot error.

My darlings, here is your . . .

CASTING CALL

Sometimes, when doing something that feels outlandish—like pitching hesitant smut—it is useful to channel a second self, an alternate identity. Are you:

> **The Sportscaster.** You call the plays as they come and make predictions based on past performances. Your tone is subdued until the action gets too hot, but even then, you are still fit for a major network. Adjusting your tie, you comment, "I'm tweaking your nipples. You're tugging my hair. I'm licking your earlobes. You're cupping my cheeks.

You know I like a little anal play. I'm primed to enter you from behind. And you're primed to take me. Here we go folks. Holy Mackinaw!"

The Metal Head. With your hard syllables and your three-finger salute, you fall asleep counting bikinis. You have a mouth like a monster truck. Your little hellcat has told you she wants it noisy. And she wants it XXX. Through a grin of gold teeth, you growl, loud enough for a capacity-crowd coliseum, "Baby, I'm your babysitter an' you're gonna ---- my --- and throbbing ---- an' then I'm gonna ---- your wet ----- until we're both screaming for mommy to come home from prison."

Dirty Harry. Your lines are the rogue heroes of the bed-room. The only dirty word you know is regret. You own nothing but a dog and a hot plate. Hand on your holster, you mutter things like, "You've got to ask yourself one question: 'Do I feel lucky?'" without flinching.

The Literate Pervert. You speak a patois of the tawdry and the numinous. You wear a fedora, know your cheeses and are vaguely married. You are usually broke. You've been mistaken for Dylan. Women are your salvation and your hellfire. You tend toward phrases like "glorious slut" and can easily quote Henry Miller's description of a vul-va in Tropic of Cancer—"An Arabian zero, the sign which springs endless mathematical worlds, the fulcrum which balances the stars and the light dreams"—while shuck-ing oysters (you stole). Deal-Breaker Alert: Henry Miller is only to be cited to women with a penchant for heavy eye makeup, vintage slips, alcohol and puppetry.

The Sweet Talker. Or are you the dirty talker's brother-at-large? An accidental bard, you make broth out of pine needles and flatten flowers between pages of Thoreau. You adore us, and you know how to express your adoration. You spend days on a collarbone, weeks on a bottom lip. You are a miraculous relic, building anticipation, the essential ember in the slow burn of any bedroom. In a world where true intimacy has become a dying art form, where language can be buckled into tacky puns, nicknames and abbreviations, tweeted and sexted, the sweet talker can be a welcome respite. You are a modern sonnet, a naughty lullaby.

Choose Your Alter Ego

The Sweet Talker

The Sportscaster

Dirty Harry

The Metal Head

The Literate Pervert

FILL IN THE BLANKS

If you are still tongue-tied, travel back to the wood-panelled living room of your youth:

I (intransitive verb) to (transitive verb) your (adjective) (noun) so (adverb) on this (piece of furniture) with your (piece of clothing) up around your (adjective) (plural noun) and my (adjective) (noun) inside your (adjective) (adjective) (adjective) (noun) right (adverb).

CHEAT SHEET:
FOR THE DIRTY-TALKING MAN

NO:

✗ Friendly Giant
✗ Cowardly Lion
✗ McLovin
✗ Colonel Kurtz
✗ Franz Kafka
✗ Bobcat Goldthwait
✗ Mike Tyson
✗ Ron Burgundy
✗ Iron Chef
✗ Boss Hog
✗ Van Morrison
✗ Silent Bob
✗ Tattoo
✗ Winston Churchill
✗ David Wooderson
✗ blood relatives

N.B.B.P.: A note on Tony Montana: Get Scarface out of your system now. Sneer the following: "Say hello to my little friend." Again: "Say hello to my little friend." Repeat as needed until expurgated.

YES:

✓ President Obama
✓ Humphrey Bogart
✓ André 3000
✓ Muhammad Ali
✓ Wolfman Jack
✓ Werner Herzog

- ✓ Peter Mansbridge
- ✓ Jimmy Page
  (the early years)
- ✓ Javier Bardem
  (except *No Country for Old Men*)
- ✓ Wayne Dobler

- ✓ Dallas Winston
- ✓ Jack Palance
  (the alive years)
- ✓ Serge Gainsbourg
  (more sober than drunk)
- ✓ Johnny Cash

LET'S TAKE IT OUTSIDE

Bush Pilots, why keep your naughty talk cloistered in the bedroom? Find a leather booth, the last seats in a movie theatre, a construction site after hours. Articulate and expound upon your fantasies. And then, like the consummate gentleman I know you are, invite your babe to do the same.

If you are still too shy, if the suit doesn't fit, pick up some erotic literature. Read it aloud. Bend your babe's ears. Bend your own. When was the last time you heard your voice wrap around something beautiful?

Tool of Seduction
EROTICA

For me a work of fiction exists only insofar as it affords me what I shall bluntly call aesthetic bliss, that is a sense of being somehow, somewhere, connected with other states of being where art (curiosity, tenderness, kindness, ecstasy) is the norm.

—Vladimir Nabokov, epilogue to *Lolita*

FOR THE BABE IN PRAISE OF DIRTY OLDER MEN

Tropic of Cancer, Henry Miller, pages 248–258.
Classic Miller: An existential hard-on, manically observant, he is at his most foul, delicate and carnivorous.

Sabbath's Theatre, Philip Roth, pages 215–235.

Now this is phone sex. (As in Nicholson Baker's *Vox*, all 165 pages of it.)

Couples, John Updike, pages 46–56, 133–138, 194–204, 312–313, 433–436.

When cheating in the suburbs was still poetic.

FOR THE SELF-MYTHOLOGIZING ROMANTIC IN TANGO LESSONS

Henry and June, Anaïs Nin, pages 81–85, 268–274.

A literary webcam, Nin's state is one of ecstatic self-portraiture. Encore, you say? Find the short story "The Woman on the Dunes" in Nin's collection, *Little Birds*.

Diana: A Diary in the Second Person, Russell Smith, pages 20–31, 61–66, 109–114.

Because your babe has always wanted to read another woman's diary. Bush Pilot Bonus: written (for your dirty-talking convenience) in the second person.

The Lover, Marguerite Duras, pages 37–41.

Draw the mosquito netting; this is the virginity scene.

FOR THE BABE IN CHAPS

All the Pretty Horses, Cormac McCarthy, page 142.

Unspeakably beautiful: love affair as ghost story.

The Collected Works of Billy the Kid, Michael Ondaatje, page 16.

How the outlaw lies with his lady.

FOR THE FAUX-PARISIAN SEX SLAVE

Story of O, Pauline Réage, the first chapter.

Metronomic prose, a château, masked men, ropes and a whip make a love letter. For some.

FOR THE FORMER GIRL GUIDE

Bear, Marian Engel, page 93.
Settle in for some genuine Canadiana. Two words:
ursine cunnilingus.

FOR THE BABE WITH THE WILTING BOUQUET

"You Have the Lovers," Leonard Cohen
"As the Mist Leaves No Scar," Leonard Cohen
"i like my body when it is with your," e.e. cummings
Moll Flanders, Daniel Defoe
For Whom the Bell Tolls, Ernest Hemingway
"I Crave Your Mouth, Your Voice, Your Hair," Pablo Neruda
"Sonnet 31," William Shakespeare
"When Man Enters Woman," Anne Sexton
"The Song of Songs," the authorized King James version
or the Ariel and Chana Block translation

FOR THE BABE WITH THE FLYAWAY HAIR
AND THE PAROLE OFFICER

*The Dirt: Confessions of the World's Most Notorious
Rock Band,* Mötley Crüe with Neil Strauss.
Page 51. Surf's up, bro; irresistible half-wit Tommy Lee dis-
covers female ejaculation in the back of his van.
Pages 113–116. Spandex, tube tops and those dark horses of
rock and roll infamy: a Champagne bottle, a tube of tooth-
paste, a telephone receiver—and a call home to mother.
Page 146. Spoiled blonde, and all id, lead singer Vince Neil
sets up sexual obstacle courses for groupies to cope with
his melancholia after crashing his wife's 240Z.
Page 238. A litter box, a leash and a collar. Meow.
Pages 344–347. First comes Pam. Then comes marriage.

Then comes your graduation from Part Two to Part Three. Congratulations, you made it! High cinq, BP. High cinq, Mistress. Can we drink now—say, at the every stupefying mention of the word bush? No. But you may sew the following badges onto the crotch of your Pilot pants: the George Clooney–Clark Gable–Marcello Mastroianni approved badge, the I Like my Dinner Spicy badge, the Certified Garter Belt Disentangler badge and the Lovely Versatile Useful Flexible Adjectives badge.

Forgive me for being so forthright, Commander Mistress. I forgive you. But can we get to the skronkin' now? Thought you'd never ask, my Beeps (represent!).

PART THREE
Takeoff

FLIGHT MISSION:
BUSH PILOTS,
LAND YOUR NORSEMAN
SMOOTHLY IN THE BUSH
AND BACK COUNTRY

A HUDDLE WITH
CAPTAIN GOODSCREW

Captain Dylan I. Goodscrew

BUSH PILOTS, YOU'RE READY. AT LEAST YOU THINK YOU ARE.
You've flirted with aplomb. You've cooked a twelve-course meal. You've entered the fantasy trade. You've talked dirty as if it was your mother tongue. Now, your babe, after an incident with the garden hose, is standing in your living room, wearing nothing but a wool blanket, her long, red hair dripping onto your rented carpet. Well done. Thankfully, she is laughing. Even better. You pluck a flower from your crop and place it between your brushed teeth. She says "aww," but it has some sarcasm to it, and this excites you. She lets the blanket slip off her shoulder. You let the flower fall. She lifts an eyebrow. You lift an eyebrow. You kiss her shoulder. She lets the blanket slip off the other shoulder. You kiss that shoulder too. And then her collarbone. And then her neck. And then her earlobes. And then, somehow, the blanket drops and she is standing like a Grecian statue inside your bachelor apartment. You look at her—

so many curves! You look at your boner—so little time! What to do now, Mistress, oh what to do?

BPs, I do not for a moment doubt you have memorably pleasured a mouth, a rack, a Lady Go-Go, a Madame Butterfly and a luscious kit, but there is always room for improvement—in our case, yours. So how to land your craft smoothly, unrushed, every time—and with your eyes closed?

From the flight deck, Captain D. I. Goodscrew:

> Smooching is pretty important. Women place a lot of value on a man's ability to kiss. From that, they glean how skilled he is in the fuck department. Kissing is an indication of give and take, grooming and experience. Then, I usually do some body stuff before making a beeline for the clit. It's all about the clit. Take the right route to get there so her bits are actually ready. Cunnilingus—I usually meditate while doing it by counting backward from one hundred. By the time I get to zero, they always come. After that? You've got a hard-on and a condom on, I like to start missionary.

It's all about the clit. That's an affirmative. Take the right route to get there. That's also an affirmative.

But that, my Pilots of the Bush, is just the beginning. In Part Three: Takeoff, here is how it stacks up: the Big O (hers), first base, second base, third base, cunnilingus, soixante-neuf, the G-spot, positions and (really, Mistress, oh really?!) rear entry.

Break.

CHAPTER 8
THE BIG O (HERS)

NOTE FROM THE FIELD:
SUPER COCK

Sam has nothing to lose. She has no house, no husband, no children and no job. There is no one to disappoint, feed, coddle or betray. Sam can smoke, get blighted and screw anyone she wants. And on this night, she will. Opulent museum ballroom. Hair in a ponytail. Vintage gown. High-tops. Sam is in the centre of the dance floor, ringed in smoke and undulating like a rare seaweed. Sam is a Yoko-esque Yes. As per the laws of nature, a man approaches. Black tie, greying sideburns, divorce. "Sam?" Opening her eyes, she instantly recognizes him as "Cookie." The head of Tripping when she was a camper too young to touch, Cookie was a sly-eyed Sam Shepard with a guitar and a notebook of poems. Cookie was the stuff of fantasy. So was Sam. "Do you still have that red bikini?" Cookie asks, bull's-eyeing. "I memorized them all."

Five glasses of Champagne, two cigars and one pornographic cab ride later, Cookie and Sam are chasing each other through Sam's apartment, playing naked hide-and-go-seek. With the moxie of a matador, Cookie pulls open the top drawer of Sam's dresser. Instead of finding Sam's old bikinis, Cookie stumbles upon what appears to be a lineup of pets looking to be adopted. In the shape of eggs, bullets, hand-held mixers, and his very own exaggerated vine and berries, a dozen vibrators growl back at him. Giving his shrinking boys a tender squeeze, Cookie laments: If only we were still up north, quoting Pony Boy, faking astronomy and staying on second base. No batteries. No outlets. No ten-inch "Super Cocks" that never tire. Sam sidles up to him. She wants him to join her secret society, and make nice with Heart Breaker, Gigolo and Meany. Cookie catches his reflection in the mirror. He is brave. This is not his first duel in the woods. He has faced down lightning storms and black bears. Surely he can face this down.

COME

Trumping even your precious orgasm is your babe's precious orgasm. Hers is your mission, your mandate, your master. You cry: Come with me. Come to and against me. Come above, below and beside me. Come because of and before me. Just come.

But of course, you do not actually say this, BP, for your babe is not your cow dog and you are not her cowboy. No. You let the curlicue of your tongue, the ramble of your hands, the wink of your Henry Winkler do your beckoning. Sometimes, it happens. Sometimes, it doesn't. Sometimes, you're not really sure either way. There was a clear vocal crescendo, a thrust of her lower quarters and climactic contractions. But wait, were those mine? Did she or didn't she? She looks happy. Or wait, is that me?

THE POWER OF MYTH

Bush Pilots, a woman's orgasm can be like the sphinx sitting at the crossroads, staring at you poker-faced while you sweat and plead to get by. It can feel like a mythic journey, the stuff of heroes. You have your canteen, your walking stick, your falcon. You have your boner, your goggles and Obi-Wan's voice in your head. You have your "Sexual Body and the Yoga of Light" training intensive. You have your Sacred Sex Intermediate Tantra workshop. You have your patented moves: Gilgamesh, the Swivel Chair and Careless Whisper. Well, lay it all down, BPs. There is something I need to tell you.

We come with instructions: our own.

Scandal!

LADIES FIRST

For all the affectionate bossing around I might do, cat to mouse, in this, your field guide to the female form, here, my minions, is the most important tip I can give you: In the delivery of your babe's pleasure (sha-pow!), you and your benevolent, highly trained apparatus are not alone. In fact, just as we, your babes, are responsible for our happiness, we, your babes, are responsible for our pleasure.

Whoa, Mistress, am I off the hook? Can I retire now and get a penile paperweight for my efforts? Can I cash in on my tenure, spend my days mowing the lawn and crack my first Busch Light before noon?

Can I singularly pursue the fulfillment of my wizardly boner and leave my babe and her lady parts to fend for themselves? "What about my orgasm?" she says? What about it? I say. I'm retired!

No, darling BP. You can't. You still have a starring role to play here; the bulletin is: Your babe's Big O is a creature of the brain—her brain. It is unleashed by her. Only once she unlocks the riddle, can you too. In short, aside from me, her experience is your best teacher.

ANTHEMS FOR A 17-YEAR-OLD GIRL

So here, Bush Pilots, is a glimpse into how we, your babes, figured it out when we had crimped hair, rainbow braces and a membership to the Rick Springfield fan club. Here, Bush Pilots, is what that self-titled debut meant to us then and what that means for you now.

That's right, Humper. Just as you were mounting the cast-iron bottom of the bathtub or sending your Slinky into the mouth of the vacuum cleaner, we too were industrious scouts, finding the heretofore hidden properties of household items: the firmness of a feather pillow, the drone of the washing machine, the rush of bathwater, the jets of the hot tub.

> I masturbated early and often, and I don't remember when I started having orgasms, but I know I was having them regularly (by myself) in high school. I masturbated with my finger and then, later—or more satisfyingly—with a pillow, and I would often masturbate for hours, coming over and over and over again.
> —Babe (ripped chiffon dress, holding a John Cheever book)

HIDING IN THE BUSHES

We found pleasure in the playground—riding the rocking horse, wrapping ourselves around the climbing pole, the rope course. We too were naturalists, following the way of the hand before school . . . after school . . . during school.

The first real orgasm came in grade six, exploratory, Jacques Cousteau style. An entire universe opened, and that's all I could do for weeks. Though a bit of a dirty, shameful secret, being such an innocent, I wasn't even sure what was truly happening. I just knew that it was so good it must be bad.

—Babe (genius IQ and a kit you could rest your drink on)

Another early bloomer credits "Judy Blume and my mom's Sidney Sheldon novels" for teaching her how to come "fairly young by myself." Our methods were as varied as we were. N.B.B.P.: They still are.

PENTHOUSE FORUM

Alone, your babe plays with pressure, motion, speed and positioning. The locus of her desire, that luxurious, long-legged nub of nerve endings, her go-go, is, as you know, designed for one purpose only: pleasure. How to make her hum? Your babe teases herself. She lies on her back, knees crossed, thighs squeezed together. She lies on her belly, legs spread apart. She stands, mons pressed against a chair back, the hard edge of a dining-room table. She ritualizes: candlelight, Serge Gainsbourg and Jane Birkin's naughty duet "Je t'aime . . . moi non plus," lube and a Gauloise at the ready. She uses your silk tie for a blindfold.

She barely makes it home from work, touching herself to unravel the taut line of a frantic day. She doesn't make it home from work— heeding the cry in the stockroom, at her desk. She comes in the front seat of her pickup truck, rocking her hips to the howl of a running engine. She comes in the back seat of a cab by rubbing herself against her jean seam. She is preternaturally discreet. She wakes up the neighbourhood.

ONLY THE LONELY?

Mistress, oh Mistress, you ask snappily, is the "bush party for one" only for the bespectacled librarian, the private-school headmistress, the bobby-pinned spinster? Is it only for babes with many, many cats? I mean, surely, it's not for babes with Bush Pilots like me whose very M.O. is her Big O?

Pilot error.

HUMPER'S INDEX

Darling BPs, the truth is, most bushes like to party. To show you just how popular and indiscriminate the bush party is, and because I know how you love your stats, the first comprehensive study in sexuality, the *Kinsey Report*, found that 92 per cent of men masturbated, while only 62 per cent of women did. Forty years later, the American Medical Association's *Human Sexuality* cites solo love as common fare (98 per cent to your 95) for women of all ages, even more so as women get older. In fact, about 70 per cent of all married women (solitaire diamond ring on or off?) are worshippers of Lady Go-Go.

Um, wicked? Yes, BP. Gold star! Your babe's body is an accumulation of her habits and preferences. Her ability to receive touch is one that she cultivates over time. If she was precociously self-aware, a propensity for pleasure having been found at an early age, your babe is more likely to be freely and multi-orgasmic (Sha-pow! sha-pow! sha-pow!) now. This early explorer is a case in point:

> I started having sex at seventeen with my first serious boyfriend, who I went out with off and on until I was nineteen and continued to sleep with off and on until I was about twenty-two. It took some time before I was comfortable enough with him to figure out how to have an orgasm with him, but by the time I was in college, I'd figured it out and I used to come a lot (at least three, often five, or even seven times) when we had sex.

Exhibit B, the recollections of yet another junior speculator:

> The first orgasm from actually having sex did not come from the first boyfriend or even the third; it came from a one-month tryst with a strapping but none-too-bright athlete from another high school who, even at sixteen, I knew was a man of little mystery. But it was this broad-shouldered man-boy who, in his white sport socks, made me come again and again, to the point of being almost comical.

Sexperts (with such provocative surnames!) Julia Heiman and Joseph LoPiccolo cite this breathy, rosy-cheeked portion of the female populace as being somewhere between 15 and 25 per cent. And the rest?

While one-third of women are consistently orgasmic, one-third are occasional and one-third are not at all.

"One third are not at all?" Whoa, Mistress, you just totally dowsed my vibe; I might have to go home and do something punishing like listen to the Dave Matthews Band. Don't do it, BP, don't do it. Your consolation round: This last camp, the "not-at-all" camp, is often optimistically referred to as "pre-orgasmic." Many babes reverse what they'd come to see as their sexual fates. Fist bump! But before you break out your backflip, Bush Pilots, as the numbers expound, some babes don't. The hard truth: Try as you both might, your babe may not find her bliss. Whoa, Mistress, can you sing "Crash into Me"?

P.S.: Marilyn Monroe, after three husbands and legions of lovers, including one pornographically dashing First Man, once confided she had never had an orgasm.

P.P.S.: Neither had Kim Cattrall, the very-much-in-heat Lassie of *Porky's*, until she met her third husband and together they penned the enigmatically titled *Satisfaction: The Art of the Female Orgasm.*

P.P.P.S.: And Marvin Gaye could not dance.

LIFE BEFORE THE BIG O

So what does that one-third look like? Angry, prayerful and in mom-jeans? No, BPs. The daughters of Marilyn come in every form—including this wildcat whose every drawled word sounds like phone sex. She sends this postcard from the edge:

> If you can believe it, I have never had an orgasm with a guy or really by myself. The only time I have been close is when I have been almost in sleep mode and I have been having an erotic dream and I am in a half-awake state. So I am still trying to figure it all out. I have been doing yoga three times a week, thinking that may help. I have taken a class about orgasms, and they tried a number of methods to try and get them (they suggested doing a lot of masturbating, we did some meditation, etc.). But nothing really worked.

What does that mean for her between the sheets? "I enjoy sex, although sometimes I feel I am close and it is a much better experience. I still don't think I have really had the full experience. God—something to look forward to, I guess." And then she adds, "I have six vibrators, including the Rabbit and the Magic Wand. Still no luck."

But wait, Mistress, oh wait: How does she tell this to her BP? Now and again, falsely. One pre-orgasmic babe discloses, "Sometimes they don't ask at all. But sometimes if they are waiting to 'go,' I say, 'Yes, I have already. Go!' With guys I don't know as well, I sometimes fake it."

Whoa, Mistress, this situation has gone FUBAR. Maybe the Big O is the fool's gold of the bedroom and I should just quit Pilot School, hang up my boner and go back to my van down by the river.

Don't you dare BP, don't you dare.

To further understand your babe's Big O—how to locate it and then multiply it—you must first fire up her libido. Really just a fancy word for your babe's desire, libido sounds as if it should be whispered with jazz hands on a leather banquette while wearing a saxophone for a necklace. Dont! No-Fly List Alert: Do not say the word aloud (e.g., "Perchance it will be the uber-boner clawing at my gym shorts that will slay your cagey libido").

The Libido Meter
READING HER SIGNALS

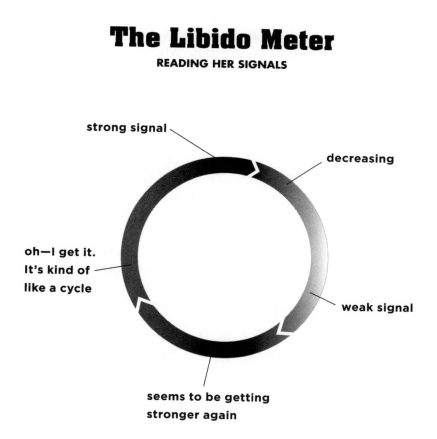

strong signal

decreasing

oh—I get it. It's kind of like a cycle

weak signal

seems to be getting stronger again

ME SO HORNY

Turbulence when approaching the Big O? Here, Bush Pilots are some practical ways to fly above the weather.

First stop? Yes, BPs, you are so on it! The bush party for one. Why? Bush awareness makes for the bush epiphany. As Captain Goodscrew says, "The best lovers are the ladies who really know their bits."

HAND IN THE COOKIE JAR

In her garter belt and black slip, your babe, lube in hand, hangs a DO NOT DISTURB sign on the bedroom door and makes uninterrupted time to explore and awaken her lady parts. What does it for her? Direct or indirect pressure? Penetration or the languorous circling of Lady Go-Go? She makes sure that she rocks (read: stokes) her pelvis as she would table-dancing at any after-hours club.

THE RECREATION DEPARTMENT

Does your babe employ the buzz of a dual-action vibrator like Rosebud or Blushy Bear? Does she use her silk scarf to skirt her exteriors? Is it this breathy sensation she responds to or the heavy tingle of a cyberskin toy? In short, your babe is left alone to question—and answer—her nether regions.

Your mission: Ask your babe to communicate her findings. Then, with your trademark BP skill, incorporate them into your sex play. Accept, darlings, your special-effects boner may not be the only way to your babe's Big O; she may have other routes. Get the coordinates—and follow them.

FLIP HER LID

Your babe fantasizes. She asks, Is that Johnny Cash waving me into his motel room, a pert girl in a wet dress already sitting cross-legged on his perfectly made bed? Is that Ronaldo hosing himself down in my backyard while doing one-armed push-ups above my stretching cat? Is that our mean contractor with the missing finger and the facial tattoo opening his steel lunchbox to pull out handcuffs? Why is Dr. Dre climbing through my window with that polar bear rug, ice bucket and ostrich feather?

Your babe uses film. What will it be: the hard run of antlers in *Les Animaux Amoureux* or that 1985 classic (complete with pajama party) *Deep Inside Annie Sprinkle*? Like you do when you run a reel of Maxim's "Hot One Hundred" across your thumping BP brain, your babe activates her senses—and in turn, her lady parts.

Your mission: Recall, BPs, in Chapter 1, that your guided tour through your babe's lady parts culminated in that fearsome air-traffic controller, her brain. Legendary. Don't piss her off. And recall, BPs, in Chapter 6, regarding your babe's fantasies: Don't fence them in. Let them roam free. And easy.

Mission Control

NOW LISTEN TO THIS

TROUBLE UP ABOVE = TROUBLE DOWN BELOW

Viagra, the boner in the blue pill, "targets genital capillaries; they don't aim at the mind." But for babes, as Daniel Bergner writes, the science indicates:

> The main difficulty appears to be in the mind, not the body, so the physiological effects of the drugs have proved irrelevant. The pills can promote blood flow and lubrication, but this doesn't do much to create a conscious sense of desire.

What does, Mistress, what does? For I will lay myself prostrate before it.

As you have gleaned from your own experience, babe for babe, we are vastly different in what turns us on and how that lust is expressed. One dynamo says, when met with her husband's advances, "Sometimes, I would rather rip my nails out." Conversely, another summons her sophomore years:

> I felt my clit was on fire half the day—I'd have the equivalent of boners in the middle of lectures that had nothing to do with thinking about sex, just a purely physiological expression of sexual excitement would take over out of the blue.

Oh why, Mistress, why must there be nail-ripping when there could be fire? To address your excellent question, we're going to take a field trip to a laboratory that looks a lot like your TV room.

MONKEY BUSINESS

On the subject of female arousal, this is what we do know—which, admittedly, after decades of determined study, is not much. Doing the research is akin to separating Siamese twins whose essential organs are bound: the splicing of hormones from brain function from the nervous system from YouTube. That said, the increasingly renowned scientist and Queen's University psychology professor Dr. Meredith Chivers has made the following surprising and instructive observations.

Instant and simplified replay: Men and women sit in La-Z-Boys with their Private Dancers wired to gauge their swelling arousal. On computer screens, they are shown footage of sex in many configurations: solo, homo, hetero, naked calisthenics, even the coupling of bonobo apes. The men respond predictably to the material that reflects their identified sexual orientation. The surprise: Women respond to everything, even the apes. Translation: Bush Pilots are turned on by what they say turns them on (hot babes, we love you!). Babes are turned on by what they say turns them on—as well as everything else (Bonobo apes, we love you?).

Um, wicked? Yes, BP. Gold star! It goes on. Whereas the men's minds were in clear accord with their manhood, the women's minds were not. Their bodies and minds appeared to be nearly estranged. The readings on the plethysmograph (butterfly) and the keypad (brain) did not correspond. Chivers summarizes: "Women's sexual interests do not necessarily match their sexual responses in the laboratory. . . . Arousal and desire do not map directly onto one another in the women—there is more potential for flexibility."

Um, wicked? Yes, BP! Gold star! Compared to your more "fixed" (sorry!) state, your babe's desire is "flexible." What, oh what, does this mean, Mistress? Must I, like a male Mary Lou Retton, get that bowl cut and indoor bathing suit and touch my toes before my babe will want to screw? No, my darlings. Dismount! It means your babe has a more democratic approach to attraction; when turning herself on, she roams a veritable sexual wilderness in her mind—boy, girl, girl-on-girl, boy-on-boy, boy-on-girl and ape-on-ape.

Like most surpluses, this is good news.

Perhaps she is closer to fire than you think. But Mistress, you ask, solipsistic as ever, so, in her mind, my babe is Bush in Wonderland—where do I and my unstoppable awesomeness fit in? Dr. Marta Meana, professor of psychology at the University of Nevada, makes the point to tuck into your Pilot-pants pocket and, like a rabbit foot, rub for luck.

Being desired is the orgasm.

Bush Pilots, let's pause and reflect on the above blazing arrow with this enlightening excerpt from Jenna (shout-out!) Jameson's *How to Make Love Like a Porn Star: A Cautionary Tale.* Light your Lucky. Get a cold one. Kick your feet up. About Victor, a teenaged Jameson writes:

> He struck me as the wild type, someone who would release my secret desire to be wanted in a seductive manner & to be treated & looked at as an attractive woman. I think he realized how much I wanted him & he came and made himself comfortable unusually close to my warm body. He made me feel like no other boy or man ever made me feel. . . . He gave me his telephone number and disappeared into the darkness. The next day I found myself alone in his room, him holding my body close to him. He gave me a few playful pecks on my arms and my face. Then the most passionate and deep kiss I have ever assumed there could be. My god. I wanted to stay here in his arms and make love to him over and over again until my body was so tired it had to stop.

Let's break it down into these ten easy steps:

1. "Wild type."
2. "Wanted in a seductive manner."
3. "Unusually close."
4. "Telephone number."
5. "Disappeared into the darkness."
6. "Playful pecks."
7. "Passionate and deep kiss."
8. "My god."
9. "Make love."
10. "Over and over again."

Now, do what Victor did. Consider it done, Mistress, consider it done.

HER BUSH IS SO BUFF

BPs, apart from the supremacy of your babe's brain in bringing about her Big O, another key consideration: the fitness of her bush.

While you tune up your man parts (Chapter 20), your babe tunes up her lady parts. In addition to the getting-it-up provocations listed above (the bush party, fantasy, film), she strengthens her PC muscle. Remedial: The PC is not a single muscle, but a cabal of muscles looped in a figure-eight formation through that prime real estate between her pubic and tail bones. If left unattended, the PC muscle can grow sluggish, developing a partiality for the track, cheap liquor, wings and sleeping in subway cars. By toning them and breathing diving-bell deeply, your babe will distribute both oxygen and blood—physiological necessities in the gathering force of her 3-D orgasm.

SEXERCISE

How to work out the lady parts? Kegel exercises. By contracting and releasing, these lady-part pull-ups will bring on and, when they begin, heighten your babe's orgasms. They can be done anywhere and anytime under the private swath of her skirt, or with toys like Betty's Barbell, named for the Susanna Moodie of masturbation, Betty Dodson. In time, your babe can step up her training with the weightier Njoy Pure Wand. This silver curve looks like a welder's steel teardrop. Bush Pilot Bonus: An interchangeable exerciser, NJoy is bent to bother both her G- and your P-spot (Chapter 2. Love it.).

Bush Pilots, this regimen is part of a larger consideration: exercise to promote blood flow. The more your babe can go to yoga, run, swim, cycle, strip, belly dance, walk, box, fence and yes, BP, strip off her vinyl catsuit while straddling your tented Pilot pants, the more she can circulate her blood—and send it, oxygenated, to her lady parts.

EXTRA CREDIT

IF YOU BUILD IT, SHE WILL COME

Here, BPs, once you find yourselves supine, is a roundup of some technical tips:

- ☞ Foreplay: The more you play before, the more likely she will come during.
- ☞ Use the toys in your survival kit; they can always (just like you!) be pulled out and turned on.
- ☞ You're such a tease. Really.
- ☞ Your babe is breathing, circulating oxygen to her lady parts.
- ☞ Your babe is contracting her PC muscles, circulating blood to her lady parts.
- ☞ Your babe is in a position (Chapter 15) that strokes Lady Go-Go or, once she has been feted, her G-spot.
- ☞ She is looking at you—even if she is picturing, say, Christopher Walken peeling latex off her body, eye contact keeps your babe conscious and present.
- ☞ Your babe wears socks when you screw. I do not jest, Bush Pilots: You want her blood to go to her go-go, not to heating up her cold feet because you, Cheap-pants, won't adjust the thermostat.
- ☞ No to Quiet Riot. Yes to "Cum On, Feel the Noize." You and your babe sound off. You moan, you gasp, you swear and, most important, you laugh.
- ☞ I'm okay (with my Bush), you're okay (with my Bush). I'm okay (with your Pilot), you're okay (with your Pilot). There is a heightened sense of mutual digging and respect. This makes for—central to the Ace screw—communication. Heed this word from one of the (so lucky!) lovers of Captain Goodscrew:

Part of the reason we could fuck for three hours during our first session is that we were just pretty straight ahead about what we wanted to be doing, what felt good, when to switch it up, what to try, when something wasn't working. I don't mean pillow talk or fantasies; I mean "Want to try it from behind now? My knees are hurting." Or "Do you need more lube?"

☞ Novelty: You screw in the afternoon rather than, like always, before bed. You screw in the hallway rather than, like always, in the bedroom. You break out an unseen, epic move. She breaks out an unseen, epic move. You get a (really nice) hotel room. All told, BPs, you stray from your usual script—setting, dialogue, genre, duration and action.

☞ No pressure. Screwing is for pleasure, not for points. You do not have goals, nor do you have a stopwatch.

Ultimate Orgasm Flowchart

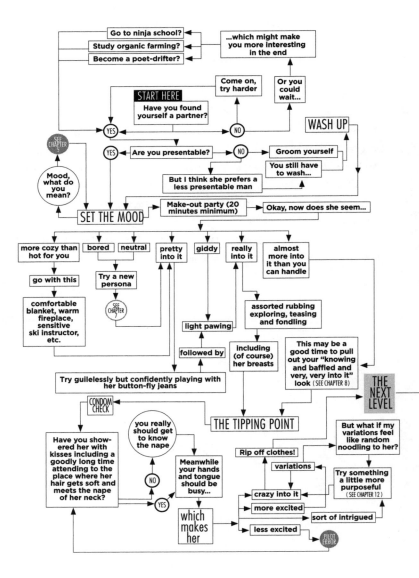

Go to ninja school?

Study organic farming?

Become a poet-drifter?

...which might make you more interesting in the end

Come on, try harder

Or you could wait...

START HERE
Have you found yourself a partner?

YES   NO

WASH UP

SEE CHAPTER 5

YES   Are you presentable?   NO   Groom yourself

You still have to wash...

Mood, what do you mean?

But I think she prefers a less presentable man

SET THE MOOD   Make-out party (20 minutes minimum)   Okay, now does she seem...

more cozy than hot for you | bored | neutral | pretty into it | giddy | really into it | almost more into it than you can handle

go with this   Try a new persona   SEE CHAPTER 7

comfortable blanket, warm fireplace, sensitive ski instructor, etc.

light pawing

assorted rubbing exploring, teasing and fondling

followed by

including (of course) her breasts

This may be a good time to pull out your "knowing and baffled and very, very into it" look (SEE CHAPTER 8)

Try guilelessly but confidently playing with her button-fly jeans

CONDOM CHECK

you really should get to know the nape

THE TIPPING POINT

THE NEXT LEVEL

But what if my variations feel like random noodling to her?

Have you showered her with kisses including a goodly long time attending to the place where her hair gets soft and meets the nape of her neck?

NO

YES

Meanwhile your hands and tongue should be busy...

Rip off clothes!

variations

Try something a little more purposeful (SEE CHAPTER 12)

crazy into it

more excited

sort of intrigued

which makes her

less excited

PILOT ERROR

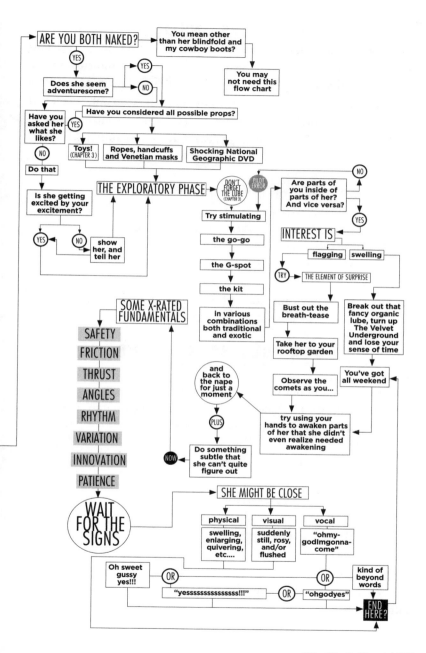

F*** MY BRAINS OUT

Now, here is the biggest calibration: After all that training (with you) and practice (on you), your babe does not, a beginner huntress with a net, chase down her orgasm. Instead, she is chased by it. Akin to the famous Timothy Leary slogan, "Turn on, tune in, drop out," she lets it and its attendant hallucinations (not unlike the sex scene montage in *The Naked Gun 2 1/2: The Smell of Fear*, but shot by Julian Schnabel) happen.

> But that doesn't mean I'm done. After one orgasm, why not have another? Once the dam has broken, the others come much faster and get more intense. Like many things in life, the third is always a charm.
> —Babe (saw the ghost of Gypsy Rose Lee)

How to multiply your babe's pleasure, BP? Repeat all of the above.

OUR COLLECTED WORKS

If your babe figures out what formations make her come, she will stick to them—and, like the following testimonials, incorporate them into your lovemaking. One XXX confessor writes:

> When I started sleeping with other guys, around nineteen, it always took me a couple of times getting together with a guy before I would be able to come with him. And then it was a matter of training the guy in how I came—on top, mimicking the way I masturbated. Later, I came in other ways, but it remains my go-to method.

While you might just get a ghostwriting credit, again witness our authorship:

I had my first orgasm at the age of eighteen—the unintended consequence of going to an all-girls school all my life. Technically speaking, it was brought on by "dry humping." Attired in a turtleneck, tapered jeans and combat boots, I straddled a boy five years my senior bearing a Pearl Jam tattoo, and through a series of pleasant thrusting motions, I climaxed. I remember feeling both pain and ecstasy at once. I didn't know if I was going to hurl all over my boyfriend or break into song.

I have grown to love this position through the years. Being on top rarely fails me, perhaps because of this distinct memory. I adore all the other combinations of lovemaking, but I usually wind things back to the "ole top pose-ish" before we wrap things up.

And again:

I never felt like my orgasms were delivered by my lovers, but that they were something I achieved in their presence. Sometimes this frustrated my boyfriends, because they felt like I wasn't really connecting with them when I came. I'm thinking of one guy in particular, my first boyfriend, who felt like I just went into a "trance" over him and also grumbled I had "surpassed" him sexually. I remember reading a passage in a Paul Theroux novel that reminded me of the way I came; the narrator was describing a woman who ground away on top of the protagonist and seemed to be in her own world.

And again:

The external kind of orgasms I discovered early, solo. Now that I think about it, I might have had the inside kind by myself first too. But they weren't as frequent with early partners, hard as I and they might have sometimes tried. Especially with a football player I sort of dated one late summer/early autumn. Tried and tried and tried and had a lot of fun. But I think it didn't happen 'til grad school on a regular basis—meaning I could choreograph things better by then. It never worked so well with guys who were overtly trying to make me come. One guy would even say, "Come, come!!!" It was useless. I hate that.

Deal-Breaker Alert: No "Come, come!!!" No "Come on." No "Hurry up." Imagine being rushed while pulling on a coat made of snowflakes. Imagine being told to quicken your step when dancing along a ledge of orchids. Imagine being prodded while finishing your recitation of the 2006 NHL draft order—backward. While some women can come as reflexively as they can count, and some women can "think themselves to climax," for others it can be like collecting eyelashes in the desert.

An orgasm is as idiosyncratic as it gets. Any pressure to perform, any stress, exhaustion, worries about self-image, booze, cigarettes, some antidepressants, antihistamines, the birth control pill, the strict upbringing, the brainwashed years, low testosterone, poor blood circulation or life without foreplay will scare her bliss away. This is true regardless of whether the bloodhounds are released by you or by her. In short, while they are both pliable social animals, your boner is in your pants, and ours is in our brains.

Sweet, Mistress. And then what happens?

EXTRA CREDIT

THE SEXUAL RESPONSE CYCLE

This term was popularized by Masters and Johnson, who filmed hundreds of people screwing in their lab and then collected their observations in the 1966 book *Human Sexual Response*. Please keep in mind that this template is the equivalent to following dance steps drawn on your living-room floor. The strokes are very broad, and by now, Bush Pilots, we know: We all like to get our rug burn a little differently.

EXCITEMENT

A Broken Social Scene concert. A bathroom stall. A backless dress. The supple adjustments of your tongue on her earlobe and one cool hand pressed against her mons. Your babe's heart starts to gallop, lending speed to her blood, which swells her lips, her butterfly, her go-go and her breasts. Her panties are wet. Her nipples, arrowheads. Her skin is feverish to the touch and her muscles coil. She feels the sensation of lifting; this is her uterus and upper butterfly, suddenly cosmonauts, ascending and expanding.

(IT'S REALLY NICE,
BUT GET ME OFF THIS F***ING) PLATEAU

You are now screwing like Eminem and Brittany Murphy (R.I.P.) did in *8 Mile*. You're a rapper; she's an aspiring model. She is pressed up—her tongue a contortion in your mouth—against the bathroom wall, and you are standing on the tips of your vintage high-tops, B-Rabbit, trying to stay the distance. Meanwhile, her wetness, her swelling, tightening and lifting continue; her uterus is pulled to its peak. You are running the periodic table across your brain.

ORGASM

The hallelujah moment wherein all of that blood and tension so pyrotechnically gathered and stored is involuntarily released. Your babe's uterus, her cervix, the first third of her butterfly, her kit and her PC muscles contract. This is to a rhythm of every eight-tenths of a second. You bust out some beats; she does too—moans, grunts, profanities, promises, confessions. It's a showdown. And then she does it, the original eye-candy, the ultimate Bush Pilot Bonus, the winning move: the back arch.

(You come. Peace on Earth.)

RESOLUTION

As you were.

P.S.: You will be happy to know this Masters-and-Johnson dance routine was updated in the *Saturday Night Fever* seventies by sexologist Helen Singer Kaplan. Not only did she streamline it by cutting the plateau and (yawn) resolution phases, she added one more sly-eyed step to the cycle. The spontaneous blowjob, Mistress? No. A word you are now all familiar with: desire—or perhaps, more to the point, desired.

Knowing and Baffled and Very, Very Into It

SOME POINTERS

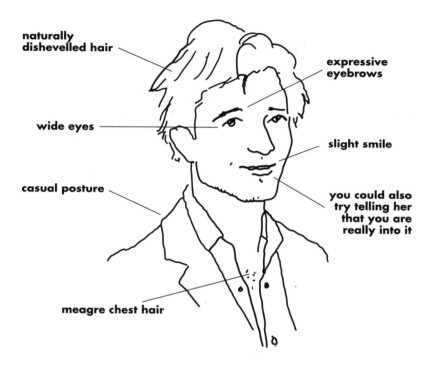

naturally
dishevelled hair

expressive
eyebrows

wide eyes

slight smile

casual posture

you could also
try telling her
that you are
really into it

meagre chest hair

SHOW AND TELL

Bush Pilots, you recognize that, in bed, your babe's brain is the best kind of tyrant. As it rules, it bends. You understand that, for your babe, sexual stimuli are varied as the psyches of the surrealists. You concede that, while you may hold the "brand new key," she unlocks her orgasm. You know that, for her, a sense of being desired is crucial. While one babe, a purr on heels, sagely summarizes it this way, "He's got to fucking love me," another very experienced madame writes:

> The best for me is the guy who understands about giving the whole process a wide berth. They pay attention to what works. They're curious—a lovely combination of knowing and baffled and very, very into it.

BPs—my Beeps (represent!)—let's end where we began. Before vibrators, before woman on top, before the acceleration of your hand, the rotation of your tongue, the precision of your Leopold Bloom, solo love was our first and most comprehensive education. Let it be yours too. Why not ask for a show and tell? Be a spy on your babe's nether regions. Be a pilgrim on her particular path to pleasure. Be her student. In a single bed, under a crisp sheet, on a long, hot afternoon.

CHAPTER 9
LOCK LIPS (FIRST BASE)

NOTE FROM THE FIELD:
MAKE-OUT REVOLUTION!

Pacing his dungeon, Jonny is despondent. He looks around at the cuffs and floggers and feels hollow. He reminisces. He misses the power ballad. He misses unhelmeted hockey hair, the eight-track player, and *The Six-Million Dollar Man*. He misses the jean jacket paired with the jean. He misses the rotary phone in the phone booth, his first house of ill repute, now obsolete, a relic. But mostly, he misses making out for hours at a time, on a velour couch, everything engorged and suspended. Jonny has a revelation. He throws his fist in the air. Time to return to our tender beginnings as sensual creatures! Time to throw down our nipple clamps, burn our spanking paddles and toss our gonzo porn! Time for a make-out revolution!

Later that night, Jonny hears a knock at his door.

Left on his stoop is a handwritten invitation, sealed with a frosted-lipstick kiss. He opens it. A make-out party—now. Jonny dons his beret and follows the directions to an abandoned warehouse by the shipyards. M*A*S*H's "Hot Lips" Houlihan steps out of the shadows. She tosses her slim, smoking cigarillo to the pavement. She crushes it under her combat boot. She motions for him to follow her. Jonny does. Her cargo pants are supremely tight. She leads him into a basement. The Simple Minds anthem "Don't You (Forget About Me)" bleeds unevenly from a tape deck. Guests are clustered in corners. Some wear fake braces. Some wear fake acne. Some compare paper routes. Hot Lips corrals everyone into a circle. She places an empty bottle of Labatt 50 in the centre. She spins it. Jonny examines the glossed mouths around him. He smiles to himself. The revolution has begun.

THE KISS-OFF

Bush Pilots, you wonder: Is she judging me through every waking moment of my life? Well, stop your wondering; she is. Can he put up a shelf level to the floor? Did he really just order a Crantini? Can he light a match in a gale? Can he kiss like Judd Nelson in *The Breakfast Club*? You, Bush Pilots, are under constant surveillance, but never so keen as during that first kiss. It is your tell-all, a taste of what is to come, a miniaturized version of your copulation station.

If your performance is weak, first base will be your last.

So let's review.

SOME PEOPLE CAN PARALLEL PARK

Some people can dance. Some can whistle nursery rhymes. Some can do all three at once. And, Bush Pilots, some people can kiss. Have you ever gone out with a woman, shared the duck confit, chocolate pudding and port, heard zing every time you looked at each other, felt an inferno in your pants, sworn she did too, headed back to her apartment thinking it could be rough and involve ropes, roommates and false promises, made out in the doorframe and been suddenly, swiftly, mystifyingly dismissed? And then she changed her number? Let me explain: You kissed like an electric eel.

Cardinal Bush Pilot truth: Sex is about chemistry, and the kiss is your first chemistry test.

CLARIFICATION

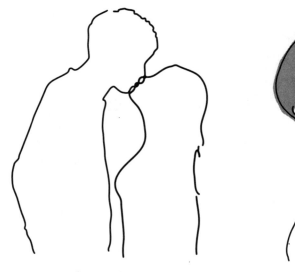

human kiss   **eel kiss**

My most recent partner nailed me with our first kiss in a bar on the Lower East Side of Manhattan. We were sitting at the bar, talking and drinking bourbon, and he just moved in, one hand cupped along my jawline, and brought it. Very hot moment, for three reasons. For one, I know that anyone who can kiss like that will likely do a proper job of fucking my brains out. For another, I am a fan of bold initiative. But third, I love kissing, and it is so disappointing that many people do not kiss me the way that I want to be kissed, because then it becomes a coaching thing. Now, in other things, coaching is great; communication is key to hearing my partner and saying what I like or want to try or whatever. That's all fine. But kissing is like a barometer tracking some sensuality-expression factor, confidence, responsiveness and style. It's one of those foundational things. And it was a hot kiss. Every fun intense thing I do with this guy now builds on that excellent, well-timed moment.

—Babe (Rubenesque, Laurie Anderson records)

THE MAKE-OUT SESSION

To prepare for the make-out session, no cigarettes and no shawarmas. Breath mints and balm-moistened lips are encouraged, but note well, your personal-hygiene products are not to be seen or tasted. We want to know you have survival skills, not cherry gloss. We want to see your toolbox, not your toilet kit. If you are on a first date and your babe asks you for Tic Tacs or "lippy," deflect. It could be a trap. Instead, rescue someone's pet. Douse a grease fire. Stack a woodpile. Ice-climb. Employ an axe, ladder or martial-arts move.

LED ZEPPELIN IV

First step: your soundtrack. King of seduction Mike Damone offers the following advice to never-before-kissed-just-shy-of-a-pocket-protector-one-man-geek-fest Rat:

> First, of all Rat, you never let on how much you like a girl. "Oh, Debbie. Hi." Two, you always call the shots. "Kiss me. You won't regret it." Now three, act like wherever you are, that's the place to be. "Isn't this great?" Four, when ordering food, you find out what she wants and then order for both of you. It's a classy move. "Now the lady will have the linguini and white clam sauce, and a Coke with no ice." And five—now, this is the most important, Rat—when it comes down to making out, whenever possible, put on side one of *Led Zeppelin IV*.
>
> —Mike Damone, *Fast Times at Ridgemont High*

But Mistress, oh Mistress, given the counsel quoted above, why is it, at the end of *Fast Times*, Mike Damone is marooned in his tight white pants while Rat is squiring the likes of luscious weirdo Jennifer Jason Leigh? Touché, BP. Touché. True, Mike Damone proves himself to be a total turd. That said, Bush Pilots, do take note of Damone's salient fifth point. In short: *Led Zeppelin IV*.

Put that throbbing mongrel rock in the tape deck of your pickup truck or the boom box hoisted on your shoulder like a fresh kill. Heed Robert Plant's hard-on tenor on "Black Dog," his vow to make his babe "sweat," "groove," "burn" and "sting"; heed the epic, suspenseful howl that is "Stairway to Heaven"—and I know it is difficult, but do refrain from the airborne drum solo unless you have evidence your babe thinks it's funny (i.e., she does it first). If she still hasn't broken it out by the second date, do so. If your babe does not laugh, Bush Pilots, take off her tragedy mask. If she is still not laughing, give her an upside-down horseshoe, wish her good luck and move on.

SOMEONE'S COMING

Now, choose your location. An element of furtiveness is essential. You must be on the verge of being caught by someone: a police officer, the parking attendant, the night watchman, your high-school custodian, the innkeeper, the barn hand, your rabbi. While the make-out session is stiffy-languid in its expression, it must have the heart-pumping subtext of a chase scene. There is the constant threat of interruption by an authority figure, your bodies pitched to the sound of their possible approach.

While there is a lot about high school we wish to forget, remember the obliviousness that surrounded you when you kissed? Resurrect it.

> I would meet my boyfriend after school and we would kiss on the subway platform or in a park or a movie theatre, garage, under a ramp. We didn't care. At curfew, I would walk through the front door with a chafed, red chin from his stubble, and wet underwear. The best was if I was babysitting my little brother. My boyfriend used to hide in my closet when my parents came home and then leave by my bedroom window. We would make out while listening for the key in the front door.
> —Babe (Eva Mendez look-alike with a houseboat named Mister)

How to update it? Bush Pilots, the make-out session begins now as it did then. Gather up what my comrade calls your "grade nine guts" and lean in for that first kiss, and then another. Let it build slowly, a gradual and sultry evolution.

STORM WATCH

The kiss is one of our first expressions of affection; it is a primal and instinctive act. Presuming its origins, Diane Ackerman in *A Natural*

History of Love writes, "We may indeed have begun kissing as a way taste and smell someone." We are all animals and—your fine fortur Bush Pilots—this is your animal kingdom. Why not follow our shaggy friends and take it outside? Bush Pilot Bonus: The rainstorm. Watch the weather; is there a storm cloud coming? Get under it. Get soaked. Think of what it will do to her dress.

TONSIL HOCKEY

Making out is an act of heightened responsiveness—an oral listening. Think of yelling "Echo!" to a cliff, and then waiting for the response. I repeat: waiting for the response. The revolutionary waits for his natural cues. Kissing is body barter. Like the best courtship, you go back and forth. If her mouth opens, open yours. If she offers her tongue, do the same. But know that this, the tongue, is the defining moment—the deal-sealer. You have stepped onto French soil. Now, everything is different—not just *th*, wine with lunch and mistresses at funerals, but the stakes. Your stakes. Use your tongue consciously, gently, rhythmically. Without being listless, take it soulfully slow. Your tongue is a Zamboni. It clears the ice between periods, your sweep making for a smooth, perfect surface.

We know our lips are choice. Conscious or not, they evoke that other sought-after set, replete with nerve endings shooting pleasure to our brains. But do add variation. Tease, nibble and suck on her tongue, her neck, her collarbone, her shoulder, her cheeks, her earlobes. Use your lips, your lashes, your fingertips.

DOWN, BOY!

The revolutionary quells his eagerness. We know you are happy to see us. Please stop licking our faces. Please stop blocking our air passages.

Please stop humping our legs. Please, no tongue before lips. Don't allow your passion to become aggression. Don't be the python darting and probing, the chicken pecker pecking, the blowfish blowing. Don't check us into the boards with your teeth. Yes, Bush Pilots, there is a difference between pressing and pinning. Gold star! Recall your creed: You are flame. You are fire.

Everyone, even men who name sex acts after themselves (the Kanye), wonders what to do with their hands in the make-out session. Stroke us, hold our hips, toy with our fingers, trace the backs of our necks, our arms, our spines, our faces, our shoulders. We love to be touched. We love to be held. Our desires are simple. Keep your eyes mostly closed. Don't stare. It's creepy as a corpse. Instead, sink yourself. Surrender.

DETENTION

The crucial element for the make-out session that truly flies is this: You only go so far.

> The pleasures of kissing are all about constraint, the sensual pushed up against a boundary, and that conundrum (getting pleasure amidst constraint) doesn't stop with adolescence. Also, kissing, in all its wilful, will-less heedlessness, can be public. You can kiss madly in front of crowds and not be stopped for indecency. Late afternoon on a train across Long Island, we are oblivious to anything but this: the whorl of mouths and tongues and saliva. A kiss, when there is no immediate possibility of going further, does not exhaust itself but can last for hours, for miles. Half-drunk, on a bridge, passed by another frenzy of commuters, we can't stop time, but we can surrender to the absolute selfishness of being this heedless together. A

kiss is never enough, but if it's all there is (and not a lay-over on the highway to somewhere else), it offers its own depth charge of immersion; it focuses attention through concentration—whether we keep our eyes open or closed, the mouth is the world we enter. When we kiss (and I love to kiss), we can be satisfied but not sated: We gorge our-selves on arousal.

—Babe (sumptuous brain and too many speeding tickets)

BPs, linger and throb in this, the most voluptuous of exchanges. Keep it at half-mast. No anticipation. No agenda. In the true revolution-ary's favourite film, *The Breakfast Club*, the Criminal asks the Princess if she has ever kissed a boy, ever had his paw hover tentatively above her Wonderbra'd breasts, while they both pray her folks don't walk in. Women have been trying to replicate this moment since they first saw Judd Nelson, in his overcoat and unzipped galoshes, stalking across the frame of the camera. We have been waiting to hear his line about how good it feels to be bad—convincingly, from you—since 1985.

Why, Mistress, oh why? Like the best doubles partner, the Criminal sets the Princess up for a winner. In a rebel-purr, he passes her the per-fect fantasy: sexiness, but bridled. Hotness, but threatened. He delivers the same rush and danger as an affair, a tidal swell, a trespassing. Bas-ket Case or Princess, it is not the Brain or the Athlete we want, but the Criminal. We want all our Saturdays spent in detention.

Bush Pilot, forgo your BlackBerry. Ignore your beeper. Rev up your station wagon. Build a rec room. Invite your parents over to pace the kitchen floor. In a world of all things virtual, be one of the rare and sexy creatures who has never forgotten the eroticism of our first carnal act. The make-out session is our sensual homeland. Bush Pilots, raise your fists in the air, spin your bottles and say it with me now: Let's make out.

CHEAT SHEET: THIS TOO IS FOREPLAY

☞ Throwing out your moth-eaten underwear
☞ Laundering your hockey gear
☞ Cleaning out the shed
☞ Organizing your tools
☞ Doing the dishes—well
☞ Leaving your beanbag chair on the curb
☞ Any form of carpentry or baking
☞ Wearing your tool belt or flour-smudged apron
☞ A temporary moustache
☞ Proficiency in playing any musical instrument
☞ Proficiency in any unusual dance move—e.g., the Robot
☞ Laughter
☞ 3-D glasses
☞ A plane ticket

LEARN HOW TO
Dance the Robot

THE STANCE

THE TECHNIQUE

Very slowly, with a serious expression on your face (improved greatly by strobe lights), allow every joint, including fingers and wrists, to move stiffly. Aim for asymmetrical randomized action with particular emphasis on the elbows. For beginners, keep feet stationary.

Imagine that you are a machine, like, for example, C3PO.

How to Wash
the Dishes (well)

A FEW TIPS

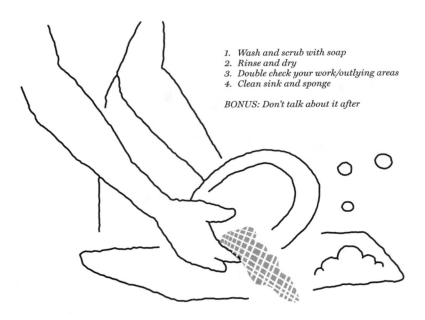

1. Wash and scrub with soap
2. Rinse and dry
3. Double check your work/outlying areas
4. Clean sink and sponge

BONUS: Don't talk about it after

CHAPTER 10
HANDS UP
(SECOND BASE)

NOTE FROM THE FIELD:
BOOBY TRAPPED!

Malcolm is a breast man. All he sees are breasts. All he wants to feel are breasts. All he wants to taste are breasts. But too often, he has to work. On this late night, Malcolm, silk tie loosened, jacket off, nurses his third Guinness, eats a rare steak and thinks about dating a mermaid. How he could keep his apartment. She could swim about and brush her hair on rocks. What language would she speak? Or would she only sing? It doesn't matter. What matters is that he could still live alone and she would be topless all of the time. *Topless all of the time.*

From the open kitchen, Malcolm catches sight of the sous-chef. She is staring at him with intent. Definitely a mating call. She motions for him to come. Never one to shy away, he does. In the kitchen, she is alone, her colleagues gone for the night. Her nametag says FLEUR. Without any introductions, Fleur leads him into the storeroom. Syrups, honeys and oils are stacked high. Under the single bulb, she unbuttons her chef coat and pulls off her white undershirt. She has tattoos up and down her arms and a tiny scar beside her belly button. Her breasts are not large, not small, but the size of Champagne glasses. Fleur looks him in the eye and unhooks her black lace bra. This is when the laws of the universe are so blissfully exacting. At last, a breast man meets a breast woman.

WHERE WOULD YOU BE WITHOUT CLEAVAGE?

The plunging neckline, the halter top, the teeny bikini, the wet T-shirt contest, *Girls Gone Wild*, the halftime show. Where would you be without Farrah, Bo, Mae West, Ursula, Dolly, Pam, Jenna (shout out!), Jessica Simpson circa *Dukes*, Suzanne Somers and your buxom babysitter? Nowhere, Mistress, oh, we would be nowhere! The breast was your first pleasure. Yes! And in high school, the breast was your first illicit bit of flesh. Oh yes! You groped, you squeezed, you nuzzled, you kissed and you sucked. Good times, Mistress, good times. Like Henry Miller's *Tropic of Cancer* and *Tropic of Capricorn*, you gave your babe's breasts nicknames: "Mine" and "Mine Two." You bought them thoughtful gifts, such as figurines and nipple tassels. You played them Iron Maiden's "Wasting Love." They listened to you. They never fell asleep. They never finished your sentences—or your beer. They never wept or slammed the door. They just sat there, all tangible love. All tangible.

We know, darlings, we know you love them. Now, let them teach you how.

TOPLESS

Many women are breast women. Why? Nipples are dense with nerve endings cleverly located along the same neurological grid as our brains and our butterflies. Lucky us! Lucky you. As Natalie Angiers writes in *Woman: An Intimate Geography*, "Nerves are like wolves or birds: If one starts crying, there goes the neighbourhood." In fact, BPs, some women are so turned on by having their nipples played with, they come from nipple play alone.

> To be clear, it doesn't happen every time; both the conditions and the participants have to be favourable. And technique is important: none of this "tune in to Tokyo" business. It has to be gradual, a slow build, rather than a sudden ambush or full-frontal attack. It's all about the crescendo, the tease, starting with a light touch, a tickle, the slightest brush of fingertips. At just the right moment, the skilled partner brings his lips, tongue and teeth into play. My full attention is now definitely on the task at hand (and mouth). I can feel it coming, I try to hold it off, struggle to bring my partner to the same level of arousal, but like the boys in high school, it's beyond my control: I reach orgasm without any other part of my body having been touched.
>
> —Babe (tortoise-shell glasses, Polaroid Instant camera)

Oh how, Mistress, how do I do this and win my babe's everlasting love—and a lifetime-of-blowjobs guarantee?

FEEL HER UP

First, BPs, you must, as always, know your babe. Just as there is variation in size and shape, there is variation in sensation. One curved-like-a-Corvette girlfriend admits that when met with extensive attention to her breasts, "I could be doing my taxes. Let's move it along. My clitoris is down below." And yet another: "My boobs, I have to say, could just as easily be earrings or Christmas decorations." Whereas, another babe (who would read your palm) offers this about her glitter twins:

> A lick on the nipple and a slight blow (but more of a slow warm exhale) onto the wet tissue is really great. Also a full, firm hand grab to the breast (or both) can be incredibly hot at the right moment during sex.

So, how to play above the belt? How to navigate the seemingly straightforward second base? As in baseball, there are rules. And, Bush Pilots, they are not yours to make.

How to Unhook a Bra

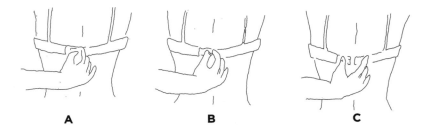

A   **B**   **C**

BUSTED!

First, no grabbing. And no "Mommy." No one wants a two-hundred-pound baby. And please, no "but-babe-it's-totally-hilarious" sound effects—e.g., honk-honk, or "U Got the Look" with your babe's breasts as Prince and Sheena respectively.

Also, if your babe's headlights are to be turned on, be prepared, BP. Her luscious halos do not want to wait while you sprint to the laundry room for clothespins. Have your props and accoutrements close at hand. Depending on your agreed play, these can include everything from massage oils to ostrich feathers, Cristal to candle wax.

ALL HANDS ON DECK

A fire roars. Seu Jorge sings Bowie's "Life on Mars." Your babe is lying, breasts bared, on your tiger-skin rug. You want to ravage her. You want to jump her pornographically ripe body. You want to take a header, bone out a mammary face-plant and then place your pulp between her pair. You pace in your Pilot suit. You kick yourself. I am not cool, Mistress. Not cool! Go to the kitchen. Fill the sink with ice cubes. Dunk your head. Hold on to your flight mission.

Now, return to your babe and, smooth as Bond, James Bond, place your warm palms side by side on her mons. (Oh, Mistress! Pick me! Pick me! I so know! Yes, it is electric. Pick me! Yes, it should end with a z. Oh! Oh! Oh! And yes, BP, it is the bunny hill above your babe's pubic bone. Gold star!) Slide your Pilot-paws between and around her breasts, your hands closing in on her nipples with every rotation. Repeat, working slowly and from the outside in. Knead and stroke. N.B.B.P.: Do not forfeit the breast for the nipple. Your approach: inclusive. Your instruction: Tease, trace and titillate.

I have big tits—and big nipples to match. The boys can't ever wait to get their hands on 'em (or their mouths). And while I absolutely love having my nipples sucked and licked and fingered and so on, they're kind of a third-gear thing. First and second gears can't be skipped. If engine-

revving is handled properly, then my nipples can be handled all night long.
—Babe (double take)

"Engine revving." Affirmative.

TREASURE CHEST

For added effect, use materials—silk, lace, fur, feathers—or massage oil.
Try that shameless hint-dropper Touch Me (suggestions from the Bush
Pilot Taste Test Lab: pomegranate mint and English lavender). You may
also use the almond oil from your kitchen cupboard. Alternately, choose
a non-staining, warming oil like the Oil of Love or, for a similar result,
submerge your bottle of massage oil in a bowl of hot water for a few
minutes before basting.

If your babe prefers less of a mess, but still wants a slide, try Knead
Me Massage Lotion or Cream. With your hand, cup her breast, fan your
fingers and bring them back and in to pinch her nipple. As mentioned,
despite our die-hard penchant for hard rock (three-finger salute!),
never confuse your babe's nipple with a radio dial; you will get nothing but static. N.B.B.P.: Pulling, rolling, clutching and twisting are only
upon request.

I've always loved sucking on a pair of tits. It's a particular
thrill of mine. Had an affair with a woman with big, papery
breasts and I loved lifting them up in my hands and licking them.
—Bush Pilot (hunter green velvet suit, skate board)

THE BREASTAURANT

With your tongue, circle the areola (the ring of skin around the nipple) until you spiral your way in to your babe's nipple. Mistress, oh
Mistress, does this tongue technique operate from the same titillating
principle as the hands-on-deck massage, wherein the prodigious Bush

Pilot works from the outside in to fire up his babe's bodacious moneymakers? Yes, it does, BP. Gold star! The ultimate homemade lubricant, your saliva, wets her surface. Kiss and suck. Suction will bring blood to the surface of your babe's nipple. N.B.B.P.: A taut nipple is a more sensitive one. As your babe is more turned on, she will likely welcome more pressure.

DOES YOUR DOG BITE?

Bush Pilots, there is a big difference between nibbling and biting. If you bite without permission, you will get bitten back. A breast is not a biscuit. Nor is it a bone. Nor is it a chew toy. If you treat it as such, you will be taken off the rack. Ask your babe what she likes. Always keep a close eye and ear to her response. What quickens her breath? What makes her moan? Let her show you—on you. You will then understand your babe's pleasure as every Bush Pilot should: kinesthetically. Kineswhat, Mistress? Oh, what does this kin-word mean? It means learning by doing. Yes! Oh yes! Do me!

Again, the more aroused your babe, the higher her body's tolerance for stronger stimulation. Timing is crucial. Some women will want nipple play early and just at the point of orgasm. Others will want your smooth palms against her pair the whole time you're horizontal. Just sitting there, Mistress, in a perma-squeeze? So easy! I could do that with my eyes closed! No, my darlings. Use your breath, your touch and your tongue; like the multi-talented BP I know you are, let variety be your creed.

YOU'RE SUCH A BOOB

No-Fly List Alert: By breath, BPs, I do not mean fog up her breasts, or pant like a dog in the back seat of a car, or gasp sluggishly like the other end of an obscene phone call, but this: You know when your babe is giving you transcendent head and she pauses for a moment and just breathes close to your close-talker and you think, I am a rich, rich man? That is what we call the breath-tease. One babe extends the breath-tease this way (take her "side note" and tuck it into your Pilot pants for every situation):

> Nothing is more sexy to me than a long exhalation close to your ear—hhhhhhhhhhhhhhhhhhh. Breath is incredibly powerful because you are succumbing to a natural desire. They go together. Also, mmmmmmmmmmmm is great. A man moaning is sexier to me than any testoterone-bound grunting. The exhalation is subtle and is instantly sexy and gets me every time. It is more than the sound; it is also the feeling of warm air on your earlobe and hair. It gives you a feeling that the man is melting in your presence. Who doesn't want to have that power?

Now, Bush Pilots, a technical note: Be aware your babe's breast sensitivity will vary throughout the month. It may also vary between breasts. That said, don't pick favourites, unless your babe instructs you to. Talk to her, especially if you want to include other elements in your play.

ICE ICE BABY

Incorporate heat and cold. Ice chips and cubes can be provocative, especially if held in your mouth, as can ice cream and whipped cream. Serving suggestion: Apply with a chilled silver spoon. Or add the element of sensory deprivation: Have your babe promise to keep her eyes closed—or loosen your Windsor knot and use your tie as a blindfold. Now, re-examine the contents of your fridge. Celluloid inspiration: that eighties tome to Kim Basinger's heart-shaped kit, *9 1/2 Weeks*. The light of the open fridge, her smudged eye makeup, his Mephistophelian charisma, the noodles, the cherries, the cough syrup, the hot peppers, the milk. Feed, pour, spread, surprise and feast on your babe. N.B.P.: Unlike those reckless sybarites, Mickey and Kim, keep all your cough syrup, Veuve and Billy Bee above the belt; absolutely no honey near the honey pot.

WAX ON

If you want to use candle wax, don't grab the one burning on your side table and say, "Babe, this is going to be so hot," because it is going to be so hot, too hot. Look specifically for candles made for body wax play. Many sex shops carry these; they are safe because they melt at a lower temperature, so there is no risk of burning your babe's skin. Let the wax pool, then tip the candle, dripping the wax with measured slowness. Be disciplined in your approach. Celluloid suggestion: For an advanced demonstration of wax and nipple-clamp play, watch Bleu Productions' *The Black Glove*. Noir, artful, starring the doe-eyed siren Sabrina and, commanding as a gothic queen, the menacing Mistress Morgana. In a word: hot. Bush Pilot Bonus: Where else can you see a woman sucking a spiked boot heel during a downpour?

THE HARDWARE STORE

If, in conversation (say, on the telephone from adjoining cars on the high-speed underwater train from London to Paris), your babe tells you she wants to experiment with toys, there is a bevy of nipple clamps and clips available. N.B.B.P.: The higher your babe's arousal, the higher her tolerance for any sensation that approaches pain.

Pain, you say, Mistress? Approaches pain, I say, Bush Pilot. Big difference. Let me explain: Nipple toys offer you and your babe a first flirtation with BDSM (bondage and discipline, dominance and submission, sadism and masochism). Aesthetically, they of the medieval metal and rubber invoke naughtiness—this being the wick of fantasy. With them on, your babe could have falcons on her shoulders, a viper coiled round her ankles and Mad Max between her legs. Practically, when employed with clear communication, these toys can speak (bossily yet intelligently) to your BPMO: your babe's expanded pleasure.

How, oh how do they work, Mistress? Clips and clamps pinch the skin, creating a bite when engaged and disengaged. To appreciate the sensation, Bush Pilot, pinch your own skin. Observe how the blood is immediately diverted away from the area being pinched and, when the pinch is released, returns. This pressure and pull can, if your babe says so, straddle her pain-pleasure divide. Try:

Butterfly Clamps. A good choice for S/M beginners, the classic rubber-tipped metal butterfly clamps, and their prizefighter cousins the heavy butterfly clamps, allow your babe to choose the pressure by tugging, depending on her preference, a metal chain or black rubber line. Like the tweezer and alligator clamps, these amenable props will not only adjust to the desired tightness or lightness, but to the myriad of nipple shapes and sizes you will undoubtedly discover—and thrill.

Clover Clamps. By contrast, clover clamps are non-adjustable—already tight, they tighten even more when pulled. Note: While the nipple has an erotic elasticity, always try the toy between your thumb and first finger. You can also experiment with placement: If the clamp is placed closer to your babe's areola, rather than the tip of her nipple, pressure is reduced; the bigger the grab, the milder the pinch.

You don't have to be into S/M play to like clamps. If you like sensation, then the vibrating, suction or even alligator clamps can be lovely—if not used with a lot of pressure. In my experience, the vibrating and weighted ones often do not stay on, unless you really like them tight.
—Babe (hoodie, name-pendant necklace)

Note: Like the cock ring around your rosie, nipple clamps have a time limit; they are a fifteen-minute workout only. Also, they should be taken off before your babe has had enough. Why? The clamps restrict blood flow so when the blood rushes back in, the intensity surges for abou ten seconds. And for your pierced babe, look for clamp that clip onto her rings and bars rather than onto her nipples. Or, if easy enough (I'm not saying you!), have her remove her hoops and bars beforehand.

Suction Toys. Some nipple teasers vibrate. Some are jewelled. Some are weighted. Some have bells. Still others create suction and, in turn, like the vacuum effect of your mouth, pressure. Made of vinyl, rubber, PVC or silicone, these cups stimulate and, through engorgement, enlarge and sensitize the nipples. Keeping them hard, these toys can be the perfect primer for your languorous play. As one babe says, "Batting them around gently can be nice."

D.I.Y. B.D.S.M.

COMMON HOUSEHOLD ITEMS THAT MAY DOUBLE AS DEVICES OF PLEASURE AND PAIN

  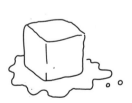 

clothespeg **feather duster** **icecube** **bullclip***

* hard-core

THE OFFICE

Bush Pilots, you can also dip into household items and raid the storeroom. Clothespins, pearls, paper clips, a fork, and a pen cap take on new life when tweezing or raked lightly over a nipple. Even a fingernail has hidden properties when circumnavigating a breast.

For the naturalist, body parts suffice. Revisit that old high-school standard the pearl necklace, or coitus a mamilla. Lube up your Midnight Cowboy and, as you would enter her butterfly, swing low and let your babe's breasts bookend you into oblivion.

A final feat: For the voyeur, what is good for her is good for you; if your babe can swing it, she can, in a turn of erotic self-serve, feast on her own breasts. Um, how Mistress, oh how do I encourage her to do this? Simply suggest it, Bush Pilots; the worst thing that can happen is she says, "No Bush Pilot, you do it." Um, okay!

STACKED AGAINST YOU

What will obstruct your commendable efforts? A cautionary word on the coconuts: If your playmate has had breast augmentation or reduction, these procedures can cause both unrecoverable numbness and oversensitivity. To think those caddish five-thousand-dollar implants can rupture, deflate, wander and leave you cold. One BP describes his night with a Barbie-shaped stripper as "plasticky and weird." That said, one king-can connoisseur says about the silicone:

> Love them. Firmer, larger, they look hotter, sexier, you feel more like fucking vs. making love.

When asked if he had to adjust his game, he said, "No, but you want to play with 'em more."

BPs, the final word: Whatever their state, treat your babe's pair with the care recommended above; as always, solicit her feedback and adjust your play accordingly.

THE SHIRT IS OFF!

What can you expect? Equally true of your pork and beans, Bush Pilots, there is a plethora of possibility—and cup size does not dictate performance. One diminutive babe writes:

> My breasts blow my mind with their potency for pleasure. I can come almost to orgasm just with breast play. Well, especially nipple play. I am probably generous to call my breasts two half-grapefruits—nope, I just cupped myself and that's about right. But ever since my old roommate with really big breasts told me she felt nothing when men fixated on her breasts, I have liked the fact of my small breasts all the more.

Unveiling the ta-tas can be as fraught or as freeing for her as unwrapping your package is for you. They are both jacks-in-the-box. Playing by the black comedy rules of nature, their news is delivered in inches and lumps and disproportion. Your F-cup compatriot's western hemisphere may be noticeably fuller than her eastern hemisphere. Like a good dinner guest, don't crowd with commentary. Instead, Bush Pilots, let your babe introduce you to her girls. Your job: adore.

CHAPTER 11
HANDS DOWN
(THIRD BASE)

NOTE FROM THE FIELD:
LIGHTNING STRIKES TWICE

Vish finds the secret key tucked under the woodpile, unlocks the door and, with a push of his Greb boot, enters. Flicks on the light. Wood panelling, wall-to-wall carpet, circa-1968 light fixtures, the chalet: It is the moustache of habitats, Burt Reynolds as a building, and with its suggestive second syllable, it even comes on to him. The smell of cedar and mothballs lingers in the air. Vish turns on the water and pours himself a whiskey.

Waiting for his girlfriend of three months, Nina, Vish picks up his Les Paul guitar, plugs it into his amp and, in an attempt to look hot but cool when she pulls in, slides open the screen doors, steps out onto the porch and plays "Foxy Lady." This is when he gets struck by lightning. A black cloud. An electrical storm. The neck of his guitar turned a mild blue. His hand too. No burns. No entry marks. No pain. Just a jolt.

Nina arrives. Jean shorts. Tank top. Bare feet. No bra. She leaps from her Datsun and strikes a hellcat pose. Vish does a reprise of "Foxy Lady." She flashes her breasts, slips him her tongue and tells him he is playing better than ever before. She even calls him "electric." Privately, he agrees. In fact, he's stunned and, inexplicably, feels the need to put on a headband. Has he made a pact with the devil? If so, where were the crossroads? Nina and Vish pull the twin mattresses out of the spare bedroom, set up a nest in front of the fireplace and, conjuring a discount album cover, recline. They make out in slow motion. And then, as they have so many times before, they tumble like teenage voluptuaries. But tonight, it only goes so far. Vish's hand slips beneath Nina's jean shorts. Fingers still abuzz, that is where they stay.

Reclining Burt Reynolds

(WITH BEARSKIN)

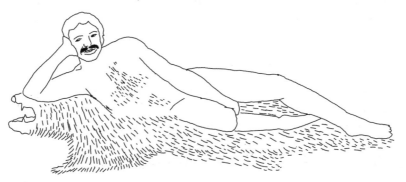

TOO COOL FOR SCHOOL

Heavy petting. Her foxy lady. Admit it, Bush Pilots: You think it retro. Like your long hair, your shoplifting, your copy of *Zen and the Art of Motorcycle Maintenance* and your virginity, you think it the stuff of high school. A muddy field. A bottle of malt liquor. Bus fare. Your hand groping your girlfriend's bra, then breasts, and then, for the first time, led south, to that sister of mercy, the butterfly in her bikini underwear. The preliminary investigation of your fingers, tentative, searching, soon to be thwarted by your tongue and finally, forever, the Marco Polo in your pants, your bookmark, your boner.

Bush Pilots, it is time to usher this grade nine act into your adult situation. It is time to go into a soundproof studio and learn its chords. Why? Read the following "sweet memory" penned by a babe (trucker hat and a ten-speed):

I really liked it when you touched my cunt through my clothing and kept your hand there, feeling my heat, containing it, communicating silently with cupped palm, strong fingers that you had me. Held. Then the gentle movement of dextrous digits playfully plying their way past buttons or zipper or buckle—I can't remember now— a little clumsy, but that's totally cute (too suave and I start getting nervous). You plunged gently into the depths of the panties you admired so much (a woman relishes this kind of specific appreciation)—the two-toned ones with the seams—and felt your way into that salty ocean, saying, "You are so wet." I loved it how you said that: hungry and soft. Getting rougher, you rubbed my clit but quickly slid on down to let your fingers slide up inside me. And then the hunt for the G-spot . . . I wish I knew how you found it . . . I wish I could educate the masses by pointing out exactly where it is . . . I can't, so my advice is this: Keep looking until you find it. Which is what you, sumptuous lover, did, and, fingers strong and pointed, fucked me with your hand, and as if that weren't enough . . . it was. I am, happily, three sweet orgasms later, very easy to please.

In? Thought so.

BACK TO THE FUTURE

Bush Pilots, the point of third base is to stay on it. But Mistress, you protest stoutly, I have so many other killer moves: the Hat Trick, the Misty Beethoven and the 2112, to name just a few! Not now, Your Hotness, not now. Tonight, you have a different sequence to complete.

Too often, your boner and your babe's mini-boner are like needles skipping over your favourite record (e.g., Bahamas' *Pink Strat*). You both know the order of the songs and you depend on hearing them that way (to make her come). But I ask: In repeating the same routine, night after night, might you be missing something? Some hidden tracks?

> I had an interesting conversation recently about being courageous with someone who has known you for a very long time. To be uninhibited. Bold. Risky. It can sometimes be more difficult than being with a stranger. That's one of the challenges, I think, of being in a long-term relationship. I'm trying to always be courageous and brave in the bedroom. To say yes to all offerings and to offer something more or new each time. And to always connect.
> —Babe (very tall feather in her fedora)

BPs, with that yes pirouetting in sequins through your brain, I tell you this: Sometimes ramping it up in the bedroom comes not in venturing forward (cybersex, a gorilla mask and a 6500 Real Doll named Jenny) but in going back.

SEXTERITY

With your hand (no longer the high-school hand that dimwittedly ted and screwed the lady parts like a pumpjack), lead your babe—in her fur hat and white panties—to your bedroom. Light your skull candle. Throw on Echo and the Bunnymen's "Lips Like Sugar."

Make out. Dry hump.

BPs, never overlook the power of this throwback combination—vintage as chamois leather and a first edition of *On the Road*. Your tongue skirts her mouth. Her tongue skirts your mouth. Your boner behind your jeans presses up against her go-go under her panties. Boner to go-go, go-go to boner. Do you read me? I do, Mistress, oh yes, I do. Over.

THE BUSH CUP

Your opening move: Trace your hand down the length of your babe's torso. Now, cup her lady parts. Not with brawn, but with confidence. Like manual floodlights, you are, Bush Pilots, igniting the area. Recall the electricity of your babe's mons, the many nerve endings that live in that cushion of flesh. Press up against them.

Slowly, pull her panties down and off. You may lift them above your head and twirl them from your second finger, then toss them aside. N.B.B.P.: Let your babe laugh harder. Lube up. Deal-Breaker Alert: BPs, to avoid the dreaded allergic reaction, please be sure to agree upon your water- or silicone-based lube before (your) hand. Also, before sexterity, be sure that your claws are trimmed and your hands are washed.

GIMME AN O

Start wide. Circle the area of your babe's lady parts, really—and this is key, BPs—really gently. Just as your babe, pre–transcendent blowjob, unzips your fly with her teeth for the duration of "The Lemon Song," your tease is her turn-on. Massage her thighs—especially, Guillaume Latendresse, that other crease you dream about, where her thighs give way to her kit. Notice its proximity to her butterfly. Return to circling the area of the bush with an aching slowness and a barely-there touch.

Dare: Talk dirty. You, dedicated Pilot of the Bush, have spent countless hours in your Bush Pilot–issue bunk, making pornographic promises to your Bettie Page pin-ups. Why not pull them out here? Still at a loss for words? Let this fantasy be your fodder.

It's gay night at the local bar. Mostly young men lit up by those bar lights that turn your eyes vampire-pale. Since this is the last place I'd ever score, I give in to some solo dancing with my boyfriends when a girl, out of nowhere, practically falls into my arms. Instantly resolute, thinking this might be my only living chance to kiss a girl in an uncomplicated way, I take her by the hand and walk us both to a less crowded part of the dance floor. We come together in a tentative, then hot, kiss, and almost right after part ways.

This drifting apart leads to several random moments of encountering one another again through the night in the bar. On the third encounter, she pushes me up against the wall. For a moment, my feet don't touch down. Almost like we are in danger and she's getting me out of the way in a hurry. I let the girl pin me to the wall with what I can only describe as this vertical energy that radiates from her pubic bone. I can feel the precise shape of it: hard and oval, and moving up and down my torso. Then, through my jeans, I feel her other hand. She palms my crotch and makes a V with her fingers and presses everywhere on the periphery of my cunt, everywhere but on my clitoris. Like she's framing it over and over, pulling and pushing her V'd fingers toward and away from me. Which makes me so hot to have my clit touched that I kiss her harder and run my hands up the length of her body. After a while, she opens my zipper

and does this same movement, with the V'd fingers, except that everything is slippery now. When her index finger finally, slowly, runs over my clitoris, starting at my anus and moving forward, it's so ready to blow. And with only a few strokes, it does, right there, into her hand, in the bar.
—Babe (Byron in a past life)

"Ready to blow." Affirmative.

GIMME A V

Bush Pilots, you may now stop circling and form the aforementioned V with your fingers. The effect of this sultry pinch? A rush of blood to your babe's lips and go-go. Remember, her go-go is not merely a playful bean to be brushed across, your fingers flicking like windshield wipers.

Pilot error.

Her go-go is an eighteen-spoked cell of sublimity. To overlook its elaborate circuitry would be tantamount to sexual atheism—or living on Frank Lloyd Wright's front porch when you have the key to Fallingwater.

How to fire up those eighteen parts? Yes, Bush Pilots! You are so on it! Gold star! Your eventual destination is a combination of the head of your babe's go-go and her G-spot. But first, continue your tour through her outskirts, namely, her lips. Some babes enjoy having their lips lightly (and this expression will probably be very unfamiliar to you, Bush Pilots) rubbed and tugged. If you are going to pull and pat the lady parts, you must ask for permission first. No-Fly List Alert: Not all babes find this form of tenderizing sexy.

GOGOGRAPHY

Now, the moment your babe has been waiting for. She has been sending you ESP messages: "My clit!" She even got her homing pigeon to land on your windowsill with this small script in his claws: "My clit!" And whoa, did you see that blimp overhead with the neon—wait, make that exploding—letters: "MY CLIT!" And did she just throw on Foreigner's "Urgent"?

s, you may now move your thumb or two fingers over the glans of her go-go. Again, and I cannot emphasize this enough, modify pressure. No one wants a hand-bang. Do not confuse your excitement with hers. It hurts.

> I was having such a good time with this guy, and then he got his hand on my pussy and then basically handled me as hard as he could. (He was the kind of guy who pumped iron to death metal.) He went ape, a kid in a candy shop. I grabbed his wrist and had to stop him. That was kind of it for him.
> —Babe (built like the Grey Cup)

PETIQUETTE

How to avoid that too common pitfall? Captain Goodscrew provides this useful barometer: "The motion is super gentle. The pressure is equivalent to stroking your closed eye." Now, try this on yourself, BPs. Do you see how any aggression makes for nothing but tears?

Track your thumb or two fingers across, up and down, above and beneath the silken hood of your babe's go-go. Ongoing note: If you need to relubricate at any point, do so (except if you hear this telltale word: ohmygodImgonnacome.[3])

If you concentrate your every stroke in one place, you could numb your babe. For added variation, lend pressure to her go-go and then retreat from her go-go. Note well, Bush Pilots: Physical titillation follows the same principle as visual titillation. Two words: lap dance. Or think of the now-you-see-it, now-you-don't lingerie of Sophia Loren as lady of the night Filumena Marturano (English translation: I Am Your Dream Bush) in Vittorio de Sica's *Marriage Italian Style*. Your absence, boys, is nearly as compelling as your presence.

---

[3] ohmygodImgonnacome hyperbole+possessive adjective + noun + contraction + verb + verb + verb (o:mygodImghunnahcum) Short for, "Oh my God, I am going to come." Loosely translated as "Don't get cute and start freestyling."

LIKE CLOCKWORK

Where, oh where should I tease my babe, Mistress? Two o'clock and ten o'clock (i.e., as you look at her lady parts, with the top of her go-go at midnight). The current sexology has deduced these points of intersection with your short hand to be the two most abundant in nerve endings. But these are mean numbers. If you really want to know what time it is, ask your babe—still in her fur hat. And whoa, are those crocheted white woollen knee socks, and a strand of pearls doubled at the neck, fingers grazing her nipples, eyes closing, lips parting?

Your babe may come. She may not come. The point is, she is primed. The result: Her G-spot will make itself known to your searching hands.

HOW TO MAKE AN ENTRANCE

A moan-ahead is not enough. Check in with your babe. This is called retrieving the owner's manual that has been lying open on your bed all night. I know it goes against your creed, BPs, but please consult it. You will find everything you need there to build your babe's orgasms, one touch—and eventually, one screw—at a time. Bush Pilots, beyond reading your babe's body and studying her breath, solicit her instruction, then ask her directly if you, the legitimate son of Hendrix, have permission to enter.

Whoa, Mistress—let me just put on my Tilley hat and matching Tilley underwear—permission? Yes, BP. You think talking, like birding, is for dorks? Watch the first sex scene of Unfaithful between former "Cherry" Diane Lane and that brooding rake, Olivier Martinez. His hands on her cheating thighs, her cheating belly. How she quivers. How they tussle. And still they talk. Bush Pilots, if Cherry and Olivier can, you can too.

TOUCHY, TOUCHY

Remedial: Most of the nerve endings in your babe's butterfly are in the first third—including, now that you have bowed to your babe's go-go,

gitive in a pencil skirt, the Bonnie Parker of the bedroom, the
.. With one hand, keep your palm hovering against your babe's
while with the other, you enter your babe's butterfly, keeping
your thumb pressed against her go-go. Important: Go finger by finger, Bush Pilot. No babe wants, nor can she accommodate, a surprise
fisting. N.B.B.P.: Your digits are to be inserted one at a time—with her
approval. No-Fly List Alert: Never use the term fingering. Like mistak-
ing threesome for a verb (e.g., "Let's threesome them ladies"), it is about
as sexy as watching you play keytar.

After a slow rotation to announce your presence, run your fingers
up against those infamous ridges on her ventral wall—what Captain
Goodscrew calls the "sweet spot"—located half an inch to two inches
in. (She may, with persistent, well-placed play, gush all over you. For
the dirt on her squirt, BPs, you may, when I say so, consult Chapter 14).

GET TO KNOW THESE
Common Signals

come hither   go away

At this point, it is all about your thumb on her go-go and fingers stroking her G-spot. Or—switch—your fingers on her g̲ and your thumb come-hither-ing Big G. And what about my other hand, so adroit and yet so aimless, Mistress? BPs, your other paw is not merely an undercover agent on a stakeout, lying in wait. Your babe's G-spot can be stimulated through external pressure as well. Whether bald eagle or Peaches' pelt, press against the point where your babe's pubic hair (or the ghost of pubic hair past) begins. Or, dive down to her perineum, or even, with your babe's explicit consent, tickle her kit.

Sticky Note for your "Sticky Fingers": You cannot, like a hosed and unknowing guest, simply move between the party in the front and the party in the back of your babe. Bush Pilots, when switching between the butterfly and the kit, you must wash your hands first. Moreover, if you are going to visit her behind—after sanitizing—recall that, like the butterfly, the kit's prime real estate is just beyond its entrance. Unlike your babe's butterfly, aside from some congenial yet ineffective mucous membranes, it does not have any of its own natural lubrication. Lube up. (For more on her hindquarters, consult Chapter 16. When I say so.)

THE WIZARD OF PAWS

You are now in two places at once. Well done, BPs! Gold star! Talk to your babe; she may want you to alternate your attentions between go-go and G-spot stimulation, or go-go and kit stimulation. If so, amble between the two, gradually working toward a sprint. Or she may want you to refocus your attentions solely on her go-go.

Again, your babe may come (and be so nice to you after!). Or she may not come. Whoa, Mistress, why would you say such a thing? BPs, I am trying to get you away from being goal-oriented in the bedroom—and in the bush. Don't have an agenda for the bush. Don't pressure the bush. Don't rate the bush against other bushes. You are not writing the *Bush-elin Guide.*

The point here is: On third base, you are uncovering new sensations in your sexual repertoire and undoing the patterns that may have unconsciously snagged you along the screw-way. Moreover, in the congress of her lady parts and your man parts, your sexterity will serve as both a Babe and a Bush Pilot Bonus.

Too often, the drive-by of the bedroom—a little cup, a little pet, a little flick—third base is sped through on the way to other, boner-based, destinations (e.g., coitus in a roadside motel—or just by a roadside). But Bush Pilots, I want you to recall, for a moment, the days shot in black and white when you and your babe had strict curfews and the same New Wave haircut. You would meet at the arcade. She would borrow your trench coat, the one with the Specials pins. Because of its bulk, you could, while rocking Pac-Man, drop your other paw down the front of her tapered jeans. She would swivel her hips, get wet and lean her head back against you. It was a beautiful, straightforward act, one that deserves a Bush Pilot revival.

How to leave third base? Quietly, and with care. Withdraw your fingers one at a time. Now end the way you began. With tenderness, cup your babe's lady parts.

Just like you did in grade nine.

CHAPTER 12

CUNNILINGUS

NOTE FROM THE FIELD:
SKIRT CHASER

Maxime is sitting at his desk, thinking about skirts and his tongue going under them and that the longer the skirt, the more suspense for his tongue. He is thinking about Amish women and the hems of their skirts, which are so long they are always dipped in mud, like in that movie with Harrison Ford. That's all he wants: to be Harrison Ford with an Amish woman. Instead, he is a teenager sitting at his desk at his summer job at the post office, licking stamps—so many stamps.

The bell rings. Maxime looks up. A girl he thinks goes to his small rural high school walks in, but with that bonnet on, he can't be sure. He licks a stamp. She nods toward Maxime. He nods back thinking Harrison Ford, so he tries to smile out the side of his mouth, but it fails. So he makes a sound like hey. The girl makes a sound like hey. He licks a stamp. And then the girl bends in half, picks up the bottom of her skirt, holds it as if it were a basket and kicks her leg up against the wall. Maxime makes a sound like er. The girl just looks at him.

He recognizes her now. She misses a lot of school—something about acting on television. Something about a prairie. Around her ankle is a key chain. The girl does not remove it, but instead stretches to open her P.O. box. As she jiggles the key, Maxime licks many stamps. The girl retrieves a thick envelope. She locks the P.O. box and her leg descends as if a train were speeding behind it. Maxime claps. He claps again. He stands on his desk and claps more. The girl bows. She locks the door to the post office. Maxime licks, missing the stamps, and then is pretty sure he smiles out the side of his mouth. The girl grabs his hand and leads him to the back, to the bigger desk, where she lies down and pulls his head up under her skirt. She seems in a rush. He can't see anything. It's so dark. He needs a lantern. To his surprise, he feels the back of his head pushed gently between her legs. What to do? Maxime pretends she is a letter, a letter addressed to some far-off place, where they raise barns and milk goats, and he only has one-cent stamps. Beside his ear, the girl's key chain chimes.

START ME UP

Bush Pilots, I see you tumbling out of your bunk in your threadbare boxer shorts, alarm clock accusatory in the corner. You club it with your Field Guide and, stubbing your toe, look down. Oh. Good morning.

You stand before your hand mirror. You put on "I'm on Fire." You call him "The Boss." You know the words; The Boss does too. He has his own bandana, New Jersey accent and denim outfits. The song ends, but still you sing "I'm on Fire." So does The Boss. You gaze at him. You recall his antics, his stage presence, his induction into the Rock and Roll Hall of Fame. You think, I should insure you. You flex The Boss. You try to high-five him, but that's a mistake. So you salute him instead, and look for a rifle to shoot in the air. Oh. Good morning.

Well, I have news for you, Bush Pilots: Love is blind. Of course The Boss deserves your adulation, but it should not overshadow that other member of your turn-on team: the more agile, the longer-lasting and even the logo of the Rolling Stones, your tongue.

THE UNCONSCIOUS

Bush Pilots, you understand the anatomical fantasia that is your babe's go-go: eight thousand nerve endings within a pelvic network of fifteen thousand. (B-O-N-A-N-Z-A.) My job is to teach you how to play that fantasia. In this regard, we are all still recovering from a wicked Freudian hangover. Sh. Everything is so loud and bright. Between the "Oedipus complex," the "hysteria" and the coke, what a sick party that guy threw. Don't you remember, BP? You spent most of your time on his couch, hypnotized and then crying, only to leave jittery and ashamed, reduced to a pseudonym (Johann) and convinced "vaginal orgasms" are the only "mature" orgasms, and the only acceptable way to tip them off is through intercourse. Damn.

THE AFTER PARTY

Now, after decades of sober scientific atonement (key parties, Annie Sprinkle and your babe's full-bodied self-awareness), we know: Only

45 per cent of babes come through intercourse, whereas more than 80 per cent of babes come through the bushjob. Eighty per cent. So, while clearly a fan favourite, you tell me, Bush Pilots: Between The Boss and your tongue, who is the real hotshot here?

One Bush Pilot (boxing gloves or, more often, a dancer's legs around his neck) puts it this way:

> It's definitely not a macho thing—like I can lick my eyebrows.
> It's more: I give a shit about making my lady feel good.

Amen.

DR. FEELGOOD

After you shave off your man-stubble and before you begin your bush-job, Bush Pilots, be sure you and your babe are safer with dental dams, latex gloves and finger cots.

Sticky Note: If you are backing up your mouth music with some of the sexterity you practised in the previous chapter, please do not strum between your babe's butterfly and her kit. If you do, fingers must be well washed between riffs.

I know, given the player stats, you and your tongue are stoked, but please do not dive open-mouthed between your babe's legs when she first walks through your door.

Do not ambush the bush.
Friend the bush on Facebush.
Send the bush a message.

Make suggestions to the bush. Make requests of the bush. Post that night's event. Give the bush a thumb's-up. Then send the bush a gift, like virtual bongos, a rose or a cupcake. (You can update your profiles later.)

The bushjob comes on the flickering heels of that fluffer: foreplay. You make dinner (Chapter 5. Memorize it.). You joke. You shine. You flirt (Chapter 4. Be it.). You spank your babe's bottom through her jeans. She spanks your bottom through your jeans. You drop the dishes; they smash and you make out and dry hump on the kitchen floor. You have been together for a month; you know she is ready for it, so you kick off your Chuck Taylors and all of your clothes except for a small purple bathing suit. You pull her into your bedroom, put on The Doors' *Alive She Cried* and pose down hilariously to "Gloria."

The Pose Down

*Muscles may not be exactly to scale

You do quarter-turns. You pop your guns. You do a javelin thrower. You do a hamstring-flex. She laughs until she is punching your mattress, but then it goes instrumental and the Lizard King speaks about Gloria's legs wrapping around his neck, and it turns serious and your babe does a pose-down too.

She is ready.

BABE ON TOP

Gentlemen of the bedchamber, ask for permission. You may be surprised by the response. For despite the bushjob's stellar reputation, I must, for full disclosure, and before you compulsively curl your tongue into the shape of a balloon poodle, balloon monkey and balloon dolphin, present its dark side.

> I'm not that into cunnilingus. I mean, I like it fine, but I'm not sure I've ever come very strongly that way. Maybe a little jolt here or there. I used to feel badly about it, and I don't think it's because the guys who have tried were all useless at it. I think I just prefer a different kind of stimulation. I've had a number of disappointed guys bringing their A-game who I've just hauled up out of there. I do enjoy it as a warmup once in a while, but it's never worked as a main event for me.
>
> This used to make me feel like I was sort of deficient— that I only really found it easy to come in one position, and one in which I was in total control, but I don't care about that really anymore. Whatever works.
>
> —Babe (performance artist, glitter eye shadow)

"Whatever works." Affirmative.

Once permission is granted, position yourselves. Get comfortable. As one Bush Pilot says about performing the transcendent bushjob:

> The key is to be comfortable. It's like what human-rights lawyers say about justice: It's important not just that it be done but also that it be seen to be done. Important not just to be comfortable but to be seen to be comfortable. Because it should be understood that you could do this all day long.

"All day long." Affirmative.

Instruction: Fetch any pillows you may need for her kit and for your knees. Depending on her preference, your babe can straddle you from above, facing you, as this Bush Pilot espouses:

> I've found the most effective position to be perhaps the least intuitive: with the woman on her hands and knees (well, knees—typically it works better if her upper body is pressed into the bed, ass high in the air). With this position, access is at its best, an openness allowing for tonguing and nibbling, decorous diddling. Don't neglect the ass, either—it's right there. Make the most of it.

Or, facing your really good-looking toes. Bush Pilot Bonus: Aside from the stellar view for you (and her), this position allows your babe to control the depth, pressure and placement of the bushjob. Moreover, while it bares her bush, it also features a possible touchdown on her kit.

> I love being on top, but turned round, if you know what I mean. Whatever that position is called. He gets the full view of all your glory, but also the rear is available for poking, spanking, etc.
> —Babe (can ride a horse through a house)

"Etc." Affirmative.

BABE ON THE BOTTOM

Alternatively, your babe can recline on her side or on her back, or even drape herself at the edge of your bed. One babe (most likely to use *billet-doux* in a sentence) confesses, "I like lying down because I'm lazy." One Bush Pilot, ever practical, concurs:

The "best" position really is the conventional one, with man between the legs of reclining woman—it allows the most manoeuvring and inspiration. But the most erotic position, I think, is man flat on his back, woman upright on her knees, perhaps holding onto the bedposts. If it's worked out, man has one hand to aid in cunnilingus and the other to caress woman's face, breasts, arms . . .

Or she can stand, in her bowler hat, thigh-highs and suede heels, up against your brick wall. Though one realist confesses, "Standing, I'm afraid I'll fall over." A Bush Pilot adds:

Standing is fun too, of course. But maybe she's not as relaxed as she could be. Not in all the right places. So the best, I'll wager, is the one where she's most comfortable. Where she can read a book, aloud or silent, or gaze at the tree outside, or dangle her arms open, resting her head on her open palms.

P.S.: A book?
P.P.S.: A tree?
P.P.P.S.: Pull yourself together, BP.

I'm calling it for a big armchair. You're kneeling in front of her. There's enough room on the chair for you to rest your elbows. Maybe both hands are free, maybe just one. It depends which way you're most comfortable.

Bush Pilots, a lot can be done with your babe's legs, both now, as you get into position, and during the service. Variations: She has one leg over your shoulder. She keeps her legs close together, to the side, spread wide or, if she is a magician's assistant, bent over her head. And remember, if you are at all anxious, relax.

We cannot do the bushjob to ourselves, so for you, Bush Pilot, the skies will almost always be friendly.

If, that is, you know how to fly them. Every bush is different; learn her customs, respect her language and, please, Bush Pilots, for the sake of your own advancement: When lost, ask for directions.

THE BUSH WHISPERER

Start in the suburbs. Don't go for your tongue solo off the top. Tease your babe, kiss her thighs, her belly, and then meander your way to the outskirts of her butterfly. Linger there.

> Most men think in superlatives, whereas with cunnilingus, it's all about subtlety.
> —Babe (in the window of New York's Standard Hotel)

Break out the breath-tease, or simply, provocatively, place your lips against hers, one paw on her mons. Use your fingers to spread her lips (your centrefold can do this as well) and massage them gently. Gently. One babe reinforces:

> Hmmmmm . . . cunnilingus. A big treat for both of you . . . very pleasurable when he's shaved. Very, very pleasurable when he's shaved. Off the charts, really. Always wonderful, provided things are soft and gentle. Even when he goes to town, he must be gentle!

Bush Pilots, always be the "spy in the house of love." Monitor your babe's arousal through her breath and the empirical evidence before you: the engorgement of her lips and the hardening of her supreme being, her go-go—or, most revealing, when she moves your head sharply like a tiller in a windstorm.

BENICIO

Lick from south to north. You may do this many times. Move to the clitoral glans (head), so reactive it wears its own hood. Be patient, Bush Pilots. You have just arrived. She knows nothing about you. No one does. You could be a con, a werewolf, Che. With slowness and subtle pressure, lick (long and languorous) and flick (short and sharp).

NO AUTO-PILOT

BPs, never phone in the bushjob. If you do, you will not get through to Bushquarters. Bushquarters will be busy. Bushquarters will give you the signal. Bushquarters will then disconnect and unlist its number. As one babe (pays for her drink in rubles) espouses, "A little variety: harder, softer, faster, slower, etc., aiming for some kind of crescendo—building up slowly instead of just doing the same thing the whole time."

How, Mistress, oh how do I do this thing you babes call "crescendo"? Circle her go-go. Now, back away. As you studied in the previous chapter, your absence is nearly as stirring as your presence. Involve your hands: Cup and massage her kit, her breasts and her perineum.

THE RHYTHM SECTION

Now, begin to lick with rhythm, alternating between short and long strokes. Your babe may rock her pelvis toward you, determining pressure and placement. Or she may lie still, processing the rush of sensation. If this is the case, offer the added element of confinement—cuffs, a rope, a scarf tied around her wrists—or suggest she keep her arms up above her head and tuck her feet firmly beneath your knees.

Be regular. Be rhythmic.
But don't be boring.
Lick, suck, flick.
Alternate between stations.

The Tongue

MULTI-DIRECTIONAL, FULLY NAVIGABLE
AND SURPRISINGLY VERSATILE

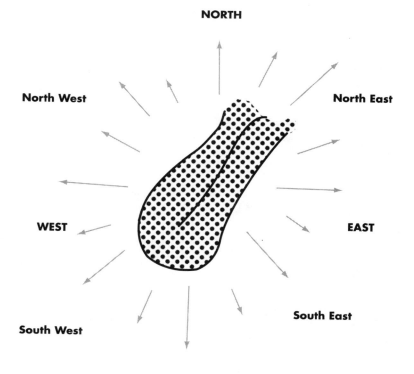

NORTH

North West

North East

WEST

EAST

South West

South East

SOUTH

HEAD

Add a new direction and track your tongue across her go-go. Begin to alternate your frictional migrations between north-south and east-west, with the emphasis on the horizontal. Why? Recall: What time is it? Two o'clock. What time is it? Ten o'clock. What time is it? Two o'clock—again. You are, BPs, by swinging betwixt two and ten o'clock, alternating between your babe's two most sensitive time zones.

To suck or not to suck? You may suck on her go-go, just as your babe would your deity (in an attic room on a day bed with the windows open). Or, penetrate the butterfly with the firm muscle of your tongue, the rest of your mouth forming an O-shape around her lips. No-Fly List Alert: If you are going to suck, do so gently. We are not your last meal. We are not the fountain of youth. We are not a spill that needs to be hoovered. Nor is there a prize in the box. We are the prizes, and we'd like to keep our boxes. So ease off on our lady parts, BPs. Heed these warnings from the Bush Club:

> **Babe 1:** Oh, absolutely no sucking!!! Once, a guy kind of sucked me down there like a vacuum cleaner. It was horrifying and quite painful.
> **Babe 2:** No mashing (it's not a potato).
> **Babe 3:** His "eating out" was ravenous, like some sort of snorvelling pig.

THE ONE-MAN BAND

At this point, her go-go is awakened. Given your sexterity, you know what comes next. In addition to your tongue's trip south, with your babe's consent, slip one finger inside her butterfly, palm up, and look for the ridges of her G-spot or "clitoral cluster" against her ventral wall. Please find it. One babe bemoans, "A finger on the G-spot is good, but they never get it right." With your other hand, press against her perineum—or inch the head of your well-lubed thumb into the entrance of her kit.

One Bush Pilot describes his set this way:

Not just your tongue, but also your lips, your nose, your eyelids, your chin, your gently curling fingers. Not just her clit but also her labia, her anus, her belly, her little hairs for tingling.

"Not just," Mistress?! Not just my tongue, but also my ears, my knees, my calves, my shoulders, my hipbones and my cheekbones? "Not just," Mistress? Oh, not just her go-go, but also her ankles, her forehead, her spine and her thumbs? Is this guy a human Swiss Army Knife? I'll give you a bushjob, while I crack open your beer, file your nails, light your fire and read your compass?! Cool your jets, BP, cool your jets. The point: Like the multitalented BP I know you are, elaborate the bushjob. There is more to it than the singular congress of your tongue and her go-go. Use all that is available to you.

Now . . .

TAKE IT TO THE BRIDGE

Slip a second finger into her butterfly. With your tongue, stroke her go-go and then, flattening your tongue, put sustained pressure on it. This can also be done with a finger, your upper gums and an oft-overlooked ridge of cartilage: your nose. This protrusion has immense erotic potential, especially when pressed up against thousands of nerve endings. Bush Pilot Bonus: Aside from her go-go, your nose is also particularly suited to tickling your babe's mons.

THE FINALE

Stay your course. Steady now. Focus on the circular and the vertical. A "Bird on the Wire," your babe is very close to coming. At this tender point, it can be the de-escalated rather than the escalated moment that kicks off your babe's orgasm. As such, provide both (except if you hear this word: ohmygodImgonnacome), go from Isaac Hayes to

Gene Simmons, intensifying your speed until, "Hallelujah," your babe thrusts her pelvis to your mouth, proffering her contractile bliss.

THE FADE-OUT

Bush Pilots, through your babe's climax, however acrobatic and prolonged her response, keep your tongue in line with her go-go until (pay attention) she indicates the end. Key: After the bushjob, don't crowd the bush. Give the bush some space. Let the bush be. When your babe completes her descent, achingly sensitive to your touch, she will, lovingly, push you away. And ask you to call for takeout.

FEEL MY HEAT

Variations on the bushjob can include temperature control. Bush Pilots, why not add an ice cube, cough drop or breath mint to your bushjob? If your babe is down with the side dishes, please make sure they are sugar free. And please don't choke on them.

Conversely, short of fire breathing, why not turn up the heat? For some hot licks, dip your tongue in hot water before going down, or add a warming lube. Like you, it heats up on contact. Like you, it responds to fanning and friction.

If your babe wants some added slide, look for a water-based and water-soluble lube—compatible with your latex gloves, condoms, silicone toys and taste buds (allergy advisory still in effect).

Or perhaps that is not what she wants at all.

EXTRA CREDIT

NOT-TO-DO LIST

✗ Say, "Isn't this 'Funnilingus'!"
✗ Say, "At the All-You-Can-Eat Bush-ay!"
✗ And then put on your pants-shorts.
✗ Work your penis so it lies suggestively against her neck.
✗ Offer a subliminal "sixty-nine . . . sixty-nine."
✗ Hump her neck when she does not get the message.
✗ Keep humping her neck because you can still totally concentrate, but who knew her neck was so warm and then hard and then so tickly and warm again.
✗ Come on her neck.
✗ Fall asleep like a neck-comer.
✗ But not before apologizing for being one.

A WORD ABOUT YOUR DROOL

After some nimble sexterity, one babe writes:

> Down came your lips, your mouth, your tongue to luxuri-
> ously lick my clit and lap up the juiciness of good loving.
> Notice that I say "lap up," as opposed to "drool on"—
> there is a growing trend out there in the world of oral
> love-giving that seems to have eager men believing that
> their role as head-giver is to "wet" the receiver. No. I can
> confidently say—and I have conferred with many a lusty
> woman on this one—if your salivary glands have turned
> my ass crack into the Mekong River, I am no longer hav-
> ing a good time.

TURN YOUR BUSHJOB INTO BUSHFEST

Bush Pilots, after a brief respite, your babe may be ready for more; the
bushjob is a brilliant way to multiply her pleasure.

> Usually my boyfriend goes down on me before we fuck.
> It's a surefire way for me to come, and right after I come,
> all I want to do is feel him hard inside me. But on this
> night—we were in a hotel room in Tokyo—he just kept
> going with the oral. And after I came once, the orgasms
> just kept happening—usually, right at the point he would
> fumble around a bit to put a finger here or there, usually
> up my ass, I would come. It happened five times in a row.
> —Babe (mistaken for Dorothy Parker)

Enticed? Here, Bush Pilots, is the key to the revelatory (i.e.,
multi-orgasmic) bushjob: time. Do not rush the bush. Take off your

stopwatches. Bust the hourglass. For once, there is no race to win, no train to catch, no game to make, no limited-time offer, no ETA. Tease your babe—not with random enthusiasm, but with preternatural strategy. Recall Chapter 1. With your tongue, nose, and fingers, focus on the highlights of your babe's anatomical wizardry: the head of her go-go, so coy under its silken hood, her mons above it and just below, her front commissure, her inner lips, her perineum, her kit and her G-spot. With her nerve endings as your landing pads, be precise, Bush Pilots: Follow exact latitudes and longitudes.

THE WAY OF THE TONGUE

Let's review: Study the bush, know the bush, friend the bush, gift the bush, talk to the bush, love the bush. And then, hale, erect, sing Bush Pilot Lifetime Achievement Award winner Leonard Cohen's "Light as the Breeze." That part about worship and being on your knees. Well we, blissed-out babes in your unmade beds, could not agree more.

CHAPTER 13
SOIXANTE-NEUF

Juliette of the feathered hair. Christopher of the feathered hair. His parents are away for the weekend, and his older brother, who is supposed to cut the grass and defrost dinner, has left without a word. His suddenly empty home, with its mirrored dining room, white shag carpet, hot tub and wet bar, appears to him for the first time in all its glory. It is the dominion of the dirty, and Christopher is now its king. He feels that noxious twinge of the bachelor. He puts on his brother's bathrobe, pours himself a screwdriver and throws Van Halen on the hi-fi. He toasts himself to "You Really Got Me." He is a virgin. His future winks, shudders and stretches out before him in a series of sexual positions that he has yet to try before he crosses over and becomes a scowl-faced condom-carrier.

The doorbell rings. Juliette, in her low-cut diner uniform, the summer sun slinking west behind her, spits her gum on the grass, kicks off her high-tops and leaps into his arms. Within seconds, they are in the sunken living room, naked and climbing over each other like a hot-breathed kennel. It is then, without warning, without signs, that Christopher finds himself on that famed Route 69. Before, it was only a rumour, whispered like a premonition between chocolate bars and menthol cigarettes. Now he is one of its initiates, one of its travellers, one of its brethren. He wonders: How to contort? How to doubly concentrate? He feels his brow furrow, his moustache grow. Surely he'll look older in the morning.

CIRCLE TIME

That old high-school favourite: the 69. Bush Pilots, I am making the assumption that all of you cigar-smoking, money-clip sophisticates are familiar with the soixante-neuf. But for those of you still playing Dungeons and Dragons and living in your parents' basements, the 69 is the position that allows for simultaneous oral sex. Like the titular configuration suggests, the 69 is when you and your babe arrange yourselves in a circle, side by side or top and bottom. While she feasts on your bangers and mash, you make friendly with her butterfly. Sound good?

Here is the hitch: Because it is a biathlete's event, the 69 has both its devotees and its defectors, in equally impassioned camps. Bush Pilots, the contentious question: Is the 69 the ultimate turn-on, or the rub-your-tummy-and-pat-your-head of the sexual lexicon? Merry-go-round or Rubik's cube? Given its gymnastics, you must ask yourself: Is the floor routine worth it? Or, like Peter Frampton, is the 69 best left in the past, where you found it in the first place?

GOOD FRIDAY

First, if your babe clenches her jaw when she comes, this after-school activity is not for you.

Otherwise, the beauty of the soixante-neuf is in its perfect reciprocity. While she teases and titillates your Joy Division, you do the same to hers, building your bliss together. For those of you I will call the Good Samaritan Bush Pilots of the bedroom—you who cannot bear to receive pleasure without giving it—the 69 is the shimmering sexual icon in a framed portrait that hangs above your rumpled bed. For the 69, you deliver pamphlets door to door. For the 69, you speak in tongues. As one soixante-neuf thumper attests: "It is gender equality. Equal-opportunity employment. Everyone wins. The only thing that confuses me is why it isn't happening to me more often." Thumper even goes so far as to say (and this may disturb sensitive Bush Pilots):

> The goal as a guy is to try to remain sane while making your lover crazy. Often, I find, the woman gradually loses concentration, and occasionally stops. This is an important victory, and despite the sad cessation of fellatio, is accompanied by grand satisfaction. This is how the 69 is won.

BLACK MONDAY

Hold the phone, Thumper. Did he really say "cessation of fellatio" and "grand satisfaction" in the same sentence? Were his eyes rolling back into his head when he said that? What kind of martyr complex is this? Herein, the turncoats denounce, lies the treachery of the soixante-neuf. While it purports to be two-for-one, it can so quickly devolve into being all-for-one.

The turncoats continue: Even if the act succeeds in going on as two-for-one promised, while she pleasures your Motorhead with the tropics of her hot mouth and pierced tongue, you can't kick back and luxuriate in images of engorged nipples and football plays. You can't revert to the empty thought bubbles of your blowjob-brain, with its neon headband, spray tan, gym bag, beach house in Malibu, gold convertible and porn-star girlfriend, Asia Carrera.

Pilot error.

YOU GOT IT GOIN' ON

Instead, you must—flooded with sensations, your breath shortening, your muscles tightening—maintain your rhythm and your focus on her go-go and surrounding butterfly. You must alternate between the firm cartilage of your nose, the swift and slow flick of your tongue, the gentle pressing of your thumb against the doorbell to her lube-moistened kit or butterfly, while visiting both her go-go (The Enlightened One) and her vulval outskirts. Bush Pilots, you must stay your course. And remember: Every course will be different. While one babe loves strong, direct pressure, another is desensitized by it. Calibrate. Listen to your "Lay Lady Lay."

As you studied so sedulously in Chapter 11, there is little forgiveness for the man who goes down distracted. Your babe is, stroke by brilliantly situated stroke, assembling her orgasm. Her orgasm is abstract expressionist. Her orgasm is a Jackson Pollock canvas. To check out halfway through its composition would be to leave the painting in the rain, to cancel out a masterpiece.

Some Bush Pilots find this—blowing while being blown—a tall order. Some say, "There is too much going on there." It is like an infomercial invention: the toaster that shines your shoes while it housebreaks your pet! The leaf blower that forges cheques while it tones your thighs! The vase that waters your lawn while it hypnotizes your dinner guests! Some Bush Pilots find this superfluity impossible to contend with. Well, guess what? Some babes do too.

OUR TAKE ON "SEXUAL MULTI-TASKING"

So hot in theory, but truthfully, in practice, after a couple of fun minutes, it's hard to concentrate on giving and receiving at the same time. Or maybe I'm just not good at sexual multi-tasking. Maybe guys are better at it—in fact, I think they are. But I always end up asking if we can take turns while we remain in, um, position.
—Babe (sly wink and a size 6 shoe)

Another near deserter bemoans, "Most of the time, it's too much work." But, she adds kittenishly, "When it does work, it really does."

So, how to make it fly? Bush Pilots, negotiate your position. For those of you who have the height differential of circus performers, finding each other's heads and tails may be difficult. As always, persevere, experiment and keep your phone lines open. Furthermore, please use that most overlooked and underrated bedroom lubricant: laughter. Straight faces are for fakers. They are like listening to Muzak when what you wanted was the live album.

BABE ON TOP

If opting for a top-and-bottom formation, most Bush Pilot proponents tend to take their cue from that inscrutable Monty Python song, "Sit on My Face." Correct, BPs! Gold star! Place your babe on top. Yes, there is the risk of smothering, but, inverted, there is the risk of a choking death. One woman-on-top practitioner adds this useful tip: "It is best if the guy has his head and neck supported with a pillow or two, particularly if a long session ensues (and, of course, this is the ultimate goal)." Bush Pilots, do not hesitate to make adjustments after the act has begun; no one wants to wake up Quasimodo.

Le Soixante-neuf

THE BIATHLETE'S EVENT

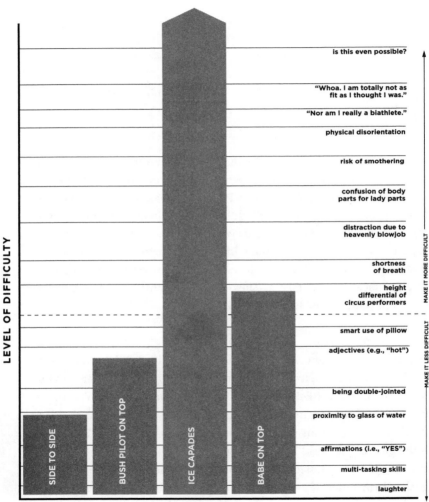

LEVEL OF DIFFICULTY

THE TECHNIQUE

SIDE TO SIDE

BUSH PILOT ON TOP

ICE CAPADES

BABE ON TOP

MAKE IT MORE DIFFICULT

MAKE IT LESS DIFFICULT

is this even possible?

"Whoa. I am totally not as fit as I thought I was."

"Nor am I really a biathlete."

physical disorientation

risk of smothering

confusion of body parts for lady parts

distraction due to heavenly blowjob

shortness of breath

height differential of circus performers

smart use of pillow

adjectives (e.g., "hot")

being double-jointed

proximity to glass of water

affirmations (i.e., "YES")

multi-tasking skills

laughter

BUSH PILOT ON TOP

Alternately, if your babe is game and starred in *Deep Throat,* you may wish to try Bush Pilot on top, babe on the bottom. One proponent describes your mission:

> He should make sure she comes first then flip around with catlike alacrity and engage in congress with her ASAP so the orgasmic onslaught keeps going.

P.S. Men do not engage in this enough.

P.P.S. Because it is difficult to pull off "catlike alacrity" while getting a blowjob.

P.P.P.S. You might get the bends.

P.P.P.P.S. That said, Bush Pilots, never presume a sexual position to be unattainable until you have tried it (with attendant humour); it is amazing how our bodies will flex and receive once they are turned on.

And again, between your kisses, communicate. Is this position purgatory or Paradise City? Is this act naughty like a night at the Playboy mansion, or baffling like trying to finish a crossword puzzle in the shower? Bush Pilots, are you being outwitted by this sex act? If so, admit it. This is not defeat. Every erotic experiment with your babe is useful information in the ongoing exchange of pleasure. Once it is acknowledged that the soixante-neuf is not for you, break the plaster cast and have a good laugh. Thereafter, move on to something more doable. Why not heed the words of the fox above? "Take turns" and trade off—or consider a final effort and adjust yourselves into the following, less tricky arrangement.

SIDE BY SIDE

The other favoured combination is 69-ing side by side. This is the porch-swing version of the soixante-neuf: lackadaisical, easy, unhurried, sunset in the background, trade winds in the foreground. Easily portable, curl up on your mattress, your carpet, your dock, the flat bed of your truck—or consider its horizontal advantage and, for the fun of it, find a crawl space.

> I'd say on your side is best. When one's on top, one's on the bottom, it places the onus unfairly on one. Or is that anus?
> —Babe (gambled her wedding ring)

An ideal starter position, side by side allows you to reach your rapture without the physical wrangling of the above top-and-bottom positions. Moreover, in being supine, you eliminate the G-force that can make the 69 so challenging: gravity. Bush Pilot Bonus: You can both choose the depth of penetration. This room for manoeuvring allows for more nuanced oral sex. In other words, how can she tease your Toto with her tongue and breath when she's busy trying to come up for air? Ditto for you, Darth Vader.

ICE CAPADES

For the truly advanced, and pathologically fit, try the vertical soixante-neuf. It looks like this: You are standing, a towering Paul Bunyan, supporting your babe, whose thighs are wrapped cobra-like around your neck. She has the sensation of coming with blood rushing to her head. A word of caution: Stay close to your bed for safety—i.e., have her shoulders on your bed's edge—and make sure your brawn can match her bounty.

The million-dollar question: how to come and pleasure at the same time? Bush Pilots, you can choose to use the soixante-neuf as a preview only. As if watching stock prices climb and fall, her orgasm should never become a pressure for either of you. If it does, defuse and move into more predictable territory. Pull her onto safer ground with the inimitable cunnilingus or a shuddering tour de vibrator.

Or, through body language and a refined sensitivity to your babe's pleasure path, you can try for that rarefied synchronicity of coming together. While this is undoubtedly a high-five moment in the bedroom, it should not be your primary goal (next step: matching tracksuits).

Otherwise, as you already know, it is a ladies-first world. After a brief howl of intermission, rest assured, Bush Pilots, unlike some of the post-coital heavy snorers we know, blow and love, she will return to her post—your post. Suggested soundtrack: the moody pluck and dazzle of the Magnetic Fields' *69 Love Songs*. This triple album should amply cover your shared oral fixation, while satisfying your need for a theme.

ADULT ENTERTAINMENT

There is an inarguable nostalgia to the soixante-neuf. Like the Hula Hoop, Chia Pets and albums on vinyl, it seems poised for a comeback. Witness its renaissance in David Cronenberg's *A History of Violence*. There is nothing like a single bed, a cheerleading outfit pulled out of storage and the scorching whip that is Maria Bello to inspire this kind of coupling. But despite its roots in a time of innocence and discovery, the 69 requires a certain sprightliness and openness. It is at once intimate and daring. It was your first foray into the acrobatic possibilities of pleasure and the body. Bush Pilots, did you have it in you then? And do you have it in you now?

CHAPTER 14
THE G-SPOT

GEYSER!

Mieko has always had good sex. She wonders if she was put on this planet to have good sex. While other mortals raise children, compose operas and explore space, Mieko's opus is her body. Her pursuit: nerve endings. She is a believer in sex for love, but mostly, she is a believer in sex for sensation.

On this afternoon, bare-bottomed, in a Ziggy Stardust undershirt and snakeskin boots, Mieko reclines on her bed like an Egyptian queen. French porn flashes from her Jetsons television (". . . oui, plus, oui . . ."). Xaviera Hollander's *The Happy Hooker* salivates from her bedside table. Body as laboratory, Mieko's hands are at play. She runs reels of past lovers in her mind: the Czech pianist with the fast fingers, the pierced veterinarian, the Finnish drag king with the impossibly perfect mouth, the Tokyo one-night stand.

Mieko can come anywhere, anytime: on top, on the bottom, on the subway—climaxing under her trench coat, a searing guitar lick amidst human busy signals. But today is a different story. Today, Mieko is flushed and fumbling. She wants to add another pleasure to her pleasure repertoire. She wants to find her G-spot. Now.

GRETA GARBO

I have told you (Chapter 1. Memorize it.), Pilots of the Bush, she can be a tricky one, that G-spot. You sit outside her apartment building. You have her photograph, a still from *Love* and your lucky autograph pen. You have a bouquet and a marriage contract. You have a glider and an island in the Bahamas. Still, she will not make an appearance—starlet of *Flesh and the Devil*, siren of *The Mysterious Lady*. And after so many days of patience and fortitude, just when you want to wave your white flag and retreat to a cardboard box under a bridge, she comes through those glass doors. But wait, is that really her? How can you be sure? She's in a turban, dark sunglasses and a shapeless overcoat. You call her name. She does not even look your way.

Perhaps, my darlings, you have been sitting in front of the wrong building, in the wrong city, in the wrong continent. Perhaps, my darlings, the quivering compass needle in your Pilot pants has misled you. Perhaps, my darlings, it is more eager than it is accurate. Gutted, Mistress. Oh, my BPs, don't be so hard on yourselves. This is a hazard common to your kind. The good news: It can be righted. Your Swedish recluse can be found.

Shred away, Mistress.

G-Spot Map

SIDE VIEW

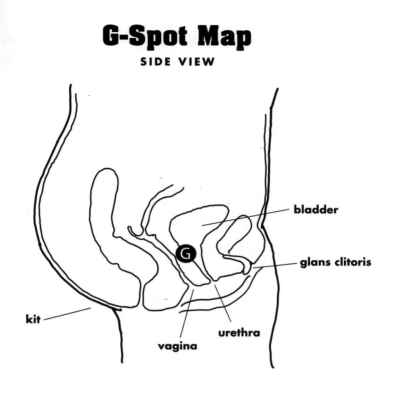

bladder

glans clitoris

kit

urethra

vagina

G-SPOT CHECKLIST

- ❏ *Anatomical understanding*
- ❏ *Mood*
- ❏ *Lubrication*
- ❏ *Stimulation*
- ❏ *Sensitivity*

- ❏ *Concentration without pressure*
- ❏ *Positioning and angles*
- ❏ *A good extra pillow*
- ❏ *Repetition*
- ❏ *Inventiveness*

HERE'S HER ADDRESS

We begin, as always, not with your Pilot-geniality, but with your babe's anatomical intelligence. Remedial: Find the urethral opening, south of her go-go and north of her butterfly. Conductor of urine, it transports her tinkle from her bladder out of her body. (Hot. So hot.)

Now, turn on your X-ray vision and picture your babe's interiors. The urethra runs an inch and a half to two inches above her vaginal canal, placing it on your babe's ventral, or front, wall.

The G-spot, like your P-spot, is the spongy tissue wrapped around the urethra. It is also known as the urethral sponge, or, because of its glandular homology, the female prostate. It is rich with blood vessels (engorgement!) and home to the paraurethral glands (ejaculate!).

A cautionary tale . . .

DON'T JOVI THE G-SPOT

One hot-blooded hound who loves burgers, single malt and the soixante-neuf (not in that order) confided, "I figure if you're having a really good time with somebody, you'll find it. In fact, I'm sure I already have." Bush Pilots, this is known as the "Livin' on a Prayer" technique. And, by using it, "You Give Love a Bad Name." Instruction: Abandon your feathered faith for my good directions.

If the G-spot is the Holy Grail of the bedroom, imagine if those Arthurian knights had had maps.

TURN ON YOUR GUINEVERE

Your babe's arousal is crucial to locating her G-spot. Why, Mistress, oh why? Her tissues will become engorged and, like the boner making a lean-to out of your Pilot pants, that ever-elusive G-spot will be much easier to find. My suggestion? Prince on the record player, plus the slow unlatching of her bra, plus a paw rolling down her panties, plus your mouth on her nether regions. Bush Pilots, as you know from Chapter 12 (crush it), cunnilingus is the perfect precursor to your G-spot quest;

despite your Captain Beefheart's goodwill, your tongue is much more likely to make her come.

Interlude.

Once your babe is flush-cheeked, cease your mouth music and find the G-spot by hand. Because G-spot stimulation requires precision, patience and pressure, pull out the lube (Chapter 3. Memorize it.).

Using one or two fingers, enter her butterfly. At about half a finger length in, on the front wall (toward the belly), there will be a ridged area, a corrugated swelling in an otherwise smooth and silky domain. Congratulations, BP! This bit of roughness is her G-spot. It may be the size of a dime, a quarter or a walnut. Like all natural formations, G-spots vary in shape and size. As one snowmobiling bedroom prophet puts it, "Women are snowflakes."

LET YOUR FINGERS DO THE WALKING

When you find her G-spot, press it firmly (nails trimmed, rings off), using a "come here" motion. Bush Pilots, given its ventral location, your babe's G-spot can also be coaxed out of hiding externally. Press down just above her pubic bone, where her (if she still has one) rug begins its roll-out. Instead of "That feels amazing," your babe might say, in a panicked tone, "I-have-to-pee!" Again, congratulations, BP! You are on the right path. After some tender and encouraging words, keep up your good work and . . .

PUT MASK AND SNORKEL ON NOW

She may ejaculate. With prolonged stimulation of the urethral sponge, the paraurethral glands (up to thirty-three ducts) grow enlarged and fill with a clear, translucent liquid. Again, your babe will feel like she has to pee. This means the urethral sponge is putting pressure on her urethra. Bush Pilots, your babe may seep or she may spurt—between two teaspoons and two cups, clear across the room.

When I discovered ejaculation, the term "sleeping on the wet spot" took on a whole new meaning. The source seems inexhaustible. When I'm fucking, I don't try to hold it in because that diverts my mind away from enjoying what is going on between our bodies, the expression on your face, the joint arousal of excellent sex. And squirting can creep up on you. I was sucking a guy's cock once and every time he hit the back of my throat, I would squirt just a bit, which hadn't happened under those circumstances before, but which was quite lovely.

—Babe (break-dancer, Scorpio)

Nectar, Mistress, totally nectar. Totally the money shot, but . . .

IS IT PEE-PEE?

No, C-3PO. The liquid's chemical composition contains trace elements of urea and creatinine—which are found in pee-pee. But it is closer in content to male prostate fluid. And yes, C-3PO, it is odourless.

"OH YES, DARLING, THAT'S IT!"

Here, Bush Pilots, is a note from the field to reinforce the importance of understanding your babe's lady parts. A friend of mine who has spent most of his adult years in a climbing gym, library or erotic embrace and is seduced as often as the puppy and baby are fawned over, finds himself at a cocktail party in London. Before the night is through, the hostess—sexy, British, and kind of Thandie Newton—has him in her bedroom. They kiss and roll around on her bed. She asks him to put his hand "down there." Ever willing, he does, and recounts:

I just sort of got in there and made sure my fingers were stroking the inner top of the canal area, smooth with little ridges, the part that feels like the roof of your mouth, and she was getting wetter and wetter, and suddenly she was like, "Oh yes, darling, that's it!" and then I was like "Holy shit!" and these high-pressure pulses of liquid started firing into my hand—one, two, three—cascading off my knuckles like an Ocean Spray ad, and I thought, "Like water from a bilge." It was like someone poured a bucket of water on our legs. We had to sleep and let everything dry off before I could go home.

THE DIRT ON THE SQUIRT

Bush Pilots, herein lies the lesson: To find that rough-edged set of dunes, you must know how to read the Braille of your hostess's body. Moreover, encourage your babe to communicate her pleasure. How, oh how do I that, Mistress—I mean, less the part about the communicating, and more the part about her pleasure? One babe (rents Winnebagos for play parties) leaves you this set of instructions:

I expect you to be delighted that I ejaculate. I expect you to cheer me on as I clear the end of a king-size bed when I squirt. I will be impressed when you look at me and say, sincerely, "I want you to soak me; just let me know what you need me to do." I will be super-impressed if you have developed a technique for cupping your mouth to my cunt and catching it all in your mouth and swallowing like a pro. My ejaculate is sweet and musty, like hay in summer. I'm not taking a piss; those warm gushes are something else, guys. Sweet release. Ask me how I do it and I'll show you. Watching is sexy and arrogance will get you nowhere when it comes to these things, but if you have new tricks to share, please do.

THE NEW PORNOGRAPHERS

BPs, I know what you are thinking: Squirter porn! I heart you! I so heart you, squirter porn! Can my babe squirt too? And if she can squirt, how can I help her squirt? Oh, squirter porn, here we come!

Um, now what, Mistress?

Get a towel. Lay down a splash mat. After the erotic preamble we grown-ups call the bushjob, use a toy, your hand or your Javier Bardem, intelligently angled to stimulate your babe's vaginal ceiling (see above, literally)—and sheathed, as per Captain Goodscrew's recommendation: "Beyond Seven is good for a tighter fit, and more useful for the squirty ladies, the juicy ladies and if you're using lots of lube." In (unmeasured) time, your babe will begin to feel she has to pee. Recall: This means her urethral sponge is weighing against her urethra. This is her signal. Your babe bears down with her pelvic muscles, devotedly toned through Kegel exercises (which maximize her capacity for pleasure and her ability to ejaculate, hop and fly). Your role? Captain Goodscrew breaks it down here:

> I just facilitate by using my fingers or my cock. Upward, inward pressure, often accompanied by clitoral stimulation, will do the trick. I find missionary works with her legs bent. She will often jockey herself into a position that's hitting her sweet spot. That's usually on the inside, toward the pubic area.
>
> The lady often bears down, and there's a pressure. I get "evicted," and my cock is forced out of the pussy right before the ejac. Sometimes it's a little trickle; sometimes it's a flood. I've had some real pro lovers that own rubber sheets, specialized pads. But a few towels work well.

Evicted, Mistress? Affirmative, BP. But Captain Goodscrew throws this very compelling bone to your homeless boner:

It's pretty hot. Plus it's kind of a fun reversal of roles to be with a lady that constantly ejaculates while I'm having orgasms but not ejaculating. There's definitely an ebb and flow to the female ejac. Some ladies have one big squirt and then clunk out (fall asleep). Some don't stop squirting. It can be a very scary experience for some women. There's some serious muscle memory and body opening that goes on. But it always seems quite cathartic and beautiful.

N.B.B.P.: Also true of you, ejaculation does not have to accompany orgasm. (Whoa, Mistress! Represent! I know, I know. Hold on to your man parts.) We will revisit this slice of revolutionary insight in Chapter 20. But because I am the Tinkerbell for your tackle, here's a preview to being a multi-orgasmic Bush Pilot. (Represent!) Captain Goodscrew writes of his "epiphany" upon discovering:

Men and women have similar physiology. It's just that men have our bits on the outside. Both genders have erectile tissue; we are both capable of orgasm and ejaculation. It's just that men have been conditioned to ejac and orgasm at the same time, and many women have lost touch with the ability to ejaculate.

SOAKER!

Even though squirting—like blinking, like breathing—has always been part of the repertoire, whether sought out or stumbled upon, it can, like any unfamiliar physical sensation, take you and your babe by surprise. One accidental tourist (knows every word, riff and lick of the Crüe's "Piece of Your Action") puts it this way:

My boyfriend and I went at it for a long, long time. He went down on me before, with a lot of finger action—up my ass, against my G-spot—making me come. We fucked. He came. And then, with his hard-on softening in me, I touched my clit. My second orgasm was taking a long time. I knew it was in there; I just couldn't find it. And then it happened. I squeezed my muscles and squirted an unbelievable amount of liquid. Like a huge gush. Way more than I ever thought humanly possible. I had squirted in small amounts before, but this was surprising. We laughed our heads off. Seconds later, I came. I realized I'd held onto my orgasm because I was afraid I was going to wet the bed. Which, in a way, I did. I have to say, it was an awesome feeling.

I have answered your second question. Now to address your first: Bush Pilots, yes, with a little reconnaissance and a lot of laundry, squirting is available to many women. What does that mean for you? Read the portentous words of this babe who "can ejaculate for miles":

Ejaculation has totally altered the way I have sex; there's no beginning-middle-climax-roll-over-and-the-snoring-begins about it.

No beginning-middle-climax-roll-over-and-the-snoring-begins. Affirmative. I'm just saying.

BPs, your babe, in her hot pants, is reading over your hirsute shoulder—again? Hey, sister, this announcement is for you—and your bush. From Captain Goodscrew:

The lady really needs to do her homework. Most of the talented female ejaculators I've met spent some time exploring their bits, and so they know how to get themselves to ejaculate. That helps a lot with timing and positioning.

Make sure you pee beforehand, and have plenty of towels. Don't get too hung up making it happen. It helps to have positive encouragement, cheerleading, being open and finding the process hot.

G-SPOTTER, I NEED BACKUP

It is true: Even you and your eager Tommy Lee can tire. In this case, toys can be handy. You will find a mass market of toys designed specifically to stimulate your babe's G-spot. Their common feature? Oh Mistress, pick me! Pick me! Just a guess, but the telltale letter G in their tarty names? Yes, BP. Gold star! And their shape; these toys have a curved tip so they can solve the whodunit of the bedroom: the G-spot. (To stock your survival kit, revisit the merch in Chapter 3.) Variations occur in properties and materials. You can choose from hand-blown glass to silicone, plastic and, Bush Pilot's honour, 18-karat gold; vibrating or non-, plug-in or battery-powered. There are even waterproof "G-spotter vibes" you can take with you—and your babe—into the bathtub. N.B.B.P.: Firm toys are better than soft ones because they don't bend when entering the butterfly. Should your babe prefer a softer toy, the built-in curve is crucial.

> Everyone has a G-spot, but it is not necessarily pleasurable for everyone. I have also met some women who don't like their clits stimulated. We are not all the same; we like different spots! I find, though, that many women who have not found the pleasure in their G-spots have either not used enough pressure (some women need a lot), or are not aroused enough or are looking too deeply (for some of us, it is very close to the opening, and most descriptions are two to three inches inside—too deep for some).
> —Babe (derby hat, seamed stockings)

THE HARD TRUTH

We're on our third pint, and here it is, boys: A loving, even incantational screw is not the most efficient way of stimulating your babe's G-spot. I am so sorry. (There's a casserole on your front porch.) Think about it: Untrained and oblivious, your zealous boner slips right by it. But, Bush Pilots (we'll have another round), do not despair. It is possible.

Remember: The directions I have given you are broad. They are based on the mean rather than the minx in hot pants, Patti Smith T-shirt and cat-eye sunglasses lying in your backyard, reading *The Pure and the Impure*. The map to her G-spot? Well, you'll have to ask her.

Respect: Her G-spot is not an elevator button that can be pushed for ascension. It is part of a larger exploration. For your babe to achieve a G-spot orgasm in lovemaking, her G-spot (and, in turn, her go-go) must already be stimulated. Once your babe is ready, here is a roundup of the best positions:

Man's Best Friend. Your babe is on all fours, with you kneeling, panting and drooling behind her. The key is for your babe's kit to be raised, allowing for direct G-spot stimulation. Even the good doctor, Dr. Gräfenberg, G-spot pioneer, writes about coitus "like a cow":

"The stimulating effect of this kind of intercourse must not be explained away . . . by the melodious movements of the testicles like a knocker on the clitoris."

Oh, no, Bush Pilots, there is something other than your "melodious" Pet Shop Boys at work here. For variations on doggie style, consult the next chapter. Erf!

Man's Best Friend

(with decorative fruit bowl)

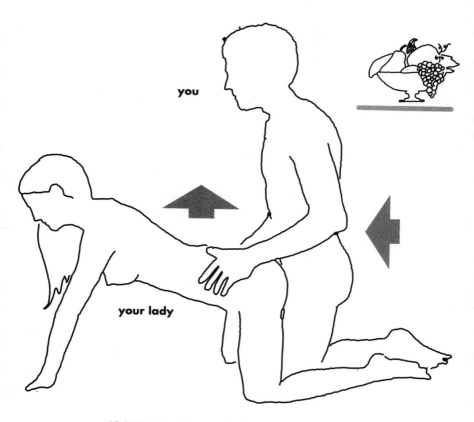

you

your lady

*G-SPOTTING: Babe raises her kit for an upward slope

CLASSIC POSITION NO.2
The Modern Missionary

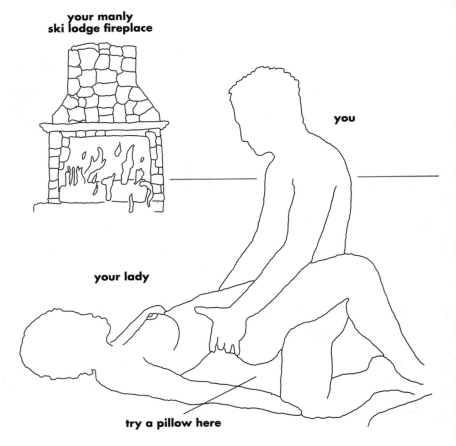

your manly
ski lodge fireplace

you

your lady

try a pillow here

**G-SPOTTING: Her hips are propped up with a pillow or two;
Bush Pilot raises Babe's derriere with his hands*

Modern Missionary. Add a marshmallow to the hot chocolate of the bedroom. With your babe on her back, prop her hips up with a pillow and place her legs over your shoulders or on the crooks of your elbows. These angles to her lower back and bass kit allow your Buddy Rich to hit her G-spot. Thrusts must be shallow.

ARRESTED DEVELOPMENT

As discussed in Chapter 1, please do not rank your babe's orgasms. Once you have excited a G-spot orgasm, go to your bathroom, scream into a towel and then get back into bed. Thereafter, do not disqualify her other orgasms. In fact, this kind of contest—little-known fact—will not only make your penis shrink, but fall flaccid permanently. And go figure: After all this, your babe may tell you nothing compares to you kneeling before her go-go.

Bush Pilots, erotic experience is determined both by physiology (your job) and by self-awareness (our job). Mieko is adding pleasure to her pleasure dome. She is a collector of sensations. Each one is essential to the next. May you and your babe take her cue.

EXTRA CREDIT

NO-FLY LIST ALERT:
YOUR GITCH, OUR PANIC

Bush Pilots, your babe is unbuckling your belt, lowering your zipper for the first time, slipping her naked foot to your crotch and pulling you free from your jeans. Cue the heartbeat soundtrack. Not only are we a mere cotton curtain away from revealing your man parts, but we are about to see your choice of underpants. Death of a Ladies' Man? You tell me.

> Don't be shy to shower first (why are men so prone to skid marks—and please keep them away from me).
> —Babe (chanteuse, strumpet and sometime caribou hunter)

Your Mankini. CLASSIFIED: TOP SECRET.

Your G-String. CLASSIFIED: TOP SECRET.

Your Jockstrap. We know you need it. But it does distress us. Remember Zach Galifianakis's furry cheeks in *The Hangover*? By wearing his J-strap to a suit fitting, he carelessly took this niche item out of range. Please limit the sporting of your J-strap to the following designated areas: the field, the ice, the court and the locker room.

Your Briefs. These are the indie underpant of underpants. Once worn by your dad, now worn by you. We find them beneath your moustache, your John Deere T-shirt and your jean shorts. We can dig them. They ride three-speeds, garden on fire escapes, drink Pabst Blue Ribbon and have a vinyl van seat for a couch. Request: If your man-ties (pronunciation: MAN-tease) are blown out or baggy, pink or grey from your confusion when met with a washing machine, please update. (N.B.B.P.: This request applies to all of your mangerie—pronunciation: MAN-zhe-ray.) For some surprise hotness, lend them to your lady.

Commando. While it startles, it definitely has its appeal. If this is your approach, please pay attention to the length of your shorts.

Your Boxers. The Bogart of the underwear set. Classic.

Your Boxer Briefs. Like the controversial colourization of *The Maltese Falcon*, the boxer brief is the updated version of the boxer. While some Bush Pilots argue it is a fashionable improvement, others cry "Vandalism!" and deride it as putting blush on the scarred face of a detective.

Underwear
SHAPES FOR MEN

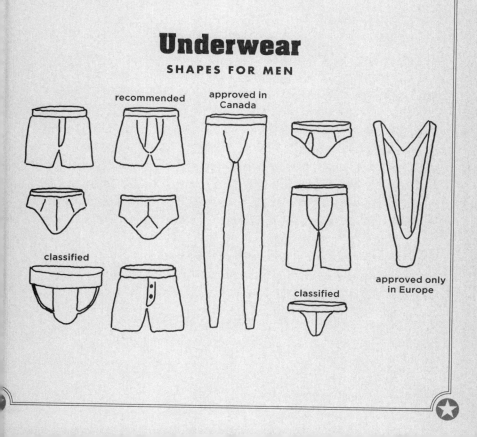

recommended

approved in Canada

classified

classified

approved only in Europe

CHAPTER 15
POSITIONS

Madeleine and Jeremy are in their van—mattress in the back, surfboards strapped to the roof, airbrushed wolf painted on the passenger door—idling at a dead stop, stuck in a traffic snarl. They are on a highway somewhere near Nantucket. AM radio plays The Beatles' "Why Don't We Do It in the Road." Yeah, Madeleine thinks, why don't we? The rain is coming down in torrents. All is obscured from view. Some might even call it biblical.

Remembering an oppressively stern but handsome priest with a Bahamian accent who absolved her unde- servedly in childhood, Madeleine is suddenly turned on. She reaches across the great divide and places her hand on Jeremy's crotch. He's in his board shorts. She thinks of Kelly Slater. She loves him. Within a blink, Jeremy's fly is open and his prayer flag is up. Madeleine licks her fingers, circles them between her legs and then straddles Jeremy. She has just gotten a brush cut and abandoned wearing panties. She feels this is part of her new daring.

They have made love in a gambling hall, a movie theatre, an ocean swell and a pet store. But this—a car wash ambience heightened by the sneering proximity of campers, cop cars, and truckers—this is fantasy lived. Head scraping the van's headliner, Madeleine rocks her body hard against Jeremy's until, to her astonishment, she comes. She has come from his touch. She has come from his tongue, but never has she come from making love. This is the first time. And it sneaks up on her, seemingly out of nowhere. It feels like divine intervention. It feels like an act from above.

DEEP THOUGHTS

BPs, you spend your days so pensive in the lady-field, wanting to know one thing—not "How can I make her love me?" but "How can I make her come?" For the unschooled Bush Pilot and his cheeky man parts—the Bush Pilot who believes he can rely on his cobra-like athleticism, killer coif and "Unstoppable Confidence" tapes—his babe's orgasm can feel like a feat for Harry Houdini. He whinges, Mistress, oh Mistress, this situation has gone lawless. I am trying everything, except for the deft angling of my boner, to solicit my babe's Big O (My Bush Pilot!) during our epic screws. What to do, Mistress, oh what to do?

Pilot error.

A Killer Coif

WARNING: This hairstyle has been primarily tested on already successful European football stars. Individual results may vary.

From studying (so hard) the symbiosis of your babe's brain and her orgasm (Chapter 8. Crush it.), you, my favourite Pilot, my pet Pilot, understand taking your babe to a bliss state is not a matter of miracles, though you can keep calling your boner that. Oh, thank you, Mistress, thank you! Did you hear that, Miracles? It is a matter of mutual awareness, communication, her air traffic controller, your "Boogie Wonderland" falsetto and—attention!—a new element: your positioning.

Here are four dance screw-tines you have, no doubt, stud-pants, been locked in before. They are the cardinal points of the bedroom. They are our greatest hits. And they have achieved their stardom and playability for very good reasons. But BPs, have you found those reasons? And have you taken them for all they are worth? Because when you do, you will turn the serviceable performance (I'm not saying you!) into the immortal and prize-winning screw (I am saying you!). You will discover your babe's lady parts are, to repurpose Dave Eggers' title, *A Heartbreaking Work of Staggering Genius.*

URBAN COWBOY

The Choreography: You lie on your back. Your babe straddles you. Giddy-up, Mistress. By keeping her butterfly close to the base of your bronco, she can stimulate her go-go through a grinding motion against your pubic bone until she reaches a clitoral orgasm. Stoked, Mistress. Wait for it, BP, there is more. By shifting your angle of penetration, a G-spot orgasm is also possible for your babe. Double-stoked, Mistress—in fact, there is a heat warning in effect. Remedial: The G-spot is located on the front wall of your babe's butterfly, only a third to three-quarters of a finger's length in. It is ridged to the touch and anywhere from dime- to walnut-sized. This means your Sundance Kid is pointed up toward you (close to your beer belly rather than forming a thumbs-up right angle to it).

CLASSIC POSITION NO.3
Urban Cowboy

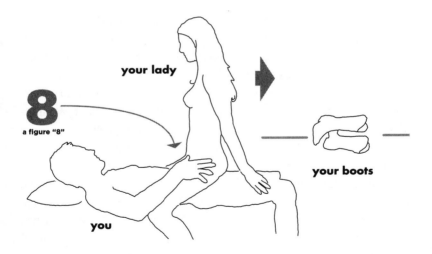

your lady

8
a figure "8"

your boots

you

*G-SPOTTING: Bush Pilot angles boner to be close to belly
rather than at a right angle; Babe leans back*

MORE COWBELL

Also recall: Pressure to the G-spot is not a sha-pow! sha-pow! To achieve a G-spot orgasm while making legendary congress, the G-spot, like your lady, must already be thoroughly primed (Chapter 14. Live it.). Suggestion: the hot licks of the bushjob (Chapter 11. Be it.) accompanied by your peerless sexterity (Chapter 10. Love it.).

Once your babe is ready and mounted, a subtle shift in angles is needed. Your babe leans back, using her hands for support, and rides your Butch Cassidy. Yee-haw, Mistress. Note well, Wild Bunch: You are both free to and have the range to play with her go-go. Do it. What works for your babe? Rocking back and forth? Up and down? The fetching figure-eight swivel of her hips?

Variations: Your babe can, in the coital version of the crabwalk, lift herself up and plant her feet beside your ears—or face your really good-looking toes to give you an intimate one-on-one with her kit. For that fan favourite, the deep back arch (Deal-Breaker Alert: Get a good grip on your babe's arms before its execution, please), relocate to a sturdy stool or chair.

A STURDY STOOL: And yes, as a matter of fact, it *is* from your parents' basement rec room bar

N.B.B.P.: For starters, choose a setting that allows your babe to plant her feet on the floor (e.g., you think bench press, small crowd, porn contract; she thinks lawn chair, Indian Ocean, new identity). Thereafter, the Urban Cowboy can be taken to the bed, the barn, the back seat of your Chevy Caprice. Or the kitchen.

CELLULOID INSPIRATION

Revisit David Mamet's 1981 film adaptation of *The Postman Always Rings Twice*. Yes, the sex begins violently (in the movie), but once it becomes consensual, it takes you through the steps.

Your babe is up against the wall. You heed her taunting. Her invitation. Her impatience. Oh, how it goads. Oh, how it smarts. You go down, all menacing-drifter gruffness. You lift her onto the counter. You pull up her skirt and slip your hand beneath her garter belt. You rub her go-go. Over her underwear. She puts her hand on top of yours. Over her underwear. You hoist yourself above her so she can undo your belt buckle and free your Frank Chambers. Concord. You spin her around so she can finish on top. Post-come, you meet her lips, a wild colt made supple (that is, until you murder her husband—in the movie).

Bush Pilots, imagine for a moment this was not on the Hollywood stopwatch, but on unlimited BP time, and Jessica had, when supine, tilted her pelvis up, even going so far as to put her ankles on Jack's shoulders so his postman could hit and awaken her G-spot. Twice. Re-enact, my BPs, but beware, the diving is deep for your drifter, and bliss can come a little too early (for you, honey).

MAN'S BEST FRIEND

We know how you love to take us from behind. Hands on our hips, kit in full view, watching your LL Cool J disappear, reappear, disappear. We know how it makes you feel like you should be wearing a gold chain with your initials around your neck, not a gold chain with ours. Doing it "doggie-style." Let's admit it: There is something truly dirty here, something about copping moves from our froth-mouthed, non-verbal, ball-licking friends and bringing those moves back home to our bedrooms, with their well-thumbed *Sunday Times* rolled up in baskets made by

Shakers. Well, the good news is that, with your Snoop angled correctly, this position, when throwing her your bone, can be hot for her too.

The Choreography: Your babe is on all fours. (I know, I know, it's so exciting!) You kneel behind her. The natural curve of her back (bow-wow!) will bring her kit into an upward slope. The key is for her to raise her kit even higher (I know! I know!), allowing for direct G-spot stimulation (erf!). With concentrated pressure from your bloodhound (ah-roo!), this breed is definitely a best in show.

But wait. Whoa. A caveat: Down, boys. My yet-to-be housebroken pups, take it easy. Capping off your babe's butterfly is her cervix. Some babes do not like the sensation of having it poked; it can make them think, not of your supreme fly-ness, but of the manoeuvring of her hairy-necked gynecologist. It can even make her bleed. If this is the case, suggest she do the moving while you hold still (you have been leashed to the bed and she is your owner and she is training you and she is a very commanding Salma Hayek).

On that note, Bush Pilots, radio in. Communicate. Try as you might, you cannot read your babe's pleasure, whether waxing or waning, in this position. However hard you squint, it is not spelled out along her spine. It is not telegraphed across her buttocks the way it is, say, across her face. Ask, listen and adjust your exemplary boner accordingly. Bush Pilot Bonus: Man's Best Friend can also be tried with your babe sitting on your lap. Or standing. And, for the truly adventurous (and fit), the Wheelbarrow is only a short step away. Your babe places her hands firmly on the ground while you grip her thighs. Yup, just like the school fair—only naked and with a different prize.

MISSIONARY

Classic as your dad's copy of *Some Girls*. Classic as an apple betty, *Saturday Night Fever*, your tartan trousers. Comforting as any decent memory. Napping in a bathing suit on a screened-in porch. Fishing for bass at dawn. Listening to eight-tracks in a boathouse. White bikini strings knotted at the hip. The missionary: It is the hug that, in sexual theatre's quickest change, turns, just like that, into a screw. It reminds us of the night we lost our virginity: strapless prom dress, a breakfast party, a backyard, grass stains, pink carnation corsage, the gel in your hair, the rented limousine after the dance, you mouthing the words to "No Woman, No Cry," a lot of panting, a lot of pressing, our four-month anniversary, condom pulled like a card trick from your tuxedo pocket. A minute, maybe two.

The missionary. I raise my Lagavulin to it. Why? It was our first dance move. Our first two-step. Yes, people think it is boring, the stride jump of the bedroom. But the truth is, we love the missionary because it allows for full body contact, for (forgive me, Sarah Silverman) mirroring—and this intimacy may be just the effect your babe needs to reach her rapture.

That said, the missionary does not place the same sought-out pressure on your babe's go-go as any of the woman-on-top (or, ahem, superior) positions. So, my Beeps (represent!), here are a few modern variations to put a new spin on an old favourite.

The Choreography: Bottoms up! Lift your babe's hips by propping pillows under her kit—or using your hands to hoist her derriere. Place her legs over your shoulders or on the crooks of your elbows. Alternatively, tilt her pelvis upward by raising yourself on your knees. These angles to her lower back and bass kit allow your preacher man to stimulate her G-spot. Shallow thrusts will do it. Meanwhile, your babe's go-go can also be turned on by:

- your virtuosic touch;
- her virtuosic touch;
- a cleverly snug fit—she pulls her thighs together, your legs relocating to the outside, or she crosses her legs loosely and swings one ankle up on your shoulder.

Note that for the modern missionary, rhythm is key and, as always, you take your conductor's cue.

While I love the feeling of my partner's cock, I do not come from it alone. I need direct stimulation to my clit for that to happen, so we make sure toys and hands are at play. We love this vibrator called the Waterdancer and a really lazy position where we're both on our backs. That's kind of our go-to.

—Babe (Marie Antoinette wig, Faye Dunaway mouth)

GOODNIGHT, BUSH PILOT

After a long day of tending the lady-fields, you crawl into bed, the handsomest-ever son of Michael Landon. But before you nod off and snore thunder, you feel a last, sentient, "let's-super-screw" flicker between you and your babe.

The Choreography: Spooning, enter your babe from behind. Try placing your top leg between hers while she wraps her top leg back and around you. You are now in a prime position to stimulate her go-go with your blazing sexterity. N.B.B.P.: Tease the bush so as not to numb the bush by over-pawing the bush. Meanwhile, toy with the depth and penetration of your Merlin-like boner, and you may just get Greta Garbo out of hiding.

your pillow   **your pjs**

CHEAT SHEET: PULP FRICTION

Here are more champion moves you and your babe can bust out during any screw-tine:

Main Squeeze. Your babe contracts her PC muscles. This is especially effective on an out-stroke as she gives the oh-so-sensitive tip of your Pierre a loving (and firm) flex.

Luck of the Paw. We can get so caught up in the congress of the man parts and the lady parts (I'm not saying you!), we can forget all about the other parts. Touch and kiss, y'all. Massage your babe's kit and perineum. Knead her thighs. Grip her hips. Lick the nape of her neck. Run your fingers through her hair. And pull her nipples into your mouth.

Sexterity. Whenever, however, 4-ever.

Rhythm. While we love the peck of your wood, remember to add some variety to your thrusts—short and quick alternated with long and deep.

Toys. Reminding you that sex is, when you get right down to it, playtime for adults. Pull your favorite props—lube and vibrators—from your Bush Pilot survival kit.

Wingmen. Foreplay and communication.

As one of Captain Goodscrew's "pro lovers" puts it (to your Pilot pants):

Direct communication is very hot. It means you give other people a chance to respond to clear signs from you about what you want, even if you are just figuring it out. Picking up on things and responding is very hot. It means you are paying attention to the whole scenario as it unfolds. Asking is hot. It means that you value the other person's experience of fucking. Enjoying your own experience of fucking is hot. It means that you're not making someone else responsible for providing your good time. Bringing your lube is hot. It means that you are confident and deliberate about what you want, you know what you like and you know what you are doing. Importantly, this does not mean having a script. It means being prepared to find out what's going to happen, and let it unfold in a respectful and safe way. And it pays to use condoms and lube that you like and are road tested for your style. And knowing your style, I have to say, is sexy.

"Hot." Affirmative.
"Very hot." Affirmative.
"Sexy." Affirmative.

HE SHOOTS . . . HE SCORES?

Bush Pilots, the days of the speed screw, the it-was-good-for-me-was-it-good-for-you screw, are over. You are living in a world of heightened sexual consciousness. Your babes know what they want and where to find it. As you read this, so studious in your boxer shorts, under your night light, Captain Goodscrew action figure clutched in your hand, babes are smoking smuggled cigars, throwing back Jim Beam from the bottle and discussing your prowess (no names, of course), much in the manner of trading hockey players. We all grew up with the rules of the rink. You know as well as we do: You will not be remembered for your charms, but for how you played the game. So Bush Pilots, get into position. We're waiting.

CHAPTER 16
REAR ENTRY

NOTE FROM THE FIELD:
THE RING-BEARER

Troy is a ladies' man, and he deserves to be. (Hint: He calls his penis "Rasputin.") But Troy's days at the bedroom buffet are coming to a sudden end. The barter of adulthood: He is trading in his little black book and his roving eye for heirloom silver and experimental jazz. Troy, despite himself, has fallen for Jesse. Sardinia. A topless beach. A sailboat. Sisters. A broken rudder. A wrench in his bathing suit. True love.

On this night, two years later, Troy and Jesse, both in expensive combed-cotton underwear, luxuriate in their Paris hotel room. Neck high in Champagne and resolve, Troy stares deep into the aquamarine eyes of his beloved and says, "Jesse, will you marry me?" Jesse blushes pink and responds in her Gauloise alto: "Yes, oh yes, I will, Troy." They kiss like baby tigers. Troy's eyes glaze over Jesse's caramel curves. Jesse's eyes flit for that famous little blue box: "Ode to Joy," carats, diamonds! Troy presents the ring. Bazooka! Jesse weeps tidily and lunges for it. Troy keeps it out of reach. Troy and Jesse scratch and wrestle. She falls back limp. Troy's hands come to rest on her luscious behind. He rubs it with a smooth underworked palm. Jesse squirms with delight. Her cheeks are their stalemate. Troy looks at his betrothed and brokers, "My ring for yours."

HOOP DREAMS

Whoa, Mistress, I totally have them and they totally keep me up at night, if you know what I mean. And then I wake up, all hooped up, and I see my babe's tail and I just think, Slay it. Slay that mighty tail. I know, Bush Pilots—or should I say, Tush Pilots. Yes, Mistress, you should! Oh, thank you, Mistress! Did you hear that? She called me a Tush Pilot! I know all about your hoop dreams. But the question is: Do you, player? Before you lace up your Air Jordans, don your Bulls jersey and step foot on your babe's back court, let's study her layout—and, if you will, Your Airness, her lines.

Send it, Mistress.

COTTONTAIL

First, recall the superlative tenderness that is the internal life of your babe's kit. Check, Mistress, superlative. The external (voluntary) and internal (involuntary) sphincter muscles greet you at her anal opening. As their qualifiers suggest, one is easily spooked, the other is amiable and may be holding a large sign with your name in block letters: BUSH PILOT. It may even be willing to carry your luggage. It may even be willing to put it in the trunk of its ride. N.B.B.P.: One of the more sublime features of your babe's already sublime kit: That reflexive internal sphincter muscle, with practice and concentration, can be coaxed into a more subdued state. By your babe.

Do you follow, BP? Oh, I follow Mistress.

BUTT . . .

My Beeps (represent!), thereafter, your babe's really good-looking anal canal is tubular, less than one inch in length and remarkably straightforward. No dips. No potholes. No blind corners. But because we are the coquettish descendants of a long line of prankster marsupials, we decided on some anatomical high jinx. For kicks, we threw in an S-curve.

Five to nine inches in length (give or take), your babe's totally smoking rectum veers toward your babe's navel (for three inches), then toward her spine (for three inches) and then back again toward her navel, where it concludes in her colon. Yes, there is a speed limit and yes, it is strictly enforced.

Keep in mind, too, Bush Pilots, my maps of the kit are historical maps. They are based on averages, not on the minx in the romper and gold boots sitting across from you on her grandmother's settee. The map to her kit? Well, you'll have to ask her for it.

Now that I know the route, Mistress—oh, I do, I swear—why must I proceed so slowly, oh why? BPs, so skittish in your Pilot pants, aside from the curvatures of your babe's rectum, her rectal walls are composed of delicate tissues, susceptible to tearing and lesions. Consequently, before you approach your babe's bottom, you must trim your Les Paul–playing claws, soak off your skull rings and be sure any toys in your survival kit are smooth, pliable and—paramount—flared at the base.

The Kit

A REFRESHER

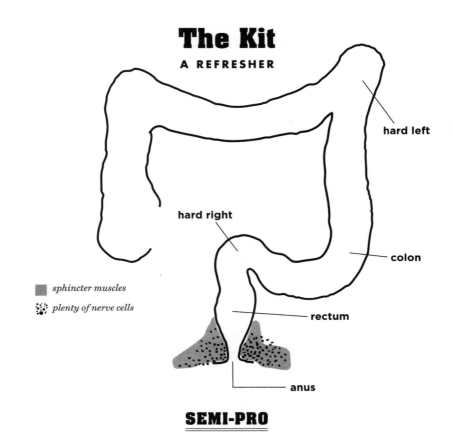

hard left

hard right

colon

sphincter muscles

plenty of nerve cells

rectum

anus

SEMI-PRO

Mistress, oh Mistress, now can I take her from behind and hump her rump? No, Booty Snatcher. Argh, Mistress. You are clever, my BPs, the proud owners of Bill Frisell albums, life-as-art arguments and opposable thumbs. You can belch the entirety of "Mary Had a Little Lamb" in one go. You can even re-enact the penguin scene from *Billy Madison*. Verbatim. You would never be the bonehead who presumes his babe's kit and butterfly function in the same way. Never, Mistress! You appreciate their divergences. Totally! You understand that, given its labyrinthine circuitry and fragile composition, your babe's kit has a whole set of cultural considerations particular to it and it alone. One of these is: lubrication.

To ride the tube,
you must overdo the lube.

LUBE OR BUST

Unlike your babe's butterfly, the Land of her Kit has no natural lubrication. Yes, it has the incidental moisture of mucous membranes, but it does not have the butterfly's elasticity, nor does it have the butterfly's elaborate sprinkler system which, when she feels fire, turns on and wets her panties. As such, it is absolutely essential to use a long-lasting lube for any kind of kit-play. I repeat: any kind. You mean like sodomy, Mistress? Yes, BP, and everything between. Between what? Between my babe's sweet cheeks? Yes, BP. A thick, water-based lube is a must. Why water? Water-based lubes, unlike oil- and silicone-based lubes, are compatible with both your condoms and your silicone toys.

To see which lube you like most, try the samplers at your local sex shop (on your wrist, please).

LAY IT ON THICK

The best lubes on offer are:

Maximus. A gel-like lube, designed specifically for the sensitive, slow-loving kit, from the sex brainiacs behind Liquid Silk. Maximus sticks—and slides. It even spares your silk sheets, your butt plugs and your beads. The only thorn: Some complain of a slightly bitter taste.

Slippery Stuff. Another heavyweight suited to the stamina of anal play, Slippery Stuff is what it purports to be and, unlike Maximus, has no taste and no odour.

Sticky Note: Bush Pilots, a reminder that when it comes to lubes there are two dirty words: glycerin and parabens. Glycerin is suspected of causing yeast and bladder infections, while parabens (antibacterial preservatives) can cause allergic reactions and, some even whisper, the odious and as yet unfounded, cancer. Both Maximus and Slippery Stuff have parabens, though they are glycerin free.

> **Probe.** Also thick and enduring, also easily showered off, Probe has the added appeal of the shortest list of ingredients out there. The only hitch: One of them is glycerin. Bush Pilot Bonus: It is paraben free.

> **Astroglide Gel.** Another contender for the slow motion of anal play, this lube is available at drug stores, but does contain glycerin and parabens.

Sticky Note: Please avoid lubes marketed specifically to "desensitize" or "numb" the end zone. If the words lidocaine or benzocaine are not enough to scare you away, consider this: It is dangerous to play if your babe cannot feel the action, gauge it and, if need be, stop it. Second, you, devoted purveyors of pleasure, are trying to arouse sensation, not dull it. Third, these anaesthetizing lubes make the assumption that anal sex hurts. Prove them wrong. Done, done and done, Mistress.

WHAT'S UP YOUR ASS?

For those of you personal-grooming types with clear plastic covering your couch, caca—yours and your babe's (undoubtedly scentless and poised)—is located past the rectum in that penthouse condo, the colon. There, it is boxed until moving time. Nevertheless, it is true: Towelling off in the locker room, you may find your Wilt the Stilt slightly soiled post-game. While there is no caca sitting in the rectum, it does travel through it and can stick to the rectal walls. What to do? Wash it off with hot water and Irish Spring, while telling yourself, If the sex isn't messy, it isn't sex—it's a board game.

While we are on it, let's address and undo the very stubborn myth that the Land of the Kit is a land of filth. It is not. Those who visit, know it is a land of enormous erogenous possibility. Meet your babe's . . .

BIG BOTTOM

The highest concentration of blood vessels (engorgement) and nerve endings (sensation) is at the puckered mouth of your babe's anal opening, or "rosebud." Happily, rosebud is Incredible Hulk–expandable; it can, if the referee sphincters consider it fair play, accommodate (from smallest to biggest!) a finger, a fist, a dildo, and your high-scoring Larry Bird—well basted, of course. Like our butterflies, the first two-thirds of the kit will respond more to your touch, while the last third will respond more to your fullness. Thank you, Mistress, chuffed.

SEXING THE KIT

Also appreciate the kit's location. While there is so much nose-pinching, border-patrolling and Boo Radley wariness around its neighbour, the colon, prospective renters miss this: Not only is the Land of the Kit mere centimetres from the butterfly, the Land of the Kit is part of the PC muscle group. These muscles form a figure eight between your babe's pubic and tailbones, resulting in a trampoline for her pelvic floor. The proof: When doing your Kegel exercises in matching leisure suits, both you and your babe will notice your kits are caught up in the flex and release of your perineal hardware.

Now, Bush Pilots, you have the lowdown on your babe's posterior: The Land of the Kit is narrow and winding. Its surrounding tissues are a convergence of your preferred currency: nerve endings. Play has the potential to be both hugely pleasurable and, given its taboo geography, deeply intimate.

> I'm all about the bum these days. Just because it's the bum and the thought of it is arousing. Lots of talking about the

bum, too. For me, the bum is the dirty naughty-girl terrain.

—Babe (Mickey Mouse hat, 1979 motorcycle)

WORD UP

How to begin? Sit down with your babe and, together, discuss: What does she want to explore? What are her curiosities, her boundaries, her hesitations? What are yours? I know, "What's next: *Star Trek* costumes and an RRSP?" Yes, it sounds like a conversation between allergic nerds in a senior's basement, but, Bush Pilots, when stepping onto new turf, communication is key. Why, Mistress, oh why?

In the wide world of sex, parameters make for permission. You and your babe must feel safe, secure and demonstrate equal—I repeat, equal—willingness before your entrée, however elaborate, into the Land of the Kit. This means no pressure, no coercion, no bribery, no extortion, no guilt trips, no ex-kits.

Talk through everything from the practical to the fantastical. What lube will you use? What positions do you want to try? How far do you want to go? Will she wear a feather cape and chains around her wrists? Will you listen to Sparklehorse? Will there be a Super 8 camera? Should you rent that cabin by the lake? And take the week off work? A sabbatical?

"VELVETY CHEEK DAY"

Finally.

Fill your claw-foot tub. Wash each other. N.B.B.P.: Hot water. Dry each other off and head to the bedroom, equipped with whatever paraphernalia you want to incorporate in your play. Fool around. You do not need to rush to your destination; take the scenic route, hook her nipples with your tongue, run your fingers up her neck to where her hair meets her skull, rub her feet and thighs and—a moment of silence, please—bow to her go-go. Once your babe gives you the go-ahead (as opposed to the gratifying yet inconclusive moan-ahead), you must follow the two cardinal rules of anal play: Lube up. Slow down.

PUT THE ASS IN MASSAGE

Lube up. Your babe can begin a sultry self-exploration (while you smoke American Spirits on your wingback chair and slide your hand down your Pilot pants) or you can, at a languid pace and with extreme care, begin to massage her derriere. Bush Pilots, be the suitor, not the intruder. You need not immediately plunge the cleft. There are two luscious Brigitte Bardot–like bulbs to be kneaded, stroked and, if she is game, pinched and spanked (Chapter 19. Thwack.).

Pleasure is hers to name. Ask your babe: What do you like? Where do you like it? Do you want more or less pressure? Do you prefer the feeling of vibration or penetration? N.B.B.P.: A tickle on the kit is a big turn-on for some, while the sensation of fullness is a fantasy come true for others.

BUGGER OFF

The killer massage to and between her prats could be enough, Bush Pilots. As one babe says, "It's all about a finger up the butt. A pinkie." Anal sex does not have to mean anal intercourse; in fact, the most common form of anal play is a finger in the receiving end while masturbating or during oral and vaginal sex. There should be no expectations here. Your babe, at this point, may be ready for her wind-down, a dunk in the claw-foot tub and the quiet return to her hot pants. Or not.

YOU'RE SUCH A TOTAL ASS-KISSER

Analingus, or its brotherly nickname, rimming (giving or getting a rimjob), is the practice of using your tongue to tenderize your babe's really good-looking anus. Revisit Chapter 12 (Love it. Be it. Crush it.). BPs, the rimjob is, in essence, the bushjob's backwoods cousin. The same sequence—and set of possibilities—applies. Friend the kit. Tease the kit.

Circle the kit. Lick, flick and suck on the kit. Penetrate the kit. Notice the availability of your paws. Continue to massage the kit, the thighs, the perineum—and, oh, what's this?—if you have thoroughly washed your hands with hot water and soap, you may even greet your babe's go-go with some of that BP-issue sexterity. N.B.B.P.: if you put a finger in your babe's kit, you cannot then put it in her butterfly without washing up in between—or (nonpareil latex-glove opportunity!) gloving it.

"I'VE MADE A HUGE MISTAKE"

Sticky Note: Bush Pilots, in the Land of the Kit, just as you would in the Land of the Butterfly, play safer or go home—to your parent's house, in the suburbs, to nurse your willy on the pull-out couch, while your mom asks "Why so sad?" and your dad plays the bagpipes.

> Kissing with mouths and then going down on a woman is fine, but moving from ass to pussy isn't.
> —Bush Pilot (frequent flyer)

BAD-IDEA JEANS

Rule: Do not switch-hit with your fingers, tongue, a toy or your Kobe Bryant between orifices—those being the mouth, the kit, the butterfly. Yes, Bush Pilots, you may make out and then carry out a transcendent bushjob. No, Bush Pilots, you may not, with your impressive yet louche tongue, move from her kit to her butterfly. You can deliver trace amounts of detritus and you can transmit (over thirty different kinds of) infection—both bacterial (antibiotics) and viral (treatable, not curable). To name a few: Hepatitis A and B, herpes, HIV, gonorrhea, syphilis, chlamydia. Yes, they sound like the daughters of King Lear or the private jets of the New York Dolls now, but they won't when coming out of your downturned mouth—on game day.

This is not to borrow the megaphone of an evangelist and single out anal sex as a disease centre. No. Bush Pilots, unprotected vaginal sex carries equal risk. Always practise safer sex (Chapter 3. Memorize it.) with the following barrier methods: condoms, latex gloves, dental dams—and, depending on your planned activity, even the Saran Wrap in your kitchen. N.B.B.P.: The only female condom is the latex-free Reality Condom. Made of polyisoprene, it is compatible with all lubricants, including oils. It is comfortable (no friction against those sensitive rectal tissues), and your lube will stick with it, rather than bolting up her backside. Okay . . .

SODOMY!

Now, Bush Pilots, what you have all been waiting for: a word about your Magic Johnsons.

Oh. Wait.

The art of anal play is an incremental one. Trailers before the feature, please.

BPs, fingers first. You can even be all thumbs—that's right, hobos, those digits you've had flagged for most of your twenties can now be put to good use. Lubricate well and circle until you find rosebud and, if your babe wants it, play with subtle penetration. One Bush Pilot offers this important instruction to your fingers and your LeBron James: "Always ask. Don't try to accidentally put it in." Foul!

P.S.: We are so on to you!

Remedial: The highest concentration of nerve endings is at the opening. Charm these little clusters out of their slumber to earn entry. Recall the rule of sexterity: one finger at a time. Insert your digits and rotate; if, after (unmeasured) time, your babe tells you she is ready for you and your player, look down. Are you ready for her? Are you con-domed? Are you greased?

FULL-COURT PRESS

Press your player up against your babe's rosebud. Before you embark, take heed: If you are going to walk the full moon, you have to be an astronaut. Ground control to Major Tom: Take it slow, slow, slower. Let your babe guide your Charles Barkley in. Communicate. Monitor your babe's response. Make sure she is breathing like a deep-sea diver. Remember: Your boner is trying to get past her first sphincter muscle; relaxation and trust are key.

> It is incredible in a sort of terrifying way. An erotically charged moment, partly because of the taboo, but mainly because it is completely new territory. Like being a virgin. Getting to be on that threshold again. It is such a vulnerable position to be in as a woman. You must totally surrender to your lover. It is a bit S&M, which isn't something I'm normally into, but in the right moment it can lead to pure, voluptuous pleasure. The feeling was that pain/pleasure edge that can be thrilling. But it needs utmost care in negotiation. It requires complete trust in your lover. It is one of the few times that the flower-gentle can actually be full of ferocity. It is not recommended for the few-minute intermission. Like with so many things, slowness is everything.
> —Babe (skinny dipping in a public fountain)

Keep your excitement in check, BPs; you are only going in as far as your babe is willing to receive you. As one babe says, "Entry must happen in tiny increments, and gently." This is not (yet) the boisterous screw with her butterfly you are accustomed to. One babe writes, "Requires more prep and goo and slow going." And yet another: "It seemed like a lot of work (the lube, the slowness of it, negotiating my partner's large penis), and I like sex to be simpler." One insider BP adds, "It's a whole different gig than the vagina." Subtext: Anal play operates at a different pace.

EXTRA CREDIT

GIRLS ON FILM

Mistress, oh Mistress, it's the last chapter in Part Three (crushing it), Rear Entry (crazed superfans!), and, well, something has come up here at Booty Camp. We thought we might see (hint) some of it during the G-spot chapter, and, well, once we got to the chapter on positions, we started to feel its hard-core (hint) absence. So now that we're all gonzo (hint) here in the back country, we have to ask you: Mistress, oh Mistress, in this our phattest, mintest read, where oh where is the porn? Sh'mon!

Bush Pilots, porn is (We don't like your apocalyptic tone, Mistress), to borrow the name of Almodovar's movie, *Bad Education*. You must know—Don't say it, Mistress!—porn is entertainment, not instruction. No! Porn is a painted clown; you don't see it pacing its trailer, without its makeup, in its regular shoes. You don't see it preparing its gags, rehearsing its script, fixing its costume. You see it only in an edited form. Imagine if we could cut and paste our sex lives? The result would be distorted. So enjoy porn's gaudy parade, but don't mistake it for schooling. Consolation: Because I heart you so, lower the blinds. I present to you one of the few skin flicks that takes you—informatively—behind the scenes: Tristan Taormino's *Expert Guide to Anal Sex*.

Interlude.

GOT YOUR BACK, BABE

After that first (sphincteral) crossover, your babe's thrusts are your guide. Continue to apply your lube, as Captain Goodscrew so eloquently puts it, "Like mustard on a hot dog when you have an exit thrust and your cock is exposed." How does it feel for your babe? One reports from the back forty: "There's this whole other dimension in the rear. The sensation is strange at first." And thereafter? "One of the hottest, naughtiest and most intimate experiences I've had."

The classic doggie-style rear entry is not advised for first-timers because it makes for the deepest penetration. Instead, the best starter positions are the spoon and the straddle (woman on-top—or, ahem, superior). Why? Your babe controls the depth and pace of penetration—and, her hands are free to play with her go-go. Variation: Your babe faces your feet, leaning as far toward them as possible. This, the Kama Sutra suggests, delays the giver's (i.e., your) orgasm.

Because of its intimacy, the missionary position is also one your babe may want to try. In it, your babe's hands are free to roam her parts. She may even wish to rotate her pelvis and contract her kit muscles to massage your Steve Nash. Three-pointer, Mistress. Bush Pilots, be attentive to her comfort. Communicate. And reapply your lube.

I think I had been put off by the negative, painful, shameful connotations of "ass-fucking." Sure, I was totally thrilled by the idea, but not comfortable suggesting it to my lady. We'd had some success with my fingers around her back door, so my lady decided we give it a try.

We set aside a whole evening, made out extensively until we were both really excited yet also relaxed. My lady did all the moving at her own pace while I manned the lube, and before long, with no pain, no awkwardness, I was completely inside her! She loved it, I loved it; the love and trust and hotness of it all was deeply and surprisingly moving. It was so beautiful and amazing that we both felt satisfied in our souls for at least a week afterward. All these previously separate feelings—horniness and gentleness, thrill and self-control, trust and taboo—they all came together that night.

—Bush Pilot (jukebox, kayak, owl ring)

LEAVE HER BEHIND

When exiting your babe's court, boys, do so slow, slow, slower—and try to time your retreat with her exhalations. Clear, Mistress, but before I do, before I must, I have one question: Might my babe come? Good question.

One babe, post-screw, writes:

It was sort of an interesting experience to share with my partner, because it was something a little off menu that we could do together that we hadn't done with anyone else, but neither one of us was that excited about it. We are both a little uptight about our anal cavities, so we ultimately stuck with what worked for us, which was most everything else.

The flipside? From the cockpit, Captain Goodscrew:

Some ladies love to be fucked in the ass. It's true. They come right away. It's great.

My Beeps (represent!), a word about your babe's Big O. All ears, Mistress. While some babes do come through anal sex, their G-spot reached and rocked to climax, most need other forms of stimulation (toys!) to be sent over the edge.

SO ANAL!

Bush Pilots, you may now loot the toy department. Premium, Mistress. Pony up in this order: butt plugs, dildos, beads. Deal-Breaker Alert: Nothing hard, nothing spiked and nothing science-fair furry. Look for sturdy, soft and pliable. The Land of the Kit can quickly become the Bermuda Triangle when it is aroused. For your "lucky bun day," may your dildo and butt plug bases be flared and your anal beads well rounded and well attached. Some inexpensive anal beads (these are not the same as Ben Wa balls) have seams that can scratch the delicate tissues of the rectal walls. Take the (nail) file out of your tool belt and shave them down.

RECREATIONAL PLUGS

Butt plugs are inserted into your babe's kit for a sensation of fullness. Start small. Start silicone. Find a well-made toy you trust. You want some flex and bend to begin. Thereafter, you may move onto harder materials like glass and stainless steel. Variations: If the butt plug vibrates, use this slender bit of buzz both on and in your babe's behind. Some butt plugs are ridged or knobbed to mimic beads, and have a flange (base ring) or handle you can turn for added intensity. Bush Pilot Bonus: Butt plugs can be used as a warmup to anal intercourse or, when inserted during vaginal intercourse, your babe's butterfly will be compressed, making the fit for your forward that much more snug.

BOOTY CALLS

Unlike the butt plug, which stays put during your play, a dildo is designed to move in and out of your babe's kit. I can totally relate, Mistress! To begin, look for more pliable materials such as vibrating silicone before Lucite or porcelain.

One Bush Pilot describes his play by play this way:

A butt plug, dildo and lube became essential accessories on the nightstand. Both rubbery toys had bases so they could stand upright on a flat surface, and wouldn't be able to slip away into the unknown. I always used the two in tandem, and I discovered a nice technique where I'd insert the plug, and then use the palm of my hand to massage the flat base while my fingers could manipulate the dildo. This motion would morph into gentle slapping, which would then escalate to a full-on spanking. My partner would frantically suck my cock while I spanked her ass and the bases of the inserted toys. This was a surefire way to generate a lot of heat and open the door to some good ol'-fashioned ass-fucking.

BEAD IT

Bush Pilots, a more advanced prop, anal beads are introduced to your babe's bottom one at a time. She makes the guest list; read it carefully. Once there, the beads may be designed to accommodate some circling and twisting. Another possibility: A thespian with a penchant for props describes her husband's use of anal beads—pulled out at climax—as "totally yummy."

HEY, BIG SPENDER

If you are burning stacks of cash in your fireplace while your babe folds fifties into cranes, ask your babe the following: Would you like your anal beads to be black obsidian or freshwater pearl? Would you like your lapidary butt plug to be jade or jewelled? And finally, would you care to sit on hand-blown glass? Sticky Note: Remember, if toys are visiting both your babe's front and back yards, they must be disinfected between trips. To disinfect, soak in boiling water, please. (N.B.B.P.: Not all toys can be boiled.) Also, anal toys should be considered "personal" to the user; if sharing, sheathe it first.

BADASS

Aside from the stink, the salaciousness, the pain, the perversion, the depravity, the fiction that anal play takes place in public parks and on skin-flick sets, yet another myth: Men want it; women don't. You approach your babe, horny, head tilted in apology for your horniness; she consents out of Betty-ish goodness or calls you a sex maniac and goes back to her crossword puzzle. Surprise: Your babe may want it as much as you do. She may even want it more than you do.

So, venture forth. Be well equipped. Be well informed. Travel safe and travel slow. You now know the ABCs of anal play. It should never hurt. It should be safe. It should be lubricated. It should be slow, slow, slower. Discover a new orifice to be wooed and worshipped—not just on your babe's body, but your own. Bush Pilots, nothing compares to, or recommends you, like hands-on experience. The Land of the Kit has an emotional component; it requires trust, care and perhaps—even that spectre of the bedroom—love.

CHEAT SHEET: FOR THE BACK-DOOR MAN

DO

✓ Bathe.

✓ Towel off.

✓ Ask for permission to enter.

✓ Use a finger or tongue before toys.

✓ Choose toys that are soft, pliable and seamless.

✓ Choose toys that are flared at the base or have a flange or handle.

✓ Be sure that anal beads are well rounded and well attached and that seams are smoothed down.

✓ Be sure your Shaq is sheathed and basted.

✓ Remember that thick, water-based, condom-compatible lube (Maximus, Slippery Stuff or Probe) is best.

✓ Start with the starter positions: the spoon and the straddle.

✓ Play by her rules.

DO NOT

✗ Neglect to trim your lengthy man-nails.

✗ Forget to soak off your knuckle rings.

✗ Slur, "I am so hammered."

✗ Josh, "I suggest it was Professor Plum, with the candlestick, in the conservatory."

✗ Do anything sudden.

✗ Use anything hard.

✗ Use anything spiked.

✗ Use anything furry.

✗ Use anything sharp.

✗ Use anything unsafe.

✗ Use anything un-sanitized.

✗ Use anything un-lubricated.

✗ Use anything anaesthetizing.

✗ Quote *This Is Spinal Tap*.

If you must get it out of your system, Bush Pilots, sing the following now:

Big bottom, big bottom
Talk about bum cakes, my girl's got 'em
Big bottom drives me out of my mind
How could I leave this behind?

—Spinal Tap, "Big Bottom"

Now that you have finished singing, well done, my darlings: You have made it through Part Three: Takeoff. Congratulations! Can we get Super Bowl Sunday–stewed now, Mistress? No. Though you may sew the following nine badges onto the crotch of your Pilot pants: the Show & Tell badge, the I-Can-Kiss-Like-That-Guy-in-*The-Breakfast-Club* badge, the Adoring the Girls Each One Equally badge, the My Tongue Is the Real Hotshot badge, the Stay the Course A Bird on the Wire badge, the As a Matter of Fact My Sheets *Are* Rubber badge, the Stroke It Like a Closed Eyelid badge, the Always In Position Always Well-Positioned badge and the Slower Than I Want to and Loving It badge. And this Bonus Badge: Burning My Mankini Now.

One final frontier to face. Pumped, Mistress. Show us the way. I already am.

PART FOUR
The Lay of the Land

FLIGHT MISSION:
BUSH PILOTS,
REMAIN AIRBORNE
IN VARIABLE
CONDITIONS AND RISING
ATMOSPHERIC
PRESSURE.

A HUDDLE WITH
CAPTAIN GOODSCREW

Captain Dylan I. Goodscrew

WELL, LOOK AT YOU, BUSH PILOTS, LOOK AT YOU. So close to graduation. And yet, so far.

Sure, you have grown from a good-natured and likeable Bush Pilot into one with a squint in your eye and a secret in your Pilot pants you like to call Omar Sharif. Your callow charm, your irreverent dress code and your Adrian Zmed–like dance moves have all been overshadowed by your Omar Sharif. You know how to ride that eighteen-spoked cell of sublimity, your babe's go-go, with your fingers, your tongue—and now, your Omar Sharif. You have turned your boyish hunger into your manly night flight, your sexual performance into your sleight of Omar Sharif. Your name has been carved into kitchen counters, pool walls and mountainsides.

And yet, despite himself and his rigorous training, Omar still feels the world is full of erotic riddles he has yet to unlock. For instance, can he make love to his lady in the back of his ride without the fuzz getting all up in his grill? Can he lower his lady's jeans and spank her to the beat of "Baby Got Back"? Can he take his lady to a play party where there may be other attractive ladies—or perhaps more simply, a play party where there is only one other attractive lady?

And, most pressing for Omar, even though he feels he is using the boner-force: he still tires. He overheats, has a surge and blacks out. Only to be shaken awake like a bandaged soldier by a beauteous nurse in some army hospital. Where am I? Who are you? What year is it? Will I live?

Bush Pilots, despite your considerable skills, would you believe there's more to learn? More badges to sew onto the crotch of your Pilot pants? More night flights to make before you—and your babe—can sing in Ozzy Osbourne and Lita Ford–like harmony, "Ace"? Here is a preview.

Over to you, Captain D.I. Goodscrew:

> I was lovers with a beautiful, smart, sexually renowned lady. She had just discovered her ability to ejaculate, and I had discovered my ability not to. We had just left our respective partners and were exploring this new sexuality with each other. She squirted about thirty times when we first slept together—and we hadn't even had penetrative sex! Eventually, our fucks were characterized by about twenty female ejacs and twenty male multiple orgasms each. We learned a lot with and from each other.

Hadn't even had penetrative sex. Affirmative. Twenty male multiple orgasms. That's also an affirmative. We learned a lot from each other. Also an affirmative.

Do you see what is possible for you and your man parts now, Bush Pilots? I see, Mistress, you say and pat Omar Sharif—or Shar, for short. I see.

Where to finish? In this, the last part of your Field Guide to the bush, "The Lay of the Land," you can earn gold captain's bars for the shoulders of your flight suit. You, Bush Pilots, can even earn your wings. (Represent!) Here's how: sex in public places, group sex, power play and becoming a multi-orgasmic Bush Pilot.

(Smoke) Break.

CHAPTER 17
SEX IN PUBLIC PLACES

THRILL SEEKER

Lisa likes to masturbate while speeding in her pickup truck, dangling from cliff edges and riding moody camels bareback across the Moroccan desert. Lisa's analyst thinks her client has a fixation with thrill-seeking. Lisa agrees.

Working as a freelance photographer, Lisa is sent on a particularly boring assignment: to document the pioneer village that lies flaccid on the outskirts of the city. Lisa brings her boyfriend, Alvaro, a coyote tracker with a ribald wit, along for the ride. While taking snaps of the tired, sunken ponies and mediocre actresses in bonnets and spectacles, Lisa is overcome by lust. She lifts her crooked aviators and scans her prim surroundings. The woods: heavily trafficked by men, sleeves billowing, carrying fake prey and axes. The grounds: overrun with lost children and sullen school-trip teenagers. Her eyes settle on a roped-off area. She takes Alvaro's always-willing hand and leads him past the NO TRESPASSING sign, knowing that lust has no sense of time or place; it is a random force. It hits like a meteor and must be marvelled at afterward, chuckwagon or no chuckwagon. There, they drop their shorts and make quick, feisty love under canvas cover. Lisa and Alvaro re-emerge to laudatory hymns, bleats and clucks, flushed in the midday light, another stunt below their tingling belts.

THE FUR TRAPPERS

Bush Pilots, sex in a public place (e.g., laundromat, discotheque, dive bar) is the work of a true pioneer. In fact, pioneers, with their starched collars, wooden teeth, pestilence and plagues, may have been the sexiest people to walk our home and native land. Whoa, easy, Mistress. Um, first name Halle? True, my bombastic underlings, yet, think on this: Pioneers launched themselves into the verdant unknown, pulling their rickety canoes up onto rugged shores to chase buffalo, spin wool and make rad outdoor boom boom. They were the original trespassers. Valiant point, Mistress, maybe we should follow the nature trails of our plucky friends of yesteryear, our petticoat-lifting foremothers, our suede pant–dropping forefathers? Maybe you should, BPs. Just say when, Mistress. When.

THE SHAGGIN' WAGON

The most popular spot for the illicit screw—and most often the first landing for the pioneering BP—is that second bedroom, the parked car. We all remember the sexual captivity that was high school; while we, your babes, roamed the halls in a Scott Baio wet dream, you smothered hourly boners in your hand-me-down Levis. How much we had to shush under our carved-up desks. Our release? What the Tom Collins crowd now calls "T.G.I.F."

Friday night. We would crimp our hair. You would shower. We would stand on our front stoops. You would pick us up. We would think, "Stud." You would think, "Babe." We would saunter toward your parents' wood-panelled station wagon. You would open the passenger-side door. We would get in and kick our suede cowboy boots up onto the dash. You would crank "When the Levee Breaks." It would speak to our E-minor teenaged souls. You would drive just over the speed limit. The car would smell like hockey gear. You would say, "Sorry." We would put on cherry ChapStick. You would think, "I so want to taste that." We would think, "I so know." Then you would slowly pull into an abandoned mall parking lot. We would smoke Benson & Hedges and split a jar of peach schnapps. We would laugh and then get serious and then laugh and then start to make out. It would feel like we were being rushed by applause. We would awkwardly vault the front seat, getting our braces and barrettes snagged on the upholstered ceiling and tumble into the back seat—which, minutes later, would receive your frantic, premature ejaculation (Don't look at me, Mistress!).

THE HYBRID

Now that you are slow-loving and come-conscious BPs (You know it, Mistress!), this back-seat screw can be recreated in a much more legendary way. Instruction: Take your Prius out of park.

> On the highway, all horned up, I started giving him a BJ, but it got so hot I jumped on top of him and he was watching the road over my shoulder—but it was sick, hot sex and at one point I looked to the side and the guys in the next car were watching transfixed!
> —Babe (wins every betting pool and has a voice to rival Tom Waits)

Sex in Various Shapes of Wheeled Transport

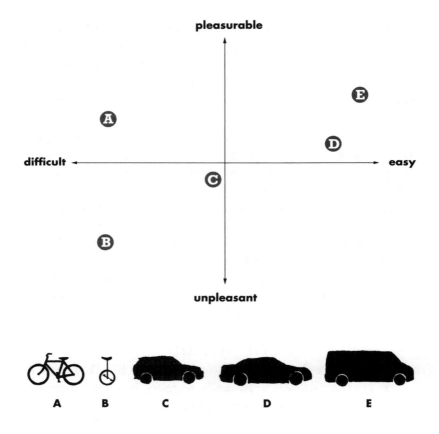

Of course, this is totally moronic and only for the glue-coloured, zombie-dusted, death-wish members of Mötley Crüe. That said, we know how much you love the iconic highway "handjob." Good times, Mistress, good times. Why not turn it around, BP? If you are in the driver's seat, able to multitask and heading home after a long weekend in

Vegas—N.B.B.P.: In an automatic vehicle—why not slip your paw under your babe's sun-faded hemline? To inflame her lady parts with your mitts, revisit the sexterity in Chapter 11. Whoa, Mistress, I'm calling for heat stroke—if you're catching my man-drift. I'm catching it, BP.

Or try the following, much safer—and still thrilling—variation. One word: customs. You and your babe are parked in that endless, anxiety-making line of trailers and transport trucks, waiting to be questioned by a surly teen in a dark uniform doing his best Laurence Olivier. You know you have no weapons and you know you have no hard drugs. Still, you are sweating bullets, illegal bullets bought with blood money. Why not let off some steam, tip your seat back and take your chances? Whoa, Mistress, are you implying what I think you're implying—e.g., my lady place her mightily agreeable mouth on my fervent man parts? I am, BP.

Be still, my beating boner.

ANYTHING TO DECLARE?

A babe with a penchant for mischief and catsuits recalls giving the kinky salute to passersby while waiting to cross into Quebec from Vermont. About her Bush Pilot, she writes:

> I thought a much more interesting way to pass the time would be to see if I could manage to give him a blowjob before we reached the booth.
>
> Of course, if he'd been asked, he may not have agreed this was such a good idea, so I casually rested my hand on his thigh and then surreptitiously moved it toward his erogenous zone.
>
> He climaxed two cars before the customs booth, and I enjoyed the thrill of flaunting it right in front of do-gooders whom I found particularly provoking. Plus there was the added frisson of being aware the only ones who could see my low-jinks were the frustrated, probing eyes of voyeuristic truck drivers.

Mistress, I'm so down with this—the erogenous zone and the climaxing especially—but may I be so forthright as to ask you: What is this "added frisson" of which she speaks? Is it perhaps some kind of supreme oral manoeuvring, a tongue-fakie kick-flip, my babe can bust out during our "risky business"? No. The lesson: In this configuration, not only does your babe get the tingles from laying her lips down in your lap, she also gets the exhibitionist charge of being watched. If, of course, that's her thing.

I will see if it is, Mistress. Mos def.

Yet another way to meld transportation and fornication? Let someone else do the driving. Rent a limo or simply board a train (Florence to Taormina), overnight ferry (Stockholm to Helsinki) or an airplane (Hawaii).

THE MILE-HIGH CLUB

To join, you must be above a cruising altitude of 5,280 feet. You must also—Bush Pilot's Honour—swear you will not brag about your tryst. Swear. If you must, tell me, like Captain Goodscrew does here:

> I fucked flying back from Holland with my lover at the time. It's all about timing. When the movie goes on and the food is served, everyone is looking forward. That is a perfect time to head back to the bathroom to fuck. Have one person go in, wait a minute, then the other person. Be sneaky, be aware of flight attendants and have a bullshit excuse ready in case they catch you exiting or departing the bathroom together.

Timing. Affirmative.

How to Have Sex in an Airplane Bathroom*

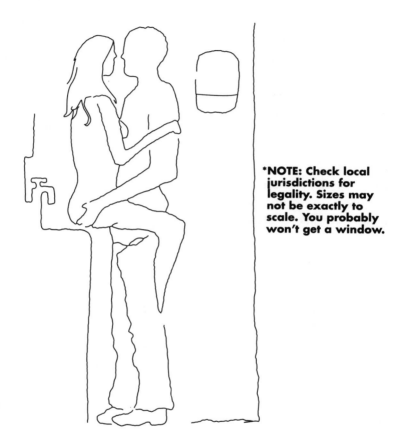

*NOTE: Check local jurisdictions for legality. Sizes may not be exactly to scale. You probably won't get a window.

The clandestine quickie can be planned or (N.B.B.P.: so very much hotter) spontaneous. Whoa, Mistress, hold up. You're saying heed my babe's lady-fleece when I don't even have my GPS with me? I am, my Boy Scout BPs. Look at it this way: Consider the reward when your babe suddenly leads you into a darkened alleyway, leaning back against the crumbling brick, lifting her halter dress to reveal a perfect, sultry bareness. Or when she follows you from the leather booth, down the hallway, past the kitchen and pulls you into the ladies' room, sidling up against the marble counter, all thighs and garters. Stand and deliver, BPs. In the contest of seduction, nothing compares to surprise. Keep your babe on her toes. Why? When you take risks and hatch adventure, you play your centre, your captain, your capital C: confidence.

The restroom is an excellent choice for the secret straddle. It is ubiquitous, with its graffiti and granite, just grimy enough, and has the practical advantage of a lock on the door. Alternatively, find an untrafficked corner in a library (Microfiche), bookstore (Crafts), movie theatre (*Battlefield Earth*), elevator, church basement, university, office tower, airport, arena, auditorium, museum, gallery, department store, greenhouse, greenroom, theme park, backstage or any place serving food and drink. Deal-Maker Alert: Parkas and frond-leafed plants serve as useful foils. As do movie sets. As do phone booths. As do smoke screens.

WHERE THE WILD THINGS ARE

Or, take it outside. Swing between the rare Elysian green of the city and its seedier corners. Be a love child of the lush and the dangerous in a backyard, public park, beach, rooftop, balcony, up a tree, down a laneway or against a chain-link fence with a freight train speeding past you.

Declare a trip to the outskirts, any outskirts. Ask your babe to pick a direction. When she says east, go east. Pack nothing but water, chocolate, condoms and a Mexican blanket. Let the drive be an exercise in anticipation, with much near-brushing of the lady and the man parts. Growling optional. Soundtrack: Remixed and Reimagined Nina Simone. Pull over when the roads get narrow and dusty and the strip malls give way to dairy farms. Behold your origins. Whoa, Mistress, are you calling my mother a cow? No, darling, I am telling you to be one with nature. Sift some dirt through your paw, kick on your hazard lights and lead your babe into the woods.

Outdoor Sex

USEFUL MATERIALS ABOUND
FOR THE RESOURCEFUL BUSH PILOT

sunset

nice clean pond

gentle patch of moss

voyeurs/ cheering section

stump

natural feather
possibly stolen from that robin

Deal-Breaker Alert: Be sure you are able to identify poison ivy, poison oak and beige families hiking back to bible camp.

Common Woodland Dangers

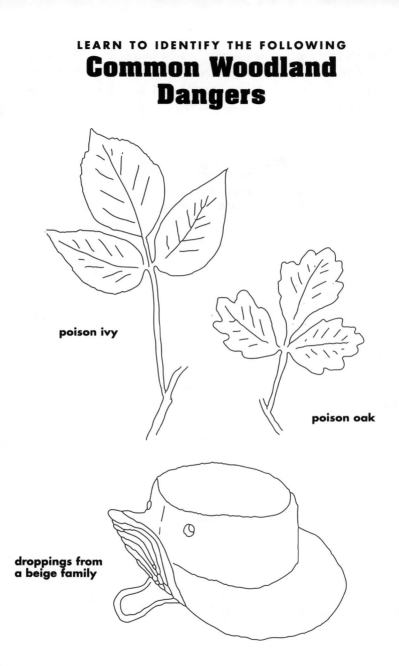

poison ivy

poison oak

droppings from
a beige family

EXTRA CREDIT

YOUR BABE DOES NOT WANT TO SEE YOU

- ☞ pet a bear cub.
- ☞ knock yourself out on a low-hanging branch.
- ☞ eat a mysterious but spellbinding mushroom.
- ☞ imitate a moose to distract a group of hunters.
- ☞ creak the door open to a sturdy-looking shack.
- ☞ ride a deer.
- ☞ climb a tree badly.
- ☞ build a "love nest" out of twigs.
- ☞ say, "What the hell could that be?" and then carefully lower your hand into it.
- ☞ bury the condom with a quick, "Compost, babe, capiche?"
- ☞ forget where you are.

Instead, BPs, for your foray into the sticks, revisit this celluloid inspiration: Sailor Ripley and Lula Fortune in *Wild at Heart*. His snakeskin jacket. Her hot, flexing body. His parole violation. Her hot, flexing body. His rendition of "Love Me Tender." Her hot, flexing body. Recall her order to get something on the radio right now, and he does and then they dance in a field? As if possessed? By her hot, flexing body? I will venture, despite his scripting of the Good Witch, this is David Lynch's only true fairy-tale moment. Why not make it yours too? Time of day: sunset.

A SCREW LOOSE

That said, Bush Pilots, desire can have no sense of direction. Your instruction: Take advantage of its suggestibility. For instance, one babe (strong jaw and matching libido) remembers making sub-rosa love under her Bush Pilot's bomber jacket at the crossroads of two busy highways, behind a molehill in an industrial park, looking at the blinking Chuck E. Cheese sign and the ashen lunch crowd beyond. (Whoa, Mistress, I was totally at that restaurant.)

A second postcard from lust-choked suburbia? Another friend remembers dropping his book bag and crawling under a Dumpster in a mall to do the foot-high, rabbit-fast missionary. And yet another, drunk on cheap vodka, got her kicks under a Salvation Army fur coat, Greyhound heading north to Anchorage. (Whoa, Mistress, I was totally on that bus.)

You see, Bush Pilots . . .

It is only when you start to think like a criminal that you can act like a criminal.

Case the joint that is the world all around you. You will see, it is flashing itself.

WE COULDN'T WAIT TO GET HOME

But, Mistress, is that a crime? Yes, my Beeps (Represent!) The Criminal Code, Section 173, prohibits the pioneer from performing "an indecent act" in a public place—if anyone can see. To that effect, BPs, look out for cops, dogs and minors. That said, of course it is the criminal aspect that serves as part of the elixir. We loved your fake ID in high school. Now we love a man in uniform. We also love a man who can outrun a man in uniform.

Public coupling is as common a fantasy as the librarian letting her burnished hair down while sucking a lollipop. For the bona fide pioneer, there is always a new frontier to cross. Imagine sex during bingo, bobsledding, exams, the Throne Speech. Imagine what JFK must have pulled off in his time. Bush Pilots, there are so many ways to shake up your sexual snow globe, but in this, the age of surveillance, sometimes all you have to do is leave the house.

CHAPTER 18

GROUP SEX: THE THREESOME, THE MORESOME (AND YOU!)

NOTE FROM THE FIELD:
BARBARIANS!

Pinstripe Nick is on business in New York. Part Hardy Boy, part Easy Rider, he is solitary by nature, six foot four with a boxer's nose and a leather briefcase. Upon seeing him, most women think "Catch." It's Friday night. The work day is done. Nick slips his tie into his pocket and finds a watering hole on the Lower East Side. Beer in hand, his eyes troll over the beautiful people: tube tops, tight jeans, longing. For a moment, he is crushed by all of the ventures he has left unexplored. He plays a slide show of his life across his brain: cowboy costume in the backyard, girlfriends, champion sprinter, girlfriends, cover band, girlfriends, university, girlfriends, lawyer. Where are the girlfriends? Where is his inamorata in Amsterdam? His madame in Barcelona? His contortionist in Osaka? Where are his tattoos, his talents? Nick wants to shock his biography. He wants to test himself. Tonight.

The bar crowds and Nick is tangled up in the banter of a small group. They invite him to an after party. He accepts. They arrive. A loft. The hostess, a former stripper with a peroxide pageboy and a pet cobra named Butch, welcomes them. The loft is sparely decorated. In its centre is a giant plush carpet, red, a sectional couch and about ten people in various stages of undress and copulation. This is a play party. With her fingertip, the hostess draws a circle on Nick's palm. She whispers, "Are you in?" He hesitates. She hovers there, between his collarbone and his earlobe. Nick has only fantasized about play parties. He looks at the hostess. Nick has only fantasized about a lot of things. He does not have to fly home until morning; his plan for the weekend: the sports section. Nick nods. The hostess leads him toward the action.

THE LAND OF PLENTY

Playing in multiples. We know how you love it, Bush Pilots. We know if it were a record, it would be the only one you'd listen to. So let's warm up with the play party's less crowded, yet still hall-of-famer cousin, the threesome. You pace your man cave, wrench in one hand, cordless drill in the other—just because. You picture the arrival of two appetent ladies in matching bikinis and fedoras. Ding-dong. Fast forward to your king-size water bed and a DO DISTURB sign hanging from your door. One lady, so very much like Dita Von Teese, pleasures your man parts while the other, also so very much like Dita Von Teese, just helps out, like some kind of sex volunteer, a candy striper of the bedroom. And then they switch. And switch. And switch again. Of course, you do all your own stunts.

IT'S TWINS!

My darling BPs, my dudes of the bush, three might be your favourite number—but do you know how to make it your lucky one?

> Finding an actual lesbian is critical. Or at least someone who's bi-curious. Logistics are important. Try to arrange yourselves so everyone has access to everyone's bits. Often, two folks will fuck and the third is helping out. Make sure you change condoms and wipe off your junk in between partners. If anyone is in a couple situation, make sure you have a good chat about boundaries and what you're comfortable with before sex.
> —Captain Goodscrew

Good news: The zeitgeist says now is the time. Alongside acid wash, yo-yos and Herbie Hancock's "Rockit," the threesome is enjoying an orifice-dizzy renaissance. Spanish *Maxim* declares the threesome the "fetish of the millennium"—what the key party was to the seventies, what anal sex was to the eighties and what *Baywatch* was to the nineties. In short, if you're curious, you're not alone. Cue the Shannon twins.

Oh, wait, hold the Shannon twins.

IT'S A BIT OF A GAMBLE

Bush Pilots, as you know from the blackjack table, anything involving numbers makes for possibilities and combinations. While the most popular version of the ménage à trois is the widely fetishized Sharon, Lois and Bram, let us not forget about the less popular and more hairy Peter, Paul and Mary and their three-part folk-alarm "If I Had a Hammer (The Hammer Song)."

THREE'S A CROWD

Sensitive viewers, be warned. When it comes to the three-way screw, cautionary tales abound; namely, being a slumped and weeping Philip Seymour Hoffman, marooned on the edge of his mattress, lonely as a man who has just been his own bachelor party, mourning the wilting epithet in his pants, while someone else feasts on the mighty curves of his gasping, white-knuckling, oh-my-God-ing girlfriend.

Or, Exhibit B: One babe remembers being in the kitchen of a stranger's house, drinking milk out of the carton before the light of the open fridge, wearing nothing but a jean jacket and trying to sober up while her crush copped her younger counterpart.

Jean jacket. Affirmative.

Herein, and always, Bush Pilots, lies the great F-word divide: love or lust. Know thyself. Is it possible for you to separate the two? That is a yes, Mistress. Can you be a runaway puppet? Whoa, Mistress. Can you screw without strings attached to your defenceless, palpitating heart? Ease up, Mistress. Can you make sex, like motocross, weekend smoking and paintball, exclusively recreational? In doubt, Mistress. Consider the question this way: Could you really watch your babe cry out another man's name (e.g., "Viggo!")?

SNAFU'd, Mistress.

One way around that, my BPs, so delicate in your flight suits, is to make your threesome an . . .

It's a perfect vacation activity (when everyone is going to disappear to different countries next week). Best if no one is actually in a serious partnership. That is, don't do it with your boyfriend/girlfriend. Jealousy will ensue. Or tears of exclusion from the third party. Do it with two others who feel playful but are unattached for the evening.

—Bush Pilot (three-piece suit, pet cockatoo)

Disappear. Affirmative. Different countries. That's also an affirmative.

THE FLIPSIDE TO THE FLING

One bi-curious babe who "loves sex and coming anyway you cut it" did have a threesome (of the Jack-Janet-and-Chrissie variety) with her boyfriend. She recalls, "It was weird and intoxicating, and it felt thrilling to be sexually devious. I made her come, and that was pretty exciting for me." But about her relationship, she adds this telling proviso:

He was a really great and fun guy, but not for me on a long-term basis. I was curious, and he was your typical horny twenty-three-year old. We had sort of talked about it as one of our fantasies. I think I felt comfortable with the whole threesome thing 'cause I knew he wasn't the one.

What if he—or she—is?

HEY BABE, WE'VE GOT HUMPANY

The perils of the odd number? For a couple to engage in a close encounter of the threesome kind, there can be no caving in to a dominant desire. This is not a place for such-is-life compromise. Both of you must want it. If your babe concedes to please you, an already uneven situation is made even more so. Pre-threesome, if, at the mention of "Sasha Grey, nudge-nudge," your babe locks you out and packs your Pilot-possessions into garbage bags, lines them up on the front lawn and labels them "TOTAL PERV," keep the ménage à trois a fantasy à un—a series of snapshots you can privately broadcast anywhere, anytime.

ULTIMATE FIGHTING

The offence is often a sense of sexual inadequacy; the sting: "Am I not enough for you?" After you answer "Of course you are," ask your babe, "What do you fantasize about?" This question should be spray-painted across your bedroom walls, and its answers, real or chimerical, allowed to prosper between your sheets, and your legs. (Chapter 6. Be it.)

READY TO HOST THE SEXUAL TRIDENT?

Stoked, Mistress. Big time. Warm up to it, BP. Hit a strip club and buy a lap dance for your babe. Venture out—top hat and tutu—to a fetish masquerade. Or, as one sartorial wizard offers, "Experimenting with phone sex might be a way of testing the waters." Engage in any activity that prefaces the idea of an interloper (e.g., Lexington Steele) in your bedroom. You and your babe must both be prepared for the disorienting body check of your paramour made the object of another person's desire—and hot (nine and a half-inch) parts.

Next step: Choose your guest carefully. A friend? An acquaintance? Someone you want to play with once? Someone you want to play with again? In the land of sexual trigonometry, it is crucial to find the right arrangement.

Thereafter, on threesome eve, establish your boundaries. As is true of BDSM play, limits allow you to surrender. Parameters equal permission. Like the knife-throwing magician and his beautiful assistant, the threesome is a "no-surprises" zone. Speaking from a place of quiet promiscuity, one decorated Bush Pilot advises,

> Decide on your target together. Maybe even consider having a safe word to say if one of you feels uncomfortable, to mean let's take a time out.

A safe word ("Hall & Oates.") Affirmative.

NC-17 OR PG-13?

You are venturing into the unknown together; have your own morse code. With your babe, devise the terms of the encounter. Will you go all the way? Or will you keep it to school yard French kissing? Or perhaps, you, Bush Pilot will simply be a voyeur. As one wolf advises:

> Penetration is not actually necessary. It ups the level of seriousness and competition and ediginess. A lot of fun can be had with cuddling and kissing and jerking and squirting.

Sweet, Mistress. Fortitude, Bush Pilot: The enemy? That famed green monster and home-wrecker: jealousy. As one post-threesome babe admits, "Jealousies are too often present." No one likes to be left shivering out in the sexual cold.

ALL CAUTION ASIDE

Bush Pilots, a telegram for you from the Land of Plenty:

> How do you start? I figured I'd be loyal and start sucking on my girlfriend's breast. That got her turned on. Sophie picked up the slack and sucked on the other breast. Then the two of them started making out. I liked that. I have my finger inside my girlfriend, and my other

hand on Sophie's lovely breasts, her back, her hair. I'll never forget the sensation of forgetting who was who—there just seems to be so much goddamned body in there. I didn't know what to do. Needless to say, I was excited. It was a smorgasbord of lips, tongues and skin. While my girlfriend gave me head, she fingered Sophie, and Sophie and I were kissing madly. It felt very, very good. It went on like this for a long time—don't remember how long, doesn't matter—we were all satisfied in the end, and I lay back in the centre of the bed, a woman in each of my arms, thinking, Now, life can be simple, can't it?

—Bush Pilot ("Beautiful Loser" and summa cum laude student of Leonard Cohen's Advanced I'll-Turn-You-Into-Everlasting-Song School of Seduction)

You're welcome.

MANATHON

Last note: orgasm control. Whoa, Mistress, are you talking to me or my babe? You, darling. Pack your Tiger (in every babe's) Woods into a warmup suit and work out your PC muscles (you'll find your training regimen in Chapter 20. Crush it.). Why? The threesome is one of the ultimate tests of your endurance. It is Everest for your man parts. With no oxygen.

I just remember having to drink a lot of water.
—Bush Pilot (can play "Valley Girl" on the autoharp)

ODD MAN OUT

Being the only man in the room is not always all it's cracked up to be; the Noah's Ark pairing off may come as a surprise. One adventurer warns:

Guys, be aware that an experience with two women can be more stressful than pleasurable. The performance pressure is doubled. And there is a lot of distraction— usually a lot of giggling. It may leave you feeling frustrated, or even excluded yourself in some way. Women have a way of bonding—it can feel like ganging up!

And the female perspective?

I tend to find threesomes overly performative . . . exhibitionism and voyeurism underwrite the entire event. I think threesomes are one of those things that one should do in order to be able to say that it's been done—like running marathons and having children. You do it so you can scratch it off the list.

—Babe ("&" tattoo between her collarbones where a locket could be)

Bush Pilots, popular wisdom dictates that in the world of threesomes, the odd man out is love. Love is what is best left behind. The threesome is for the playfully unattached (fits my description, Mistress), for those who want to watch and be watched (copy); it is stumbled upon and not planned (same). But popular wisdom has led us astray before (e.g., Coldplay, Mistress? Gold Star, BP!).

Heed this Pilot's post-threesome state: "The great thing was, the next morning my girlfriend and I were more turned on to each other than we had been in weeks. We snuck off to the spare bedroom and fucked like dogs all morning." BPs, we invent our relationships as we live them, and maybe your relationship is the one with the space and lucidity to accommodate anything—or anyone.

The Threesome

WHAT SORT OF BED DO YOU NEED?

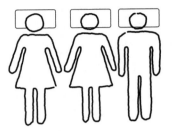

800 *recommended thread count for nice, delicate sheets*

standard North American bed widths

99 cm	*single/twin*
137 cm	*full/double*
152 cm	*queen*
193 cm	*king*

crazy European widths

210 cm	*emperor*
240 cm	*Caesar*

THE MORESOME

I'm an exhibitionist, so I'm fine with people watching me. Plus since I fuck for a long time and I'm often fucking very squirty ladies, that can attract a crowd. I was fucking a friend on what was a gynecologist's table. There were little stirrups for her ankles. Anyhoo, she was quite the prodigious ejaculator. I mean, like, she would squirt a good four feet. They brought out a mop and a bucket eventually.

—Captain Goodscrew

Bush Pilots, in the wide world of sex, the play party is its team sport. Whoa, Jim McKay. Seriously? Play party? Who has play parties anymore? Didn't they die off with sideburns, Corvettes and my uncle's checked pants? Didn't they die off with glam rock, mesh and utopian experiments? No, BPs, they didn't. So get your gear out of storage. Dust it off. Throw it on. The play party is still fair game. It has its own rules and its own rewards. It has its own star athletes. From suburbia to the Sunset Strip, sexual decathletes abound. Are they swingers with dentures who say things like, "Don't panic, you're organic"? No, darlings. They're your future babes. And they're team players. The question is: Are you?

PRETTY PLEASE WITH BRIDGET ON TOP?

First stop: orgy porn. Whoa, Mistress, why not just break that cumbersome fourth wall and start at the Playboy mansion? I could warm up with Holly, Bridget and Crystal. Before a fireplace. While an Alsatian keeps watch. And Hef grins from his leather divan at my adroitness. After all, Mistress, I was roundly chastened (read existential yard sale!) by your lecture on Porn School (bogus!) in the chapter on Rear Entry (heck yes!) and figured this would be my best educational tool, so to speak.

Touché, BP, touché. Reality check: In the exaggerated realm of fantasy (sucking on a Playmate's toes while another dangles her D-cup in your palm, while another rides your Randy "Macho Man" Savage—Shucks, Mistress.) porn is a useful prompter in answering: Do you want the play party to be fact or fiction? Do you want the busy experience of group sex, or do you instead want to submit yourself to surrealist Leonora Carrington's assertion, "Imagination will save you"?

ATHLETE OF THE YEAR

Bush Pilots, I present you with the 1972 classic *Behind the Green Door*, starring the babe who put the chic in porno chic, Marilyn Chambers.

Her first act: She drives a red convertible on a winding country road in a toque and leather coat. Her second: She drinks a beer solo on a hotel rooftop. Now this, Mistress, is foreplay.

N.B.B.P.: Not only does Marilyn Chambers look like Patty Hearst, but she gets kidnapped. Deal-Breaker Alert: This 1970s act of wearing masks and, with your Broseph who has a car, abducting a woman against her will is no longer cool. The same is true of the pre-show mime.

A soon-to-be-screwing audience, looking cast by John Waters, is ushered into a small theatre. Meanwhile, our "lovely child" is massaged by a nurse. Her body is real, in breast and bush. It has not been shaved, pumped and tanned. It has not been donated to porn-science. Gloria is brought out on stage, stroked and kissed by a posse of raven-haired women. Unlike the pina colada mix and coarse come-ons of present-day smut, the only script here is her moans. The music begins. What else, but a heavy bass line.

What else indeed, Mistress?

Enter: a man in white stretch pants with the crotch cut out, led by his Jimi Hendrix Experience, which we are sure he could play behind his back. He even wears a sabre-tooth necklace. BPs, Gloria never utters a word. I will take her cue, save to say that Marilyn Chambers is the ultimate orgiastic athlete. Her performance is so flawless you are reminded of who she was before this movie: the Ivory Snow mom, 99-and-44/100-percent pure.

THE HOST WITH THE MOST

Porn may placate your curiosity, sending it back to its cage. Or it may do the opposite. If so, here Bush Pilots are some guidelines for hosting a play party.

Bated breath here, Mistress, bated breath.

All right, BPs, hold on to your flight missions. First manoeuvre:

Draw up your guest list. According to one guru, "A play party is like a dinner party. Find the right mix of people." Start small. Yes, eventually, you can stage your play party for one hundred under a full moon on a downtown rooftop, but for now, invite eight to ten friends and, as one experienced BP says, "You want a private environment."

Observe the suggestion of even numbers. Also observe: The play party is a sexual happening, a planned event. It is not the jam band of the bedroom. It is not a Phish concert, only shorter.

> It is not about free-for-all sex with strangers, but respectful communication around sexual experience (from first BDSM experiences to play with familiar partners).
> —Babe (cue "Hot for Teacher")

RSVIP

One team player puts it this way:

> The parties I attended were very careful about including open-minded, positive people.

Not that they are not "open-minded and positive people," but in making your place cards for your play party, BP, I implore you: Stay away from clergy, professional acquaintances, neighbours, strangers, the goon on your hockey team, blood relatives, your in-laws and your ex. Recruit only those who have expressed an interest in attending a play party or have some level of experience in the scene.

CONDITIONS OF CONDUCT

Spell these out explicitly beforehand. One Bush Pilot provides this report from the field:

> Before the actual event, there's an email that goes out that is the riot act of acceptable behaviour at the party:

no aggression, always use protection, you're allowed to say no, etc.

But what, Mistress, oh what is this "acceptable behaviour" of which he speaks?

CHEAT SHEET: BUSH PILOT AS HOST

- ☞ Clothing is optional.
- ☞ Participation is optional.
- ☞ Safety is not.
- ☞ Drinking is allowed.
- ☞ Drunkenness is not.

Sticky Note: Participants must be capable of making coherent decisions—e.g., Yes, I want to screw you, and then you. And possibly you.

My Beeps (represent!), a few technical tips: Have extra bathrobes and throw pillows on hand. Have your guests arrive together. Thereafter, lock the door. If a guest leaves, they cannot come back. Which would really be their own fault, wouldn't it, Mistress? Gold star, BP!

ROOM SERVICE

One renowned host remarks, "Facilitating fantasy is like filling drinks." Bush Pilots, as you know from lifting your neighbour's antiques for the night to dress up your bachelor apartment, seduction begins the moment your guests step their stockinged feet through your door. Create the voluptuary's version of a funhouse. From the spare room with the black light, restraints, Korean massage stick and swing, to the candlelit bathroom with an ostrich feather, robe and sitar, to the master bedroom bedecked in *Eyes Wide Shut* chandeliers and play party–noir sequined masks, make for destinations.

How to Rock a Bathrobe

sunglasses (big)

turned-up collar

cigarette (unlit)

stolen from cool hotel in L.A. or Morocco

distracted and/or hip hop attitude

your man goblet

Throughout your lair, lay out a proliferation of the true player's combined comfort suite and security guard: lube and condoms. Bush Pilot Bonus: Consult Chapter 5 for what to lay out on your dining room table (other than yourself, of course).

SCREWING BY NUMBERS

I was terrified the first time I went to a play party. My background was straight white married guy, and so it was a bit of a shock to see BDSM and the pan-sexual free-for-all. By my third party I was pretty comfy with it. It's definitely a scene. Within the group there are twinky gay dudes, BDSM folk, hard-core lesbians, bi-dudes, transgender, plenty of bisexual ladies and a few straight dudes.
—Bush Pilot ("the Underwear Burglar," troubadour)

If you find a four-leaf clover and then receive an invitation to a play party (after you gamble and quintuple your bonus), go prepared. Captain Goodscrew, who, at a play party, tends to "fuck two to three ladies for a long time" (I can so relate, Mistress!) packs the following in his carry-on:

I have a little sex kit in a mic (microphone) case that has plenty of Crown & Beyond 7 condoms, a fuck rag (towel) and Liquid Silk lubricant. I usually wear a tank top and fancy CK (Calvin Klein) underpants. I bring a six-pack of Grolsch and some weed (an illegal narcotic).

N.B.B.P.: Observe what he does not pack. "It is best to not have a partner."

CHEAT SHEET: BUSH PILOT AS GUEST

☞ Know the conditions of conduct.
☞ Know your limits.
☞ Articulate them.
☞ Know that you can say no to anything except safety.
☞ Be conscientious about your own playing.

- ☞ Establish clear consent; insist the play be verbal.
- ☞ Stay sober.
- ☞ Know participants tend to pair off.
- ☞ Know it will not all be hardcore.
- ☞ Know that, for some Bush Pilots, sex cannot be abstracted from love.
- ☞ Know that, for some Bush Pilots, you may go as far as footsies.
- ☞ Know that, for some Bush Pilots, it is okay, just this once, to mistakenly walk home in women's pants (capris excepted).

Whether hosting a play party or playing in it, the essential element is a safe environment, one in which every player can pursue his or her pleasure, whatever form it may take (Perchance me, Mistress?). That said, you may be more enticed by the idea, preserved in the no-fault insurance of your cerebellum, than the actuality of group sex. However buffed, bodies are messy—especially given their vulnerable, nail-biter tenants.

Bush Pilots, I know, when you think "play party," you think: It's just me, the freighted-of-lip, wistful-of-eye BP, dapper but doomful in a dinner jacket with a bunch of strippers and a circus performer who, given how she bends, cannot possibly have a spine. With my virile melancholia, I will be the centre of attention. The babes will look at me and think, Screw me through your tears. And I will screw them. I will in fact be the only man there to screw them. And then, when I need a break, they will screw each other. And I will watch them and marvel at the fact that I am surrounded by hot, tanned, toned, expert screw-machines.

Sorry, Hansel.

Pilot error.

REPLY ALL

That is not how it goes. As one reality-struck player put it, "Play party sounds sexy" but in truth it's "you and a bunch of ordinary Joes you see on the subway every day." Another BP offers, "I would never hang out with these people if it weren't for the sex."

Fantasy involves a portal, a passing through, an initiation. Gloria goes behind the green door and comes out a voodoo child. Pinstripe Nick walks into the action and changes the rating of his slide show. And you? The play party can take place in the unparalleled bacchanalia of your brain—or for keeps, on an intimate's triple under-padded kilim carpet beneath glass lanterns, while three half-strangers watch from astride a camel saddle, stroking each others' thighs and nipples. What will it be, Bush Pilot? Sidelines or scrum?

CHAPTER 19
POWER PLAY

NOTE FROM THE FIELD:
I WAS MADE FOR LOVING YOU

Thwack. Sol is standing at the edge of the medieval banquet table he stole from a theme restaurant he used to work at. It is the only furniture in his apartment. His girlfriend, Charlotte, the front woman of a Kiss cover band, is bent over it, still in her makeup from a gig earlier that night. She is singing "I Was Made for Loving You" in her French accent. She is pantsless, her body a supple bracket bent over the hardwood as Sol's palm circles her ass. Thwack.

Twenty years earlier, Sol was a boy in Chicago making snow forts in his backyard. Between the ice-glazed lawn furniture, Sol built perfect igloos. Inside them, he imagined playmates, bashful but willing, tugging down their K-Way pants to reveal virgin bottoms. Sol imagined his palm and the echo of its clap as he spanked them. Sol imagined his playmates calling him sir.

On a winter afternoon, feeling especially sucker-punched by adulthood, Sol met Charlotte. They were in a bookstore. He had heavy eyeglass frames. She had a cheetah coat. He had a polyamorous lifestyle. She could shatter a glass with her high C. He was often in the back of a limousine, women's undergarments bursting from his pockets. She was often in the back of a limousine without undergarments. They talked. They giggled. They played peekaboo between the stacks. They made love under his parka. They got kicked out of the bookstore. They raced home to his place, up the long flight of stairs, past the birdcage, and, before unlocking the door, Sol said, "I would like to tie you to the pipes in my apartment and spank you." Charlotte replied, "I was just going to ask you to do that." And then, door creaking open, they looked at each other and, at the same time, said, "Finally."

PUT YOUR HANDS IN THE AIR

No, BPs, power play is not when Stu "The Grim Reaper" Grimson is in the penalty box and there are only four men on the ice. Oh Mistress, pick me! Pick me! And no, darlings, power play is not when Eddie Van Halen, shirtless and Cheshire, shreds it on "Eruption" with his tiny, tiny teeth. Good guesses. Power play is a different kind of talent. It is another word for that whispered set of letters BDSM (bondage and discipline, dominance and submission, sadism and masochism) and all of the erotic acts that lie, ready to pounce, between.

Gnar, Mistress.

IT WAS A DARK AND STORMY NIGHT

First, my gimps, let's attend to common misconception. The shackles-clamps-and-caning world of BDSM is not a room in a condemned building wherein the windows are tinfoiled and Marilyn Manson is salivating in a leather trench coat grumbling "slave" while dragging his snakeskin whip across the cement floor, as death metal plays through a loudspeaker. That is, unless you want it to be.

Second, whatever your shared fantasy, BP, before your babe throws on her tail harness and you break out the blindfold, your BDSM must be SSC (safe, sane and consensual). Consensual means "agreed upon without coercion." In other words, there is no taunting, no bullying, no steering. Peer pressure died with your last badly rolled joint, your last faint moustache, your last premature ejaculation (Don't look at me, Mistress!). You know your desires; your babe knows hers. You negotiate and set your limits together. There is no room here for miscommunication. Not to scare you, but by entering the after-hours amusement park that is BDSM as a dom or sub novice with a rock-hard question mark in your Pilot pants, you could seriously hurt someone you love— or yourself. On all fours. Fettered as if by an indulgent farmhand. In a gas mask. And kitten tail.

> It's when we're doing sexual things that we figure out what we want. Sometimes those discoveries can be freaky, which is why, psychologically, BDSM carries risks for folks without the resources or support they need.
> —Bush Pilot (Thelonious Monk in his headphones, *The Unbearable Lightness of Being* in his hand)

Third, you and your babe are, by entering the after-hours amusement park that is BDSM, enacting its safe approximation. I cannot emphasize the following enough: If you are careless or ill prepared, things can go very wrong. Working around major arteries and air passageways, there can be no shortcuts and no improvisation. This is not MacGyver. This is not Tool Time. This is uniquely skilled and detailed play. Please do not skimp on the quality of your equipment. Do not flout the rules of safety. And never leave your bound babe unattended. The BDSM world is not one you, sensual travellers, stumble upon, but one you blueprint, source and build together, whip by well-placed whip.

With that warning loudly sounded, we are going to focus our lens on what is commonly a Bush Pilot's first foray into the BDSM world, a simple, classic, yet deeply sexy act.

A GOOD SPANKING

Talk to the hand, Mistress. Schooling it, BP. We know how you love the sight of our full moons. We know how they make you howl. But do you know how to spank them? Yes, Mistress, oh yes, we do! Give us a chance! Hitting the skins is not the primitive whack of the schoolteacher. Nor is it the punishing swat of the circa-1962 parent. Nor is it the rambunctious, well-intentioned lunar landing of the beginner Bush Pilot. Instead, spanking rides that provocative fissure between pleasure and pain. There are sweet spots. There are rules. And there is range. For instance:

If you slap a hide high, Cowboy, you will get what you deserve: a bucking bronco.

Of course, BPs, your babe bent over your knee, you will be neither the cattle baron nor the chaw-spitting coot. You will be the conscious, sensuous sir—for only then will you convert your snow dome into your pleasure dome. Clear? Yes, Mistress, clear. Did I ask for an answer?

BEFORE HAND

Like any percussion, there is enormous latitude to spanking, from the in-the-moment hand yowl (Dealt it, felt it, Mistress) to a premeditated spank with toys and attendant role-play (Amped, Mistress!). Establish: Before you hoist your ping pong paddle, can your babe go home with red marks on her derriere? Can you? Spanking can bruise BPs, and be warned, if toys are involved, spanking can cause cuts and welts.

Set the stage. Does your babe want candles lit and the hard-on melancholy of Solomon Burke, or does she want you to put "Devil Inside" on repeat, pop open your hard suitcase and pull out a leather paddle while she inches her PVC mini dress up and bends over until her fingertips touch the floor?

> I wanted to do something with my lover at the time that was, well, adventurous. And I was bored with the usual stuff. Sometimes one wants to become something else, someone else.
> —Bush Pilot (painter, studio space in a friend's garage, steady leather-clad girlfriend)

What will it be, Bush Pilots: fact or fiction? Are you simply adding the new dynamic of domination-submission by dealing a spank to the kit while making love? Or are you speaking in a thick Russian accent, wearing a Biltmore and going by the name Igor? If so, settle on a loose script before show time; no one wants to be left stranded on stage.

Most important, always secure a safe word in advance; if the play proves to be too much, you or your babe can, upon the utterance of "Spandau Ballet," hit the gong. Forgive my highlighting of the obvious, Mistress, but why not simply say "stop"? Good question, my incorrigibles. This is the only time in your sexual play when you or your babe may speak those universal words for "quit it"—e.g., No, Don't—and not mean them.

Power play is an interesting refuge for us from the regular world. I work a stressful job where people's livelihoods are in my hands every day. Although I'm supposed to be tough, I am almost always called on to play "good cop" to male colleagues. I think that's part of why I usually take the dominant role. It's so refreshing to call the shots, give directions and ask for exactly what I want—and get it.

When I talk to my partner about power play, he says he enjoys giving up power. It's exciting for him to let everything go, and know that I'm in charge, and it's okay. And it's a delicious anxiety, not knowing exactly what will happen, but that he can trust me to check in and to be aware of his boundaries.

—Babe (descendant of courtesans)

Check in. Affirmative. Be aware. That's also an affirmative.

YOU'RE ASKING FOR IT

But Mistress, oh Mistress, you bite your bottom lip, how do I begin to tell my babe I want her dress up like my babysitter circa 1978 and drape herself over my bar stool humming "How Deep Is Your Love" while I spank her with her hairbrush? Or how do I tell her I want her to crawl around the house in small leather shoes with a leash in her mouth while I pat her bottom and she barks and whines and I call her "Lady" and then make her eat bacon from a bowl on the floor?

BPs, you must immediately gather up your shoulder-hunching shame, your cloistering belief system and your gnawing fear. Wrap them up in muslin. Dig a deep hole and bury them in your backyard. Make headstones for them, bring them flowers, talk to them, sing them traditional Irish songs, but get them out of your bedroom. Decide: My childhood is not a ghost but a sheet with holes cut out for eyes. It has no place here. The point: It will do nothing but stifle your desires. Point so taken, M. May I call you M? No.

> One of the most powerful lessons I learned about sexuality was that, sometimes, I needed to shake off my upbringing. There were times I needed to be rough, I needed to be in control. Not at my behest or wishing—at hers. It started, as these things so often do, with spanking.
> —Bush Pilot (gold dollar-store sunglasses, whistles in his sleep)

Before your babe can bare her behind, you must articulate what it is you want to experience.

In *Whipsmart: A Good Vibrations Guide to Beginning S/M for Couples*, poker-hot dominatrix Mistress Morgana reminds you:

You only deserve what you are able to ask for.

Um, okay, Mistress, this is between us, right? Right. I want to lick the mud off my babe's riding boots. And then bite her toenails. And be used as her footrest. And be blindfolded by her pantyhose. And trampled. And spanked. With her riding crop. While I neigh. Plaintively. Pony-like. But there is no way I will ever tell her that. No way. All right, BPs, at ease. Let's update Morgana's assertion: You deserve much more than what you are able to ask for; in truth, between the sheets, no one asks for nearly enough. How to make up the difference? If the thought of cataloguing your XXX-factor (Chapter 7. Rip it.) makes you quiver in your Pilot pants, why not let some erotica do your dirty work?

EXTRA CREDIT

HIT THE BOOKS

Spank Me: The Art of the Spirit. Boasting an elegant vintage aesthetic, this illustrated book offers up countless iconic spanking scenarios that can serve as your starter fluid.

Spanked: Red-Cheeked Erotica. Short stories anthologized by Rachel Kramer Bussel. Let their ink do your talking.

Taboo: Forbidden Fantasies For Couples. Edited by Violet Blue, this fiction collection goes far beyond spanking and can serve as fodder—or filler—for your more roving wishes.

Alternatively, BPs, find the work of American writer Mary Gaitskill of "Secretary" fame (from the book *Bad Behavior*) or rent the 2002 film of that name. It will, in a single sniffle, be perfect, nerdish company to your every errant desire.

COMING ATTRACTIONS

Your preview: Lithe masochist Lee Holloway, played by that Miranda July-esque "I am a fawn and I am filthy" slice of genius Maggie Gyllenhaal, makes spelling mistakes. Her boss, Mr. E. Edward Grey (played by James Spader in tones as hushed as commentary at Wimbledon) reprimands her scattered brain. He orders her into his office. Forehands and backhands ensue—and between them, could it be, a score of love-love? Bush Pilots, you will need: a law firm, a long hallway, a heavy oak desk, a typewriter, a red marker and one polka-dot blouse. For me, Mistress, or my babe? Only you can answer that, darling.

Or consider, and lift, this Bush Pilot's strategy: He and one of his playmates, within days of their first encounter, made a list of their fantasies, involving everything from a milk bath to a rubber whip, *Last Tango in Paris* to a chastity belt, a photo booth to a tickle fight with James Franco. I'm just saying. Deal-Maker Alert: With your babe, crawl under the covers, and with notepad and pencil in hand, make your own agenda for naughtiness; missions completed, scratch them off—one at a time.

I have said it before and I will say it again: The crucial point here is that, whatever your method of communication, you and your babe must have trust and transparency. It is only when your expectations are clear and your safe word ("Milli Vanilli") is settled that you can play with abandon—and accuracy.

> When I talk about spanking, I always say slapping. I haven't found the right word, maybe, because "slapping" sounds violent, but "spanking" sounds infantilizing to me. I think it might be difficult for people to try this, because it can feel really uncomfortable to hit someone, even when they are telling you it's okay.
>
> —Bush Pilot (rock climber, DJ)

AMAZING GRACE, HOW SWEET YOUR KIT

Bush Pilots, you have established your parameters for safety. You have set out consensual terms. You are ready for action. Pumped, Mistress. I know.

Choose your position. Will your babe be standing in her lace-up stiletto platform boots, bent over the kitchen table, or lying on your lap? Once you are both in place, warm up the kit. Pet and rub the kit. Respect the kit. Prepare the kit. Orbit before making your lunar landing. Stroke the area you are going to spank, moving slowly as zero gravity. Eventually, depending on your babe's preferences, perhaps even pinch and squeeze the kit. You may not be the one on your knees, but this, Bush Pilots, is your place of worship. Act with accordant reverence. Why?

NEUROTRANSMITTERS

Oh! Oh! Oh! Pick me, Mistress! No, BP, these are not tracking devices your babe's father keeps in your babe's shin. Good guess. Oh! Oh! Yes, this is a chemical release that occurs in her brain, allowing her to pull (not unlike most other waking moments) the pleasure from the pain. And yes, they peak just before she does. Gold star! One sub-agent of this process is that poor man's opiate, endorphins. Bush Pilots, appreciate: By making sure your knee-socked sweetheart is duly aroused, by enchanting all of her nerve endings, her endorphins will clamour together in a pain-relieving rush and she will find the satisfaction inside the sting (not to be confused with that shrimp-coloured bass player—the satisfaction inside that Sting will be decoded in Chapter 20). Deal-Breaker Alert: Do not drink and spank. Alcohol not only increases your willingness to "sing" William Shatner, it also separates your babe from her ability to gauge sensation and your ability to create it.

HIT YOUR MARK

Bush Pilots, do not go high, to the side or centre court. This can be especially painful for you as it puts pressure on your glitter twins. Instead:

Aim for the curve where the kit gives way to the thigh.

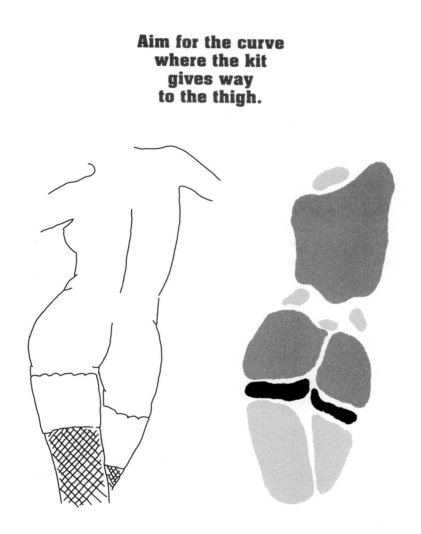

WHERE TO SPANK, WHERE NOT TO SPANK

Nope
Yes
Ideal

N.B.B.P.: Be precise. Be safe. Avoid the tailbone, the neck, the kidneys, the backs of the thighs and the backs of the knees. And please, Bjorn, while we still love your terry-cloth headband, no aces, no smashes and no grand slams. Also, begin with a predictable, metronome-like rhythm; your babe does not want to be startled by your sudden channelling of Neil Peart on "YYZ." And please: Stroke, tickle and rub her kit between spanks.

When your babe is ready and gives you the go-ahead, you may employ different pressures and props. Bush Pilots, be alert to one thing: her responses. Ask your playmate what she prefers—the bite of a wooden hairbrush or ruler, or the dullness produced by your heavy palm or paddle? If she is willing, diversify. Be conscious of your part; like any good percussionist, you are anchoring the band.

COOL IT

Remember, Bush Pilots, this kind of power play is not necessarily incremental, nor is it consistent. Every day will be different. One day, your babe may want tender; the next, she may want tough. As always, take her cue.

> Spanking is really intense. You generate an intense situation. It can get quite athletic.
> —Bush Pilot (leisure suit, soundproof bedroom)

What follows your workout? A cool-down. For her. Return to stroking and rubbing your babe's derriere. If needed, use Arnica gel, an anti-inflammatory homeopathic cream that can be applied topically to soothe any bruises.

DO YOUR HUMPWORK

My students, my captives, my playthings, there is only so much I can teach you. This book is about flying the bush, not about flying the flogger. If you and your babe are ready for a different kind of inter-stellar travel—i.e., one that includes riding crops, whips, straps and canes—before you gleefully break out your props, read *The Compleat Spanker* by Lady Green. Or, for a complete blow by blow, rent Zen Buddhist powerhouse *Nina Hartley's Guide to Spanking*. Remember *Boogie Nights*: the cuckolded, moustached everyman William H. Macy, woeful and suicidal, pacing while his wife, a hard-bodied bit of cruelty, humped every nearby hunk? That is Nina Hartley. With 650 dirty movies to her credit, she deserves a star—or three Xs—on the sidewalk in front of your house.

FLY ZONE

Re-entering the atmosphere: Of course, experience is the best educa-tion; the pro spanker allows himself to be the spankee. The top plays the bottom. I am playing the bottom, Mistress—my babe's bottom. No, darling. Remember Chapter 10? How could I forget it, Mistress? The clamps, the wax, the pearl necklace. Remember the term kines-thetic? I do. Wait, I don't. Bush Pilots, the best way to learn is to do it yourself. You mean get spanked, Mistress? I do, BP. No guts, no glory, Mistress? Bull's-eye, BP. Though perhaps this is not such a stretch for you. Perhaps this has been your fantasy all along: a wooden spoon at the flour-spattered kitchen table. Your babe in a see-through apron. An unlit cigarette dangling from her lipstick-ed mouth. Eyes painted like Sophia Loren in *The Millionairess*. Naughty. Naughty. Naughty boy.

DREAM SEQUENCE

To reiterate, by spanking your babe or by being spanked, you are not throwing your last penny into the weirdo wishing well. You are not, my red-blooded, bush-loving BPs, one step away from bee stings and man-nequins (unless of course, that's your thing). Whether you are dealing a hand or being dealt one, you are not deviant; you are merely soliciting your sexual charge differently than you did the night before and the night before that and the night before that.

> We'd always been open to trying different sex toys and different ways of doing things. When we negotiate it now, it's during the phase of foreplay where we're teasing each other and talking about what we feel like that particular day. We've moved away from assuming that sex means making out, then oral sex, and then vaginal penetration, and started to think more creatively about what we feel like in that moment.
> —Babe (coonskin cap, tenor guitar)

Moved away from assuming. Affirmative. Think more creatively. That's also an affirmative.

Sex begs to be in a state of constant reinvention. Will she wear the torn nylons, or the feather headdress? Will you rent a bungalow at the Chateau Marmont or sneak into a gazebo in the park? Will she play Sister Rosetta Tharpe or Slayer? Sheepskin or sandpaper? Butt plug or dildo? Catsuit or night nurse? Master or servant? Try her leg here, your thumb there. Harder. Softer. Slower. Faster.

With power play, you and your babe significantly up the ante. You examine and then ditch all of your inherent notions on how you make love. You undo patterns. You abandon recurring roles. This isn't simply an inversion of your late-night program; it is your chance to ask yourselves one simple question: What are we willing to do for pleasure?

Never forget to play, BPs. We all had our forts to dream in.

EXTRA CREDIT

PACKING FOR THE DUNGEON

We're not patient enough for rope bondage or some of the intricate and beautiful things that some people do. Our gear is pretty simple: a pair of nice padded handcuffs and some vinyl tape. Vinyl tape sticks only to itself—it's amazing.
—Babe (bombshell, cat named Umlaut)

So you and your babe are ready to play in the BDSM way? Here, Bush Pilots, is a list of eight items to put in your hard silver suitcases before you and your babe head, smothering smiles, into your pleasure chamber—be it damp basement with naked light bulb, burnt-orange bedroom with Victorian couch or motel in Havana with sweat stains and ceiling fan:

The Silver Suitcase

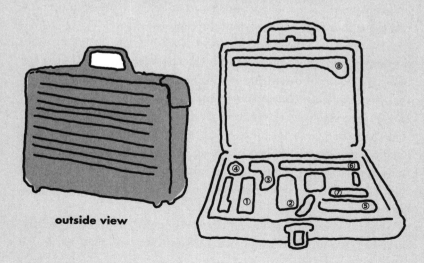

outside view

1. Bondage rope   2. Wrist cuffs   3. Blindfold   4. Collar   5. Harness   6. Feather tickler
7. Whip   8. Quiver crop

TO THE DUNGEON!

(Crack of whip!) Packed your silver suitcase? (Crack of whip!) Good. (Feather tickler.) So broke you are stealing bouquets for your babe from graveyards? (Crack of whip!) Do not despair, poor sod, I have some ideas for you too. (Feather tickler).

BONDAGE ROPE

Oh Mistress, Mistress, you won't believe it: I have some leftover twine in the tool shed! No, Bromeo. Your ropes must be soft and pliable—e.g., hemp. Reason: You do not want to chafe your babe's skin and thereby lose your passport to it. Usage: While rope can be traced slowly as tectonic shifts across your babe's breasts and butterfly, it can also be employed for "not-much-I-can-do-here-but-submit-to-your-transcendent-bushjob" binding.

Often when we think of bondage, we think of fettering her wrists and ankles. We think of shrinking her into submission. But you may also spread your babe's wealth, evoking that first foray into bondage, that oldie but goodie: your teenaged babe's wrists tied to your parent's brass bedposts. The same can be done to her ankles. Note: This position makes for your sub's extreme southern exposure.

Tie me up, tie me down, Mistress. Not so fast, Bush Pilot. Before beginning your rope course, consult the one offered by the Elmer the Safety Elephant of the BDSM world, Jay Wiseman. A perfect primer, the *Erotic Bondage Handbook*'s emphasis is on that one non-negotiable—you guessed it: your safety.

Thereafter, you may move on to the classic, *The Seductive Art of Japanese Bondage* by famed educatrix Fetish Diva Midori. The positions are decrypted through precise diagrams and instruction. Bush Pilot Bonus: Presto, boner. Doe-eyed bottoms are shot by charmed photographer Craig Morey.

Living on ramen noodles and grass clippings? Tempted as you are, do not do it yourself with a curtain sash, nylon stockings, tie or belt of the finest silk, velvet or leather, the long laces from your baskє shoes or her boxing boots. Deal-Breaker Alert: These materials tighten and become difficult to undo, risking nerve damage (indica᎐᎐ by tingling and numbing). Instead, use the braided nylon rope coiled in your garage (or, I know it pains you, but go to Ace Hardware) or the rope a bell-sleeved magician with the Cowardly Lion's hairdo would use in his magic tricks. If using for fettering rather than dragging, you, Doug Henning, will need between ten and twenty-five feet of it. Bush Pilot Bonus: Slip a pair of woollen mittens over your babe's hands so you both know she cannot untie your knots. Snowstorm optional. Safety not. Rule (namely, the two-finger rule): Be sure you can fit two of your fingers between your babe and the rope. No "This is a knot we'll never be able to undo, babe!" Instead, cheat that effect and tie a quick-release (Don't look at me, Mistress!) bowline.

TIE A HELPFUL KNOT
The Bowline

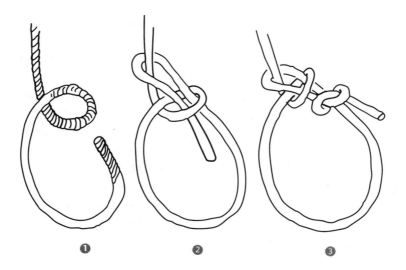

1   **2**   **3**

Also: Your blunt-edged bandage scissors (available at a drug or medical supply store) are close at hand—as are you. I said it at the beginning of this chapter and I will say it again: Never leave your bound babe unattended. Ropes are doubled to lessen the constriction. Lastly, nothing near the neck (other than the collars listed below), nose or mouth. Ever.

LEATHER WRIST CUFFS

Usage: Another prop that plays with restraint. Fasten these updated Wonder Woman cuffs together with buckles (or clasp) above your babe's head, behind her back or before her heavenly bush. Pro: These cuffs are easier to release than your knotted hemp rope, but will achieve the same "Not-much-I-can-do-here-but-submit-to-your-blazing-sexterity" wish for confinement. Con: None. Purpose:

Giving up control makes for giving into sensation.

Option: ankle cuffs. Best worn with black heels, scuffed soles, hardwood floors recovered from shipwrecks.

Thinking of selling one of your kidneys? Even if you are playing Jimmy McNulty, no metal cop-issue bracelets (these tighten and cut into the skin; they are also dependent on you not losing the key). Instead, return to the do-it-yourself bondage listed above.

N.B.B.P.: Always choose materials that will not burn or bite her skin.

LEATHER BLINDFOLD

Yes! I love a blindfold, Mistress, love it! Good news, my darlings, we do too. Why? Our most common fantasy (no offence) is screwing someone other than you. This blindfold makes it possible. Every time. In your babe's (temporarily blinded) eyes, you can be a sultan, a master, Marlon Brando, without having to change out of your hockey jersey. Sticky

Note: The blindfold can go on in conjunction with any of your other BDSM gear, but it is removed first, before the manacles and nipple clamps.

The effect: With your babe's sight hindered, her other senses will compensate, mobbing her nerve centres like moths to the light. BDSM plays with restraint (ropes and cuffs) and sensation; in this case,

Inhibition of one sense makes for the enhancement of others.

Storing your bar tips in a box under your bed? Anything adjustable you would wish to have against your eyelids can serve as a blindfold: namely, scarves and their smooth brethren, sashes and ties. Still in a bind? She can always grow her bangs Feist-like or wear your terry-cloth headband or bandanna.

LEATHER COLLAR

Usage: Dress-up. Classic BDSM fetish wear that spells, "S-U-B-M-I-S-S-I-V-E," this collar reminds you and your babe: Never underestimate the anticipation that can be created simply by dressing for the occasion. BPs, we all know how visual you are in your lust (wisp of a dress, microscopic underwear, cleavage). Stoke it—Already stoked, Mistress—with this collar that has the appearance of a space-age necklace fit for an Egyptian empress. It elongates your babe's neck and seduces your eye. Want to go further? For your "Sit, girl, here, girl" fantasy, find a leather version with a D-ring for a leash.

Submitting to science experiments for cash? Go Sex Pistols and fetch a studded dog collar. Or simply have your babe lightly wind a black ribbon around her neck until she looks like she just walked out of one of Henry Miller's *Tropic of Cancer* bordellos in Paris. N.B.B.P.: The two-finger rule is in play.

HARNESS

Usage: Dress-up. Effect: Giddy-up. Recalling the scorching Charlotte Rampling in 1974's *The Night Porter*, this leather fetish wear has the appearance of a holster or abbreviated suspenders. Here's how it works: Picture a U-shape in right angles. Belted just below your babe's bra level, the harness both frames her breasts and obscures her nipples—making you wonder, even though you might be the one holding the reins, who is the slave driver here. Just a guess, Mistress: not me.

Rather than reins, you may also "whoa" your babe and pull back with any of the binding devices listed above. Variations: The harness can be worn by your babe nude, with tuxedo pants, a cop hat or as leather lines of flirtation on top of a prim, high-collared white cotton dress. I'm just saying. Mascot for a fast-food chain? Your suspenders—or sauce—can achieve the same sculptural effect.

Sticky Note: Tempted as you both might be, no sugar near her sugar shack. The Pretty in Pink discount alternative: Your babe can make her own fetish confection by cutting strategic holes in her bra and mismatching panties.

FEATHER TICKLER

Usage: Sensation. Brush and graze it against your babe's bound and blindfolded skin. May I suggest (if it's not too much for you) starting with her inner thighs? Thereafter, tease her breasts, her bush, her neck, her hipbones and—your bottoming babe lying in an instructed starfish on your hard mattress—her kit. This bit of boudoir brightness is composed of whisper-thin ostrich and tougher turkey feathers. Unlucky birds, lucky Bush Pilots.

Permanent garage sale? Short of trapping a pigeon, approximate the sensation with a clean feather or set of feathers; a French maid feather duster will more than suffice. In fact, for sensory play, even your toothbrush will do.

LEATHER WHIP

Bush Pilots, you must be well versed in whipping safety before you come close to your babe with this thing. Prerequisite: Jay Wiseman's *SM 101: A Realistic Introduction*. An excellent resource for BDSM beginners, Wiseman's book takes you through the basics: communication, negotiation, safety and techniques for bondage and flogging.

N.B.B.P.: Whipping, like spanking, is rhythmic, incremental and not to be done against the tailbone, neck, kidneys, backs of thighs, knees or near any joints. In BDSM play, you are not cutting through the CAUTION tape, but pressing up against it. Also know that your willingness to play—and your babe's too—will shift with your emotional and physical weather. Deal-Maker Alert: Following the same principle as your safe word, employ the BDSM traffic-light code to keep your scene safe: "Red" means "stop"; "yellow" means "slow down"; "green" means "go." Just to be clear, Mistress, are these flags or T-shirts? Neither, BP. They are verbal commands.

Green light, Mistress.

Akin to the (coming soon!) quiver crop, the leather whip delivers an unexpectedly full range of sensation, from the heavy thud to the biting sting. It follows the same architectural blueprint as a cheerleader's pompom but is made of lithe strands of black leather—a knotted bulb between its nipping ends and its sure handle. Equine fantasy: The whip's tail-like shape evokes the stables of Catherine the Great—horse lover, reputedly. Her stallion, specifically.

Mowing lawns for beer money? See below for your alternatives to the quiver crop, but accept: Nothing in your domicile can substitute for an S/M whip.

QUIVER CROP

Usage: Spank. Spank. Spank. Spank. Spank. Tease. Repeat. A totem for your rough trade, BP, this prop so encapsulates the erotic experience, it should be hanging on the brick wall above your unmade bed. Nothing packs quite so raw a sting and so supple a softness as this leather crop with its flared, chicken-feather finish. Its name says it all.

Busking as a one-man band with an upturned sailor hat at your bare feet? A sting can safely be created by any slender cut of wood, from your drumstick to your chopstick. The feather chaser can come from the already-mentioned soft props of sensory play. Revisit your duster, and if you must, your pet peacock. Kidding.

Dog-walking? Bush Pilots, best for your budget, and for your bedroom, the following verbal bondage—for S/M starters—surpasses all.

Your words: "Hold still."

Priceless.

P.S. Now switch.

EXTRA CREDIT

A SELECT LEXICON OF FETISHES

Seven years into a casual-sex relationship, my part-time partner interrupted our regularly scheduled coitus with the announcement that she was going to have a breast reduction. My sexuality had always been based around a powerful fetish for a body type that she matched to a T, or more accurately, an impressive H. I had been completely focused on her chest all those years, and now I had to be creative and think outside of the bust. I started concentrating on her behind, which suddenly had a strong resemblance to her former front. Anal sex was already a part of our repertoire, but now it took on a deeper significance.

—Bush Pilot (most likely to call from the shower)

Because you want the correct term for your consuming obsession with your babe's high heels, her ballet bun and her wet suit. Because your babe loves the sound of a polysyllabic word other than amortization, interception or Astroturf coming out of your mouth. Because you know: In order to get what you want, you have to ask for it. BPs, I hereby give you two things: permission and a lexicon.

First, a fetish is when a "prop, body part, scene or scenario" usurps your babe as your love interest (your Easton hockey stick, winning poker hand and signed Jethro Tull poster do not count). The fetish, not your babe, is what you pursue. It is what tips you over into benediction. Your babe may wear it or possess it, but the fetish, like a spoiled, cartwheeling baroness, holds your attention and dominates your desires.

THE DOCTOR WILL SEE YOU NOW

The psychology is thus: A fetish is thought to be borne out of two sexual cycles: childhood and, more commonly, adolescence.

These formative time slots (one impossible to remember, the other impossible to forget) can provide unconscious training for the fetishist. BPs, you masturbate with a sable wrap (doraphilia) and want to be mounted by a Venus in furs? Could this desire originate in the childhood tradition of falling asleep in your mother's lap on the plush red upholstery of her ottoman? Or could it be from your first encounter with the neighbour's daughter, her lifted Laura Ashley dress, your dropped wool pants, your two eager bodies hell-bent—while your parents dined downstairs—under a pile of silver fox coats?

Heel, Bush Pilot!

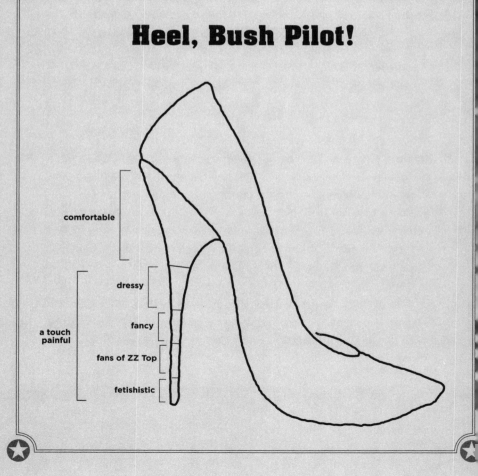

comfortable

dressy

a touch
painful

fancy

fans of ZZ Top

fetishistic

I LOVE YOUR LEDERHOSEN

The object can be inanimate: the smell and squelching sound of a rubber mackintosh raincoat against your babe's naked skin (rubberist); her silk (hyphephilia) underwear, the panties she sports while jogging (mysophilia), sent to you, priority, in the mail ; an ice-coated dress stepped into by your blue-lipped babe (psychrocism); her nine-inch stilettos (altocalciphilia) furiously pumping a gas pedal at a red light, spiking a birthday balloon, dangling precariously from flexed toes or lined up in your private, mirrored closet. I'm just saying.

I LOVE YOUR EYEBALLS

The object can also be a body part: her curved instep, her plump set of toes (podophilia), her tiny, raspberry-like breasts (mastofact), her ample, pocked buttocks, her strong, aquiline nose (nasophilia), her clean-shaven legs (crurofact), the fleshy bulk of her navel, the heavy swing of her hair. The fetishist's appetite will evolve from watching his babe wind her curls between her fingers to braid-cutting—as the name suggests, he mates his orgasm with her new haircut.

GET YOUR FREAK ON

BPs, the expression of desire is as peculiar as we are, whether the object is robots (androidism), blow-up dolls (Dames de Voyage), screwing the produce department (sitophilia), being bookended by pregnant (cyesolagnia) twins, bites (odaxelagnia), tears (dacryphilia), shoulder-length opera gloves, belly-dancing, a silver dog mask, a birch flogger, the tickle of a duster behind the ear, being baby-powdered by an obese and uniformed night nurse after she slowly wipes your bare buttocks, pinching and cooing all the while (autonepiophilia)—or, most unusual, the self-explanatory, John Money–termed, picket-fenced normophilia. Arrest those people.

FUNHOUSE

Yes, the world of fetishes—plushies and cat play, penny loafers and pie-throwing—may seem impenetrably strange to you, BP. But look at it this way: Like the eccentric in the room (Casanova, Sid Vicious, Baudelaire), a fetish possesses its own particular, if canted, truth. Example: You rescued a wooden ladder from your grandfather's barn and have not understood until now why you immediately propped it up against your bedroom wall to watch your babe climb it. And climb it (acrophilia). Fetishism is the ouzo version of desire; it is desire distilled. So, just when you want to wince and turn away, pause for a moment, retrieve your playfulness and curiosity, and swear you will never overlook where you might find your naughtiness—and, more important, where you might find your bliss.

CHAPTER 20
THE MULTI-ORGASMIC BUSH PILOT

RAIDERS OF A LOST ART

Ben loves his penis. He thinks it gallant and able. Sometimes, his girlfriend calls it "Big Ben." This pleases him to no end. Yet despite his girlfriend's pleasantries, she leaves him for Thailand—something about a "pilgrimage." Big Ben finds himself single and looking for love. While drinking a Stella in front of the Final Four, Ben reads an article in *Hello!* and finds out Sting is not only a rock god but can make love for an entire afternoon. Ben and Big Ben are instantly depressed. After shotgunning the rest of the case, feeling ashamed, listening to the *Rocky III* soundtrack, screaming "Eye of the Tiger" into the mirror, then almost sobering up, Ben enrols himself in a workshop called "The Multi-Orgasmic Man." He does not tell his roommates.

Years later, Ben stands at the peak of a snow-capped mountain wearing a loincloth. Women in sequins and slingbacks gather in the surrounding wood. They are breathless. It was a long walk from Ye Olde Cock Tavern. They whisper. They light smokes. They look for the bar. The rumour is Big Ben can drain a glass of red wine with his Winston. The rumour is he can retract his pool boys in a fight. The rumour is Big Ben has trained himself to survive the most gruelling combat of all: modern love. He has made a pilgrimage; now, they will too.

UM, WHO THE HELL IS THAT GUY?

My loverboys, my libertines, let me be the first to break the news. Let me be the first to tell you and your good-natured members: There is a new man in town. He is not tall or dark or handsome, neither a swarthy shipping magnate nor a billionaire athlete. Oh no. His skills are otherwise: secrets, old as seaweed, old as dirt, old as sex itself. They are the teachings of the ancient mystics that have travelled through time to transform an otherwise excitable southern hemisphere into a natural wonder, a combustion of accomplishment. His cape does not hang round his neck. No, it hangs round his wombat, and it reads MOBP. He is the tortoise 'tween the sheets; he is the new Wolverine. Meet the Iron Man of the bedroom. Meet the Multi-Orgasmic Bush Pilot.

You never know when he may appear, or in what form: the karaoke-crooning trucker, the toothless surfer or, most injuriously, your babe's last lover. The barbell in the bedroom has been raised—by a Slinky of remarkable staying power. And it's springing up everywhere. In the days of yore, a smooth talker with an excellent hairdo who outlasted the halftime show earned bragging rights. No more. Bush Pilots, drop your comb, drop your French class, drop your Pilot pants. It is time to turn your lightning bolt into an electrical storm. It is time to embrace the multi-orgasmic way.

THE OLD MAN AND THE BUSH

I am a multi-orgasmic male. That means I am capable of having orgasms without ejaculating. No popping means I have no agenda. I can have sex indefinitely.
—Captain Goodscrew

YOUR SUBSCRIPTION TO THE NEW PORKER

Before we proceed with your regimen, Bush Pilots, let us first clarify your flight mission: The MOBP comes—and comes again and again— without losing his wood between rounds. You scoff? Hush, young one. Observe. Let us go back three thousand years to the founding fathers of the Art of the Bedchamber. Let us then cross-correlate their techniques with those of your captain, Captain Goodscrew, who, when gripped by momentary shyness before entering a play party, tells himself:

Wait a minute. I look great naked and I fuck for three hours.

You shall soon understand the wisdom of their ways. Cue the pipa. Okay, cut the pipa.

LESSON ONE: EJACULATION VS. ORGASM

The Taoist Don Juans—and your ejaculatory babe—teach you, BPs, that orgasm and ejaculation are separate phenomena. They are physiological processes independent of each other. Translation: Just because you sneeze doesn't mean you have to fart. For Captain Goodscrew, this was a revelation. Here is how he stumbled across it:

> I attended several female ejaculation workshops, where I learned that ejaculation and orgasm were exclusive events. It's just that men are conditioned to experience both at once, and most women have lost touch with the ability to ejaculate. I realized that men and women share physiology, only men's bits are on the outside.

But what, Mistress, oh what does that mean for me and my studious, if exquisite, boner? Good question, BP! It means orgasm is good; in its contractile heaven, it is an energizing sensation. Ejaculation is bad; it is an expulsion of seminal fluid that serves as the pot brownie of the bedroom. Orgasm is an otherworldly set of pelvic pulsations accompanied by exclamatory cries of "yes," "mercy," "God," "I totally love you" and, finally, "I totally love me." By contrast, ejaculation starts as a neurological reflex in your spine and ends in a fishpond in your pants.

As soon as you pop, it's game over.

—Captain Goodscrew

Cue the theremin.

LESSON TWO: YOUR MORTAL ENEMY, THE MRP

Bush Pilots, once your swimmers are loosed, you are felled by that aggressive opiate known ominously as the male refractory period. In other words, you roll over and play dead. The MRP is the mortal enemy of the MOBP. Why? Meditate for a moment on that post-ejaculatory sleep. How deep. How dark. How so like the afterlife. Meditate now on the amount of energy you must have spent to fall into that black hole. What if you had, rather than plummeting into the void, diffused your dragon-like power?

Your Enemy

AND HERS TOO

The Taoist master and physician to the Yellow Emperor, Peng-tze, threatens you this way (flashlight pointing up toward his chin): After spilling his life force, a man "is thirsty and his limbs feel weak and stiff. In ejaculating, he enjoys a brief moment of sensation, but then suffers long hours of exhaustion."

The MOBP does not. The MOBP comes without expulsion. And so, the MOBP comes again. How to hold your fire, Serpico?

LESSON THREE:
DEEP (AND I MEAN DEEP) BREATHING

During sex, I try to time my breathing to my partner. Or at least be on the same page. Breathe really slowly. Time your breathing with your thrusting. There's a beautiful rhythm to a couple breathing and fucking. Music helps. Something without vocals or that is not distracting. Everyone fucked to Massive Attack back in the day. I like Ratatat.

—Captain Goodscrew

How to Breathe

TAKE CONTROL, GO DEEP, GO MYSTICAL

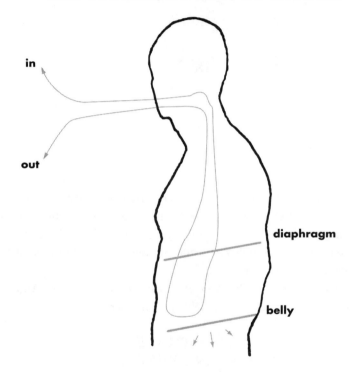

Bush Pilots, the MOBP huffs and puffs without blowing his house down. Breathing deeply slows your rocketing heart rate. Acting as a corporeal industrial fan, it circulates your mounting mojo—an essential step toward staving off your point of no return and expanding your orgasms. Rather than panting into your pecs, direct elongated breath to your diaphragm. Your inhalation makes new space for your pinwheeling sexual energy to go to. Your exhalation relaxes you—and your convivial sidekick.

N.B.B.P.: Breathe through your nose, please, as opposed to your mouth, Darth. Your nostrils act as filters, distilling, moistening and heating the air. Also, add a slight constriction to the back of the throat. Called ujjayi breathing by the yogis, the hissing sound will aid your focus, allowing you to stay in the present moment without having to recite Joe Montana stats.

> When I was younger, I would think about gross things like Vietnamese pot-bellied pigs to prevent orgasm. Now I just decide to ejaculate or not. I trained myself by doing breathy-jerky-offy exercises. I also had lovers who were interested in exploring female ejaculation and male multiple orgasm. It was like we switched traditional roles. They would squirt twenty or thirty times and I would have non-ejac orgasms twenty or thirty times.
> —Captain Goodscrew

Oh, twenty to thirty times, is that all, Mistress? Because after screwing for, like, eighteen hours, I usually come, like, ninety-four times and my babe squirts, like, eighty-six times, and then we levitate and glow in the dark and look a lot like unicorns. Cool your jets, BP. I can't, Mistress! I can't! I am not down with this whole twenty-to-thirty thing! Here, my Beeps (represent!), is the next step in your regimen . . .

LESSON FOUR: GET A WRISTBAND FOR YOUR JOHNSON

Locate your pubococcygeus muscle—your PC, or sex, muscle. When you're in the john, press pause on your pee-pee; alternately, enter your end zone with a well-lubricated finger and pull up on your pelvic hardware. You will feel a tightening around your finger and may experience this thought bubble: How did it come to this? Do not fret, BPs. You have found the brawn beneath your spring-loaded snake. Gold star!

Recall BPs, like your babe's, your PC muscle is not a single muscle but a muscle group. A sex-muscle group just waiting to be buffed in my stylish Pilot pants, Mistress? Correct, BP. Slung between your pubic bone and your tailbone, the PC muscles are why you have a flexing floor party every time you come. Yes, but Mistress, how does my stupendous man-strength add reverb to my orgasm?

As one recent MOBP convert says, "It is all about your plumbing." When you contract your PC muscles, you clamp the prostate gland; this, in turn, stops ejaculation. The advantage to this extracurricular activity: Unlike breaking out your barbell, you can boner-build anywhere, anytime. The world is your dojo. Please note: This is a no-hands activity. I.e., You can take your finger out of your bum. Repeat this exercise thirty to forty times a day. Start with two reps of ten, for five seconds each. With practice, increase your reps and hold slightly longer. If you are at all confused about this exercise, ask your toned lady friend for a demo. Code word: Kegel.

Your eventual goal (shimmering in a distant haze wherein January Jones stretches naked and purrs, "Come on, Bush Pilot, come here"): controlling ejaculation through contraction.

> Once I learned how to manage my ejaculation reflex, I was able to move subtle sexual energy in my body from explosion to implosion.
> —MOBP (guitar tech, adobe house in the desert)

LESSON FIVE: THE TAO OF WANKING

> I find I'm good for about forty-five minutes to an hour of penetrative sex before I need a breather—water, pee, rest.

It also helps recirculate my chi, which is all concentrated in my nether regions. Sometimes I'll do a bit of yoga to circulate that energy. Then back at it. I've done up to six sessions in a day. That's usually with a real pro lover or at a sex party and I'm trying to show off.

—Captain Goodscrew

Oh, forty-five minutes, is that all, Mistress? What a chump! And six sessions! Puh-lease! I'm on my seventeenth session today and I haven't taken a break for water or peeing or a rest—hah!—except to conduct a rousing yoga demonstration for a bunch of pros at a sex party they paid me to go to. Excuse me, Mistress, I have to start my next session. Number eighteen, hop on to my perma-boner! Don't mind the stiffness!

All right, my darlings, all right. Patience. Becoming an MOBP is a slow, step-by-step process. Now that you are rocking your deep breathing and your man-Kegels, you can add this exercise to your regimen; it will be unfamiliar to many of you, but I'm sure you'll get the hang of it. Jack on, jack off: Unfold your Perfect 10, grease your Gibson and get down to it.

LESSON SIX: HARD TO BEAT

The key: Be the watchdog over your own arousal. Monitor your breath, your pelvic muscles and your heart rate. Recognize the signs as you approach ejaculation, and practise "falling back" rather than forward.

Men tend to let the arousal dictate when ejaculation occurs, but as you become more and more comfortable in high states of arousal, and you couple that with the ability to move the sexual energy up instead of out, you can begin to have orgasms without ejaculation.

—MOBP (you'll find him at Le Crazy Horse)

Through masturbation, the MOBP becomes boner-vigilant, carefully surveying what the Taoists call the Four Attainments: lengthening, swelling, hardening, heat. My BPs, you want to stay between stages three and four, hardening and heat. What does this mean, Mistress, oh what does this mean? Not to boast, but how can I possibly be hard without being hot? Keep your kingly erection, but don't let your breath quicken, your muscles coil or your dukes of hazard come in for a group hug. You may have noticed that when your testicles crowd, you are ready for your credits to roll—just when your babe wants a second episode. The MOBP knows when to make pit stops on his way to the pleasure dome. He stays stiff by staying cool.

Whoa, Mistress, can you toss me that bass guitar? I'm feeling a little "Under Pressure." Roger that, BP. Relief is here. A friendly reminder: Your babe's pleasure is not solely dependent on your sprightly man-parts. Ergo, the rest of this book.

Phew.

Also, BP, becoming multi-orgasmic is a stop-and-go technique, hitting the red light ten to twenty seconds before it turns green. If you feel that tingling sensation just before you come, then come—and don't sweat your awesome sauce. One seasoned practitioner puts it this way:

> There's a point at which a man is going to ejaculate, no matter how much he concentrates and clamps and does whatever. Controlling your PC muscle you can control how close you get to that point of no return, but once you've crossed that line, you don't have brakes and shouldn't try.

LESSON SEVEN: DON'T THROW IN
THE KLEENEX

Bush Pilot, if it is taking your tackle time to be convinced of the difference between ecstasy and emissions, cut yourself some slack. You are undoing years of erotic hardwiring. That said, one MOBP travels back in time to remind you of life before sperm:

I got a *Sports Illustrated* Swimsuit Calendar in my Christmas stocking, and was understandably fascinated by it. I felt myself under this strange obligation to do tribute to each of the people in the calendar, and so would keep going after my initial orgasm until I had another.

Remember when you were eleven and alone in the TV room, on the brown corduroy couch, under the afghan, staring into the turquoise eyes of Heather Locklear as Officer Stacy on *T.J. Hooker*? You, pipsqueak, could achieve this seemingly Herculean feat. It was possible then, it is possible now.

One of the most exciting aspects has been the fact that sex does not end with his orgasm; we can continue to play and stimulate each other until he is completely spent, which can take quite some time.

—Babe (break-dancer, lives above a bowling alley)

LESSON EIGHT: THE BREAKING POINT VS. THE PRESSURE POINT

Grasshopper, you have practised your breathing. You are pretty sure you could snap a board with your penis. You have turned your PC muscle into a PC-muscle six-pack. While some dudes want to walk around with no shirt on, you want to walk around with no pants on. (Check this out, Matthew McConaughey. Eat my shorts. Oh wait. I'm not wearing any shorts.) You have masturbated yourself into a state of heightened arousal-awareness. Now, it's happening. You're in bed and she is a Grade-A smoke show.

Here are some consistently helpful tips and reminders to help you delay your crossing into climax.

Stop what you are doing. Now, return to Lesson Two. Stall your swimmers by lengthening your breath and visualizing your sexual energy move from your man-tropics into other, cooler parts of your body.

You need to stay relaxed (in an almost meditative state). The secret is to breathe deeply, move slowly and as you feel the sexual energy expanding in your groin, you sip it or suck it up your spine and spread it out and around your body.
—MOBP (rode his bicycle from London to Japan)

Return to Lesson Four. Call security. Contract your PC muscle group, bringing in the brawn to tame your unruly prostate.

Find your million-dollar point. Legend has it this acu-pressure point was either named for making the MOBP feel like a million dollars or for the fee a savvy Taoist master was paid to tell you its CLASSIFIED: TOP SECRET loca-tion. (You will find my banking information in the ap-pendix.) But because you're my Beeps (represent!), here goes: Also known among us grown-ups as your taint, it ain't your kit and it ain't your Klondike, it is that firm bit of flesh between. Not too close to your hair-dusted bum and not too close to your lovely balls, but midway, give that no-man's-land a firm Scout's honour. With three fin-gers across, press down as if taking its pulse. This will dam your waters—or, at the very least, delay their ap-proach. Deal-Breaker Alert: BPs, it is of utmost impor-tance that, through practice, you find the techniques that work for you. One MOBP says, "Every time I press my taint, I pop," whereas another BP puts it this (very achievable) way:

I was having sex with this girl and I had a full-body orgasm with nothing coming out. It blew my mind. I hallucinated. I started reading the books. I masturbated in horse stance. I even slept with ugly girls—like they suggested—to get my stamina up. I just couldn't get to that multi-orgasmic level. But the three-finger thing totally rocks my world. So I just do that.

P.S.: "Horse stance" is that attractive bowleggedness we assume when mounting our equine friends—and sometimes just our friends.
P.P.S.: Those Taoists, so mean about the ugly girls.
Our horsey BP's very sage conclusion:

I found something that works for me, so I don't need to go any further.

But if you do want to go further (and do naked calisthenics with January Jones) . . .

Press your tongue up against the back of your teeth.
Like your breath, this will circulate your energy.

Lift Captain Goodscrew's approach to penetration.
It's useful to know that the frenulum, or tip, of the penis is way more sensitive then the base. It's useful to penetrate very deeply. That means most of the pussy-to-cock friction is on the base of the penis.

MRP vs. MOBP

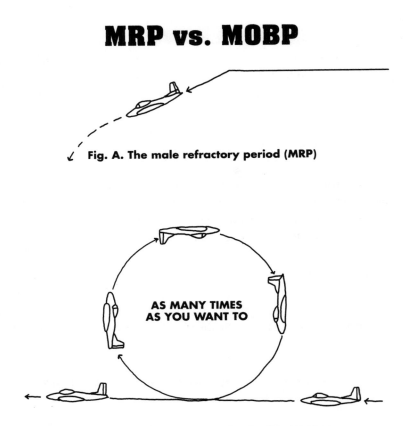

Fig. A. The male refractory period (MRP)

**AS MANY TIMES
AS YOU WANT TO**

Fig. B. The multi-orgasmic bush pilot (MOBP)

BUT WHAT OF PLEASURE?

Will my orgasms be as mind-blowing if I can't sign off on them, Mistress? Yes, my darlings. Here is one babe's eyewitness account of her MOBP:

> He throws his head around a lot when he's orgasming.
> It's quite spectacular and expressive and it's amazing to

watch, these waves of who knows what taking over his body. So we have to make sure that we're far enough away from the wall or any hanging lamps that he doesn't give himself a concussion. Who wants to worry about that when you're fucking someone who is going to be orgasming for twenty minutes straight? Not me.

According to the multi-orgasmic missionaries, your orgasms will not only be as good but better; evolving, through practice, into full-body orgasms.

Whereas before I could have one type of orgasm (sometimes great sometimes not), now I can have several orgasms over about an hour. Some of the most powerful orgasms of my life, and some that are more subtle. It certainly has changed the way I make love. I no longer have to worry about ejaculating too soon, or how good my one orgasm is going to be. In fact over 75 per cent of the time, I don't ejaculate, I try to peak as many times as possible (try to get to the point where I feel like I am having a continuous orgasm), and then I let my lover determine when we stop.

—MOBP (after "a lot of reading and a lot of practice")

Captain Goodscrew describes it this way:

When I do have a non-ejac orgasm, it's pretty obvious because I slow down a bit, my eyes do funny things and then I'll start back up again. It's more heady and releases some powerful endorphins. Once I get into orgasm mode and my cock is all contracting, I'm in another blissful universe. It's a place I can only get to with sex.

N.B.B.P.: While Captain Goodscrew pauses at the forty-five-minute mark, he is a veteran. My instruction to you: At your boner's twenty-minute mark, soften slightly. You don't want your babe to have to bring out the smelling salts.

BUT WHAT OF DEATH?

> When a man squanders his semen, he will be sick, and if he carelessly exhausts his semen, he will die. And for a man, this is the most important point to remember.
> —Sun Ssu-miao (T'ang Dynasty physician), *Priceless Recipe*

The Taoists argue that the non-ejaculatory way is the healthful way. Ejaculation exhausts the loving Bush Pilot, depleting his life energy. Because of its effect, the Taoists prescribe limitations to your emissions based on age, condition and even the season: e.g., the MOBP may ejaculate more in summer than in winter, and more on vacation than during times of stress. One MOBP comments on the frequency of his ejaculations:

> I'm pretty careful about when and how often. In the summers, or if I'm very active, it's more often: three to four times a week. The winters, three or four times a month. It's connected to my immune system and energy levels. I've noticed I can become lethargic and dull-witted if it's too often. Conversely, if it's not often enough, I will become irritable and obsessed with sex.

Whoa. Seriously, Mistress? Three to four times a month! Insane. Three to four times a week! Total death wish. What can I say? It's his "life."

Yes, I hear you, my darlings. It sounds extreme, perhaps even paranoid, but what I want you to take away from those spook Taoists and make your own is this:

SCREWTOPIA

Here, BPs—turn your boners way up—is a report from the field by a babe (narwhal tusk on her wall, nothing but Champagne in her fridge) who follows the multi-orgasmic way:

I think about the scripted sex of my early twenties, and it's like thinking of eating Kraft Dinner for the rest of my life. What I look for in a sex partner is the no-single-script part. The total variety of experience that is possible when you let go of the script. Not that there are no scripts at all, it is just that there is a plurality of them—some you find, some you make up.

Sometimes you find yourself on a path that your partner knows and likes, some new position that feels good that you hadn't thought up before, riding this rise and pause and rise and downshift of physical and sexual intensity in this open-ended way that's still focused and directed. It's about pleasure with another person, and that runs an incredibly wide range from kissing to watching them masturbate to good, old-fashioned pounding to, well, some interesting constellations of limbs and bits.

But the great thing about being a long-session gal and being with someone who is multiple, and the great thing about not just being hungry for that one moment of getting off together, that I think robs you of other kinds of pleasure, is that you get to play each other's bodies and arousal like an extended remix. It's more like going to a rave than saving the last dance.

Word.

Bush Pilots, to date, our sexual equation has amounted to a rocket launcher of a hump that lasts as long as recess and sends you and your babe both into orbit—for six seconds. She comes. You come. Good night.

We have been living in a state of sexual somnambulism too long, my sleeping beauties. It is time to wake up. Of all the ancient secrets of the East—yoga, Zen, miso—the best one is this one: the multi-orgasmic screw. Much in the way that fast food is losing, mouth by mouth, to slow food, fast love is losing, bush by bush, to slow love. Bush Pilots, do not be the last caveman. Kick off your animal hide. And see the light. And when I do, Mistress . . .

WILL I TOO BE CALLED STING?

No, my darling. But if you build it, there is a better chance she will come. And come again. We live in a world sinking in information about her Big O. But what about yours? Imagine if your one-hit wonder (I'm not saying you!) were a medley (I am saying you!), your bliss-sprint a marathon?

Replace your babe's cry of "Oh my God" with "Are you God?"

Bush Pilot, the slow draw is the sure fire. As the Taoist masters said three thousand years ago: Lay 'er down. Legends of the Screw, I know you have it in you.

Well done, my darlings, you have made it through Part Four: The Lay of the Land. Congratulations! May we please get loaded now, Commander Mistress? No. Though you may sew the following four badges onto the crotch of your Pilot pants: the I Once Outran a Police Officer badge, the I'm a Team Player and I Like to Party badge, the This Spanker Is Going Pro badge, the I Have Been to Screwtopia badge.

One last test. So ready, Mistress. Bring it. Consider it brought.

PART FIVE
(Your Wings)
Graduation

FLIGHT MISSION:
BUSH PILOTS,
AFFIX YOUR WINGS TO YOUR
HEADBOARD, NOT TO YOUR HEADLINER—
THOUGH SHE WILL BE LOOKING FOR THEM
IN BOTH LOCATIONS.

YOUR FINAL EXAM

Bush Pilots, bedroom eyes on your desks, five minutes on the clock. You must score a perfect twenty points to proceed (to your lap dance with Rollergirl in the Champagne room). Here we go. Multiple (orgasms!) choice:

1. Which bowl does your team most want to win?
    A. Rose Bowl
    B. Sugar Bowl
    C. Cotton Bowl
    D. Bush Bowl

2. Spot the porn within the Metallica.
    A. "No Leaf Clover"
    B. "Harvester of Sorrow"
    C. "Welcome Home (Sanitarium)"
    D. "Cum on My Tattoo"

3. You are sharing a taxi home on your first date. You:
    A. make eyes at the driver.
    B. put a beer sleeve on your boner.
    C. discuss the genius of nu metal.
    D. pay the fare and invite her up to your rooftop for a single-malt Scotch and a Cuban cigar.

4. The Bush Pilot will find the most nerve endings in his babe's:
    A. eyelashes.
    B. roommate.
    C. go-go.
    D. really sensitive mouth on his boner.

5. The G-string is:
    A. lingerie.
    B. what comes after the F-string.
    C. what Kenny G calls his man parts.
    D. what you pull on to light up the G-spot.

6. An appropriate nickname for your babe's go-go is:
    A. mini-me.
    B. C-Rod.
    C. flock of seagull.
    D. none of the above.

7. The two cardinal rules of anal play are:
    A. Rush her kit, then split!
    B. Lube up. Slow down.
    C. Tap on it, then run, shouting, "Turtle!"
    D. Lube down. Slow up.

8. Which of the following must you and your babe decide on before your S&M session?
   A. Your Thunderdome theme
   B. Your safe word
   C. Your life insurance policy
   D. Humiliation and suffering

9. Kegels are:
   A. German for tablets.
   B. for ladies only.
   C. a total hoax.
   D. strengthening exercises so you can lay down the drum solo from "Moby Dick" with the flexing musculature of your man parts.

10. When flirting, the following is of utmost importance:
    A. Your Clint Eastwood–like body language
    B. Staring at her breasts without blinking
    C. Exposing your chest tuft and pubic tuft in one clever outfit
    D. Being able to lick your lips and unzip your Pilot pants at the same time

11. Bush Pilots, open your survival kits. Which of the following items is most important?
    A. Your condoms
    B. Your condoms
    C. Your condoms
    D. Your condoms

12. Which of the following best describes you, Bush Pilot, during a threesome?
    A. You call your babe "Vibe Killer"—but considerately, like in a stage whisper.
    B. With your babe, you agree on a safe word and boundaries beforehand and you follow the plan accordingly.
    C. You "accidentally" lock your babe in the bathroom and hump the other woman quietly out of respect and loyalty.
    D. You give the women equal attention, repeatedly crying, "Check me out!"

13. Spot the porn among the kung fu.
    A. *Dance of the Drunk Mantis*
    B. *Yes, Madam 5*
    C. *Lady Whirlwind*
    D. *Fists of Fury*

14. Your babe tells you she wants to ejaculate. You:
    A. display your innate sportsmanship and challenge her to a shooting contest.
    B. bring her to orgasm and then stimulate her urethral sponge with toys and fingers.
    C. gamely put on your rain poncho.
    D. tell her it's physiologically impossible and then make a sound like *fhhf*.

15. Your babe loves the soixante-neuf and you don't. You:
    A. show off your communication skills and make a legible sign reading BLOWJOB OR BUST.
    B. ask (in a Welsh accent) if you can take turns.
    C. submit and whisper "sacrifice" throughout.
    D. rage at your "ineptitude" and quote *Hamlet* from inside the kitchen cupboard.

16. Your babe buys the Hitachi Magic Wand and comes for the first time. You say:
    A. "Fhhf."
    B. "Traitor."
    C. "Finally."
    D. "Let's get some attachments" (in a Welsh accent).

17. Your babe wants you to talk dirty. You:
    A. swear on a continuous loop, but you are pretty sure it evokes Ginsberg's "Howl."
    B. quickly catalogue her library and habits of speech as a starting point.
    C. too shy, pull out your own tattered copy of *American Psycho*.
    D. understanding the wily ruse in her request, simply repeat, "Talk dirty."

18. Your babe confesses her most bizarre fantasy. You:
    A. worriedly call her parents, her elementary school principal, her boss and then the police.
    B. secure an elephant, a dictator and a Neapolitan ice cream cone.
    C. give her the silent treatment for weirdness.
    D. confess yours (in a Welsh accent).

19. The libido is:
    A. a Swiss circus troupe.
    B. a maker of dirigibles.
    C. the name of David Lee Roth's yacht.
    D. a fancy word for your babe's desire.

20. You invite your babe over for an aphrodisiacal feast. You:
    A. slay a rabbit before her stunned eyes.
    B. present your boner on a plate with a little sprig of parsley.
    C. play Creed, calling it "food for the soul."
    D. clean up, serve oysters and screw indefinitely.

21. Bonus question: What is the only thing you cannot give your babe?
    A. A respite from your ability to fart on command
    B. "Ew" in your camo pants-shorts and mock turtleneck, memorizing Coldplay's "Vi-jh-va La Vi-jh-da"
    C. Self-awareness
    D. Props

YOUR REFERENCE LETTER

To Whosever Bush It May Concern,

This letter confirms your prospective Bush Pilot completed the intensive *How to Be a Bush Pilot: A Field Guide to Getting Luckier* training course and graduated with his wings.

As his chief instructor, it was my privilege to observe your prospective Bush Pilot's competency evolve markedly over the course of his training regimen. With study and practice, he parlayed his passable lay—the very common Woodpecker—into the very uncommon Indefinite. In his study groups, he proved in his interactions with others to be an effective communicator, demonstrating leadership and flexibility in his ability to both take and give direction.

During his innumerable test flights, your prospective Bush Pilot executed his aerial manoeuvres with precision, energy, innovation, competence and an exceptional commitment to his craft. Displaying remarkable interpersonal skills, he was always keen to attune his craft to higher performance in lower altitudes.

He was awarded MVBP (Most Valuable Bush Pilot) and presented with both the Condom in the Dark and the Seventeen Times in a Really Nice Hotel Room badges. A final attribute worth mentioning: Upon graduation, your prospective Bush Pilot could sing Boston's "More than a Feeling." Note perfectly.

Should you require any further information, please do not hesitate to contact me.

Regards,

Commander Mistress

COMMENCEMENT

Bush Pilots,

Unlace your combat boots, drop your flight suits and get yourself a glass.

Congratulations. You made it. You didn't think you would. So many nights of locking yourself in your bathroom with your babe's schnapps and crème de cacao, crimping your hair and quietly singing Nazareth's "Love Hurts."

Of course, we never doubted you.

You studied and sweated and dared yourself. You accepted that jerky is not an aphrodisiac and that the woodpecker is an idiot bird. You farted elsewhere. You stopped soaking your shirts in Drakkar Noir. You memorized the fifteen thousand nerve endings in your babe's lady parts. You gave them their due. You did push-ups with your tongue and pull-ups with your fingers. You talked dirty to your swimsuit issue until you were hoarse. You recognized that the G-spot is not an emcee, the kit is not to be surprise-mounted and sex toys are not for inferior dorks. You came to understand that a moan is just a moan. You reassessed your package. You stopped calling him Simple

Jack. You trained him. He took over your weight closet. He pumped. He flexed. He conditioned.

You evolved from a man with a few patented moves—the Mechanical Bull, the Steve Holt! and Holding Out for a Hero—into a man with unparalleled technique. Your sexual willingness became your sexual prowess. Your medieval sword: a light sabre. Your name is written in lipstick across bathroom walls, tattooed to backsides and held hushed on the ends of tongues. Leonard Cohen pictures you when he meditates. So does Jenna Jameson. So does your babe. You have more sex. You have better sex. You have epic sex. You are a certified Bush Pilot.

But sometimes, just for old times' sake, you serve us beef jerky, frozen peas and Five Star for dinner. In camping pots. And then you put on *Led Zeppelin IV*. And then you sing the wrong words to "When the Levee Breaks" while doing a really slow head bang. It gets to us. We fool around in your sleeping bag. It goes well—so well you get to try out your new, patented move: the Ace. Just this morning, you drew the steps and mailed them to yourself to copyright them. Phew.

We knew you had it in you.

Somewhere.

Bush Pilots, for now and always, I salute you and I say:

We love you. We really do.

May you find blue skies above your head.

And may the Bush be with you.

YOUR WINGS

(you've earned them)

ENDNOTES AND BONUS TRACKS

(BECAUSE, LET'S FACE IT: WE JUST CAN'T SAY GOODBYE)

PART ONE: UNDERSTANDING THE INSTRUMENTS

CHAPTER 1: THE LADY PARTS

The Federation of Feminist Women's Health Centers, *A New View of a Woman's Body: A Fully Illustrated Guide* (West Hollywood, Calif.: Feminist Health Press, 1991), in Rebecca Chalker, *The Clitoral Truth: The Secret World at Your Fingertips* (New York: Seven Stories Press, 2003), p. 96.

Natalie Angier, *Woman: An Intimate Geography* (Boston: Houghton Mifflin, 1999), p. 63.

Ian Kerner, *She Comes First: The Thinking Man's Guide to Pleasuring a Woman* (New York: ReganBooks, 2004), p. 51.

Alice Kahn Ladas, John D. Perry and Beverly Whipple, *The G-spot and Other Discoveries About Human Sexuality* (New York: Henry Holt, 2005), p. 88.

Cathy Winks and Anne Semans, *The Good Vibrations Guide to Sex* (San Francisco: Cleis Press, 2002), p. 19.

Betty Dodson, "In Bed with Dodson and Ross, Part 1," episode 19 of *On the Minds of Men: Uncensored Sex Talk with Dr. Lori Buckley* (http://personallifemedia.com/podcasts/218-on-the-minds-of-men#ep19).

Martin Portner, "The Orgasmic Mind," *Scientific American Mind*, April 2008, p. 27.

Norman Doidge, *The Brain That Changes Itself: Stories of Personal Triumph from the Frontiers of Brain Science* (New York: Viking, 2007), p. 97.

Marta Helliesen, facilitator of Brain Sex workshop at Good for Her, personal correspondence with author.

CHAPTER 2: THE MAN PARTS

K. Winston Caine, Perry Garfinkel, and the Editors of *Men's Health* Books, *The Male Body: An Owner's Manual: The Ultimate Head-to-Toe Guide to Staying Healthy and Fit for Life* (Emmaus, Pa.: Rodale, 1996), p. 258.

Winks and Semans, *The Good Vibrations Guide to Sex*, p. 172.

"The World's Biggest Penis," episode 3 of *Penis Envy* (Channel 4 [U.K.], February 1, 2006).

Mary O'Connell, "Phallus in Wonderland," *Ideas* (CBC Radio One, August 6 and August 13, 2007).

Dr. Robert H. Stubbs, personal correspondence with author.

Dr. Robert H. Stubbs, "Penis Lengthening: A Retrospective Review of 300 Consecutive Cases," *Canadian Journal of Plastic Surgery*, Summer 1997, pp. 93–100.

CHAPTER 3: TOOLS OF THE TRADE

Sears, Roebuck and Company catalogue, 1918, in Rachel P. Maines, *The Technology of Orgasm: "Hysteria," the Vibrator and Women's Sexual Satisfaction* (Baltimore: Johns Hopkins University Press, 2001), p. 19.

Nina E. Lerman, Ruth Oldenziel and Arwen Mohun, eds., *Gender and Technology: A Reader* (Baltimore: Johns Hopkins University Press, 2003), p. 110.

Natalie Angier, "In the History of Gynecology, a Surprising Chapter," *New York Times*, February 23, 1999.

Tristan Taormino's Expert Guide to the G-Spot, DVD, directed by Tristan Taormino (Los Angeles: Vivid-Ed, 2008).

Michael Castleman, author of, among other books, *Great Sex: A Man's Guide to the Secret Principles of Total-Body Sex* (Emmaus, Pa.: Rodale, 2008), personal correspondence with author.

Michael Castleman, "Sex Toy Story" (http://www.mcastleman.com/page3/page40/page25/page25.html).

Vern Bullough, "The Condom," in Russ Kick, ed., *Everything You Know About Sex Is Wrong: The Disinformation Guide to the Extremes of Human Sexuality (and Everything in Between)* (New York: Disinformation Company, 2005), p. 291.

PART TWO: TURN ON

CHAPTER 4: FLIRTATION

Diane Ackerman, *A Natural History of Love* (New York: Random House, 1994), p. 262.

CoCo La Crème, facilitator of Flirtation 101 workshop at Good for Her, personal correspondence with author.

Social Issues Research Guide, "SIRC Guide to Flirting" (www.sirc.org/publik/flirt.html).

Nicole Krauss, *The History of Love: A Novel* (New York: W. W. Norton, 2005), pp. 72–74.

CHAPTER 5: APHRODISIACS

Isabelle Allende, *Aphrodite: A Memoir of the Senses* (New York: HarperFlamingo, 1998), p. 131.

Allende, *Aphrodite*, p. 130.

Andrew Dalby, *Food in the Ancient World from A to Z* (New York: Routledge, 2003). p. 128.

Diane Ackerman, *A Natural History of the Senses* (New York: Random House, 1990), p. 169–171.

Emma Moore, "Top-Shelf Treats," *Wallpaper*, July 2009.

JoAnn Baker, Erica Orloff, *Dirty Little Secrets: True Tales and Twisted Trivia About Sex* (New York: St. Martin's Griffin, 2001), p. 76.

Theresa Crenshaw, *The Alchemy of Love and Lust: How Our Sex Hormones Influence Our Relationships* (New York: Pocket Books, 1997), p. 55.

Chris Kilham, *Hot Plants: Nature's Proven Sex Boosters for Men and Women* (New York: St. Martin's Griffin, 2004), p. 184.

Patrick Faas, *Around the Roman Table* (Chicago: University of Chicago Press, 2005), p. 68.

Adam Goodheart, historian and travel essayist, Washington College, personal correspondence with author.

CHAPTER 6: FANTASY

Nancy Friday, *My Secret Garden: Women's Sexual Fantasies* (New York: Pocket Books, 2008), p. 100.

Anne Carson, *Eros the Bittersweet* (Normal, Ill.: Dalkey Archive Press, 1998), p. 10.

Daniel Goleman, "New View of Fantasy: Much Is Found Perverse," *New York Times*, May 7, 1991.

Valerie Steele, *Fetish: Fashion, Sex and Power* (New York: Oxford University Press, 1996), p. 58.

CHAPTER 7: TALKING DIRTY

Vladimir Nabokov, *Lolita* (New York: Vintage Books, 1955), pp. 314–15.

Henry Miller, *Tropic of Cancer* (New York: Grove Press, 1961), pp. 248–58.

Philip Roth, *Sabbath's Theater* (Boston: Houghton Mifflin, 1995), pp. 215–35.

Nicholson Baker, *Vox* (New York: Vintage Books, 1992).

John Updike, *Couples* (New York: Knopf, 1968), pp. 134–37, 255–59, 311–14, 402–9.

Anaïs Nin, *Henry and June* (San Diego: Harcourt Brace Jovanovich, 1986), pp. 152–54.

Russell Smith, *Diana: A Diary in the Second Person* (Emeryville, Ont.: Biblioasis, 2008).

Marguerite Duras, *The Lover* (New York: HarperPerennial, 1992), pp. 37–41.

Cormac McCarthy, *All the Pretty Horses* (New York: Vintage Books, 1992), p. 142.

Michael Ondaatje, *The Collected Works of Billy the Kid* (Toronto: Anansi, 1970), p. 16.

Pauline Réage, *The Story of O* (New York: Blue Moon Books, 1993), pp. 3–52.

Marian Engel, *Bear* (Toronto: McClelland & Stewart, 1976), p. 93.

Leonard Cohen, *The Spice-box of Earth* (Toronto: McClelland & Stewart, 1961).

e. e. cummings, *100 Selected Poems* (New York: Grove Press, 1959).

Daniel Defoe, *Moll Flanders* (New York: Modern Library, 2002).

Ernest Hemingway, *For Whom the Bell Tolls* (New York: Scribner, 1940).

Anne Sexton, *Selected Poems of Anne Sexton* (Boston: Houghton Mifflin, 1988).

Ariel Bloch and Chana Bloch, trans., *The Song of Songs: A New Translation* (Berkeley, Calif.: University of California Press, 1998).

Mötley Crüe with Neil Strauss, *The Dirt: Confessions of the World's Most Notorious Rock Band* (New York: HarperCollins, 2002), pp. 51, 113–16, 146, 238, 344–47.

PART THREE: TAKEOFF

CHAPTER 8: THE BIG O (HERS)

Website of the Kinsey Institute for Research in Sex, Gender and Reproduction (http://www.kinseyinstitute.org).

Dennis Coon and John O. Mitterer, *Introduction to Psychology: Gateways to Mind and Behavior*, 12th ed. (Belmont, Calif.: Wadsworth, Cengage Learning, 2008), p. 371.

Claudia Dey, "The Hard Truth: Kim Cattrall, the Notorious Sex Fiend of the Small Screen, Dishes on What She Really Looks for in a Man," *Toro* Magazine, October 2005.

Dr. Meredith Chivers, personal correspondence with author, June 17, and November 16, 2009.

Daniel Bergner, "What Do Women Want?" *New York Times*, January 25, 2009.

Jenna Jameson with Neil Strauss, *How to Make Love Like a Porn Star: A Cautionary Tale* (New York: ReganBooks, 2004), pp. 262–63.

Mantak and Maneewan Chia, *Healing Love Through the Tao: Cultivating Female Sexual Energy* (Huntington, N.Y.: Healing Tao Books, 1986), p. 41.

Timothy Leary, *Turn On, Tune In, Drop Out* (Berkeley, Calif.: Ronin, 1999).

Angier, *Woman: An Intimate Geography*, p. 278

Winks and Semans, *The Good Vibrations Guide to Sex*, p. 30.

William H. Masters and Virginia Johnson, *Human Sexual Response* (Boston: Little, Brown, 1966), p. 78.

Helen Singer Kaplan, *The New Sex Therapy: Active Treatment of Sexual Dysfunctions* (New York: Brunner/Mazel, 1974).

Winks and Semans, *The Good Vibrations Guide to Sex*, p. 31.

CHAPTER 9: LOCK LIPS (FIRST BASE)

Ackerman, *A Natural History of Love*, p. 251.

Chip Walter, "Affairs of the Lips: Why We Kiss," *Scientific American Mind*, February 2008.

CHAPTER 10: HANDS UP (SECOND BASE)

Angier, *Woman: An Intimate Geography*, p.75.

Paul Joannides, *The Guide to Getting It On!: America's Coolest and Most Informative Book About Sex for Adults of All Ages* (Waldport, Ore.: Goofy Foot Press, 6th edition, 2009), p. 224.

The Black Glove/The Elegant Spanking, DVD, directed by Maria Beatty (1995 and 1997, New York: Bleu Productions, 2003).

CHAPTER 11: HANDS DOWN (THIRD BASE)

Chalker, *The Clitoral Truth*, p. 54

Fire in the Valley: An Intimate Guide to Female Genital Massage, DVD, directed by Joseph Kramer (Oakland, Calif.: The New School of Erotic Touch, 2004).

The Best of Vulva Massage: An Anthology of Erotic Touch, DVD, directed by Joseph Kramer (Oakland, Calif.: The New School of Erotic Touch, 2009).

Chalker, *The Clitoral Truth*, pp. 67–69.

Justine Dawson, teacher of Orgasmic Meditation at One Taste San Francisco, personal correspondence with author, December 2, 2009.

Denyse Beaulieu, *Sex Game Book: A Cultural History of Sexuality* (New York: Assouline, 2006), p. 145

CHAPTER 12: CUNNILINGUS

Kerner, *She Comes First*, p. 94.

Tristan Taormino's Expert Guide to Oral Sex, Part 1: Cunnilingus, DVD, directed by Tristan Taormino (Los Angeles: Vivid-Ed, 2007).

Violet Blue, *The Ultimate Guide to Cunnilingus: How to Go Down on a Woman and Give Her Exquisite Pleasure* (San Francisco: Cleis Press, 2002), p. 121.

CHAPTER 14: THE G-SPOT

Betty Dodson, *Orgasms for Two: The Joy of Partnersex* (New York: Harmony Books, 2002), p. 82.

Deborah Sundahl. *Female Ejaculation and the G-Spot: Not Your Mother's Orgasm Book!* (Alameda, Calif.: Hunter House, 2003), p. 189.

Cathy Winks, *The Good Vibrations Guide: The G-Spot* (San Francisco: Down There Press, 1998), p. 47.

Nice Girls Don't Do It, film, directed by Kathy Daymond, 1990.

CHAPTER 15: POSITIONS

Sheri Winston, *Women's Anatomy of Arousal: Secret Maps to Buried Pleasure* (Kingston, N.Y.: Mango Garden Press, 2009), pp. 259–62.

Lou Paget, *How to Be a Great Lover: Girlfriend-to-Girlfriend Totally Explicit Techniques that Will Blow His Mind* (New York: Broadway Books, 1999), p. 179.

Ancient Secrets of the Kama Sutra: The Classic Art of Lovemaking, DVD, directed by Brad Armstrong (Los Angeles: Vivid Entertainment, 1997).

Annie Sprinkle's Amazing World of Orgasm, DVD, directed by Annie Sprinkle and Sheila Malone (Oakland, Calif.: Ero Spirit, 2007).

CHAPTER 16: REAR ENTRY

Sadie Allison, *Toygasms!: The Insider's Guide to Sex Toys and Techniques* (San Francisco: Tickle Kitty Press, 2003), p. 52.

Joani Blank with Ann Whidden, *Good Vibrations: The New Complete Guide to Vibrators* (San Francisco: Down There Press, 2000), p. 37.

Jean-Luc Henniq, *The Rear View: A Brief and Elegant History of Bottoms Through the Ages* (London: Souvenir Press, 1995), p. 170

Tristan Taormino, *The Ultimate Guide to Anal Sex for Women* (San Francisco: Cleis Press, 2006), p. 90.

Douglas Haddow, "Pornocalypse Now," *Adbusters*, May/June, 2009.

Anal Massage for Lovers, Vol. 2, DVD, directed by Joseph Kramer (Oakland, Calif.: Joseph Kramer Productions, 2005).

The Better Sex Guide to Anal Pleasure, DVD, directed by Mark Schoen (Hillsborough, N.C.: Sinclair Intimacy Institute, 2004).

Jack Morin, *Anal Pleasure and Health: A Guide for Both Men and Women* (Gardena, Calif.: Aaron Blake Publishers, 2008), p. 69.

Tristan Taormino's Expert Guide to Anal Sex, DVD, directed by Tristan Taormino (Los Angeles: Vivid-Ed, 2007).

PART FOUR: THE LAY OF THE LAND

CHAPTER 17: SEX IN PUBLIC PLACES

Canada. Criminal Code, RSC 1985, c. C-46, s. 173 (1) ("Indecent Acts").

CHAPTER 19: POWER PLAY

Nina Hartley's Guide to Spanking, DVD (Adam & Eve, 2006).

Whipsmart: A Good Vibrations Guide to Beginning S/M for Couples, VHS (San Francisco: Good Vibrations, 2002).

Lady Green, *The Compleat Spanker* (Emeryville, Calif.: Greenery Press, 1997), p. 47.

Jay Wiseman, *SM 101: A Realistic Introduction* (San Francisco: Greenery Press. 1996), p. 53.

——*Jay Wiseman's Erotic Bondage Handbook*. (Emeryville, Calif.: Greenery Press, 2000), pp. 46–48.

Midori, *The Seductive Art of Japanese Bondage* (Emeryville, Calif.: Greenery Press, 2001), p. 32.

Joannides, *The Guide to Getting It On!*, p. 224.

American Psychiatric Association, *Diagnostic and Statistical Manual of Mental Disorders: DSM-IV* (Arlington, Va.: American Psychiatric Publishing, 1994), p. 526.

Brenda Love, *Encyclopedia of Unusual Sex Practices* (London: Greenwich Editions, 1999), p. 109.

Brenda Love, "Cat-fighting, Eye-licking, Head-sitting and Statue-screwing," in Russ Kick, ed., *Everything You Know About Sex Is Wrong* (New York: The Disinformation Company, 2005), pp. 122–28.

Violet Blue, *Fetish Sex: An Erotic Guide for Couples* (Los Angeles: Daedalus, 2006), pp. 122–26.

CHAPTER 20: THE MULTI-ORGASMIC BUSH PILOT

Douglas Wile, ed., *The Art of the Bedchamber: The Chinese Sexual Yoga Classics Including Women's Solo Meditation Texts* (Albany, N.Y.: State University of New York Press, 1992).

Mantak Chia, Maneewan Chia, Douglas Abrams and Rachel Carlton Abrams, *The Multi-Orgasmic Couple: Sexual Secrets Every Couple Should Know* (San Francisco: HarperSanFrancisco, 2002), p. 4.

Bob Findle, school director of The Body Electric, personal correspondence with author.

Khadijah Caturani, "Every Sperm Is Sacred: The Tao of Sex in Ancient Asia," *Ego*, June 13, 2005, http://www.egothemag.com/archives/2005/06/post_3.htm.

Chia et al., *The Multi-Orgasmic Couple*, p. 12.

Daniel Reid, *The Tao of Health, Sex and Longevity: A Modern Practical Guide to the Ancient Way* (New York: Fireside, 1989), p. 296.

Al and Pala Copeland, owners of 4 Freedoms Relationship Tantra website (http://www.tantra-sex.com), personal correspondence with author.

Ancient Secrets of Sexual Ecstasy, DVD (Higher Love Video, 2006).

ACKNOWLEDGEMENTS

To the many ladies and gentlemen who answered my call for XXX-confessions: If this book is a power ballad, your stories are its refrain. I hold my lighter high in the air for all of you—especially for you, Captain Goodscrew.

To Cory Silverberg, certified sexuality educator, sexuality guide for About.com, and co-founder of Come As You Are, for close reading and kingly support.

To my intrepid research assistant in her leather pants, Janet Dey, and to the unblinking librarians at the Toronto Public Library.

Along with the cited authors and interviewees, this book is much beholden to Dave Bidini, David Bowie, C & Y Cinema, Claire Cameron, Michael Castleman, Meredith L. Chivers Ph.D., Jason Collett, Kevin Connelly, Jonathan Garfinkel, Adam Goodheart, Paul Kennedy, Kevin Lacroix, Dr. James Maskalyk, Hilary Martin, Duff McDonald, Janet Morassutti, Alisha Piercy, Christine Pountney, Damian Rogers, Martha Sharpe, Russell Smith, R.M. Vaughan, Christopher Wahl, Jeff Warren, Carl Wilson, the brilliantly resourceful staff at Good

Vibrations in San Francisco and at Good for Her in Toronto, particularly founder Carlyle Jansen.

To my righteous Bros who let me into their lady-heavy lexicon.

To the Godfather of the Bush, Derek Finkle, and to the editors I worked with at Toro magazine: Pat Lynch, Micah Toub, Melanie Morassutti and Godmother of the Bush, Heidi Sopinka.

To Anne McDermid for good wine and good counsel.

To my comrade, Jason Logan.

To the team at HarperCollins, especially my editor, Kate Cassaday, for brainpower and hilarity.

To my husband, Don Kerr (guitar lick), my son (drum solo), my parents, my sister, my Kerr family, my people, I thank you.

BP,
I'm going to miss you too.
CD